Dyslexia

Dyslexia

Third Edition

Gavin Reid

continuum

A companion website to accompany this book is available
online at: http://education.reid.continuumbooks.com
Please visit the link and register with us to receive your password
and access these downloadable resources.
If you experience any problems accessing the resources, please
contact Continuum at: info@continuumbooks.com

Continuum International Publishing Group

The Tower Building	80 Maiden Lane
11 York Road	Suite 704
London	New York
SE1 7NX	NY 10038

www.continuumbooks.com

First edition published 2005, London
Second edition published 2007, London
This third edition published 2011, London

British Library Cataloguing-in-Publication Data
A catalogue record for this book is available from the British Library.

ISBN: 9781441165855 (paperback)

Library of Congress Cataloging-in-Publication Data
A catalog record for this book is available from the Library of
Congress.

Typeset by Pindar NZ, Auckand, New Zealand
Printed and bound in India by Replika Press Pvt Ltd

Contents

Introduction

This new third edition of *Dyslexia* incorporates all the advances in the field of dyslexia in both research and practice. Policy developments in the UK have resulted in a much brighter picture all round in terms of awareness of dyslexia. The UK government report 'Identifying and Teaching Children and Young People with Dyslexia and Literacy Difficulties' written by Sir Jim Rose (June 2009) is expected to have a considerable impact on the learning outcomes of children with dyslexia in the UK.

The report provides an up-to-date picture of the nature of dyslexia and literacy difficulties, and of the evidence on interventions for tackling it. The report accepts that there is a need to develop better access for schools, parents and children to the advice and skills of specialist dyslexia teachers, who can devise tailored interventions for children struggling with literacy, whether or not they have been identified as having dyslexia.

In the UK, teachers can now apply for Training and Development Agency (TDA)-funded places on specialist dyslexia training, leading to the award of Approved Teacher Status (ATS) or Associate Membership of the British Dyslexia Association (AMBDA).

The UK government department, which incorporates the TDA Department for Children, Schools and Families (DCSF), endorsed all of the recommendations in the Rose report, including one supporting the training of teachers in specialist dyslexia qualifications. The aim of this training, according to the DCSF, is to build capacity within the schools system and improve access to specialist, high-quality support for pupils with dyslexia. It is expected that teachers obtaining specialist dyslexia qualifications with the support of Government funding from the TDA will work across schools to support other staff and pupils.

This progress seems light years in advance of the situation that abounded when I wrote my first book on dyslexia in 1993. At that time the priorities were to lobby government for recognition of dyslexia, to develop an awareness of dyslexia among teachers and to promote extended specialist training in the field of dyslexia. Although the priorities might still be very similar to what they were all those

1

years ago, the progress that has been made to meet these targets has been considerable. Today, governments themselves are taking the initiative – although, it must be remembered that much of this is due to the early work and the ongoing lobbying of dedicated parent and teacher groups.

There has been significant progress in the scientific field regarding the nature and origins of dyslexia – particularly in genetics, where a number of possible genetic permutations associated with dyslexia have been identified. In other areas, too, our understanding of the reading process and the skills associated with language and learning have been revisited many times, and intervention strategies have been revised and contextualized for learners with dyslexia. Indeed, it has been recognized that many of the strategies and programmes long advocated for children with dyslexia can be useful for all. This has been acknowledged in government reports on reading in the UK, US and New Zealand, and more recently in the New Zealand literacy benchmarks, which should have a big impact on providing support for children with dyslexia in Australasia.

It is encouraging that in most countries there has been recognition of the need to develop policies for dyslexia at both national and local levels. There are some excellent examples of policies for dyslexia in the Republic of Ireland and Northern Ireland, and other countries further afield, such as New Zealand and North America. I mention the Republic of Ireland as an example as governments there have shown a dedication to dealing with dyslexia at all levels, and the rhetoric of policy has been supported by the essential follow-through in staff-development programmes and classroom practices.

Having presented courses on dyslexia in over 60 countries, in every continent, I have noted the progress and desire among practitioners and policy-makers to establish and develop knowledge and expertise in dealing with dyslexia in the classroom. It is impressive to witness the endeavours of individuals in some places with few resources (such as Africa), who are attempting to ensure that there is adequate training and knowledge in schools in relation to dyslexia.

At the same time it is equally impressive to note how in other countries, such as Scotland, dyslexia and other specific learning difficulties have been seen as a government priority area and supported with funding to enable innovative intervention, research and training programmes to be developed. This pattern has also been seen in many areas of the US, too numerous to mention in this introduction. In Tennessee, for example, the Tennessee Center for the Study and Treatment of Dyslexia at Middle Tennessee State University has been developing training programmes for teachers since 1993, as well as offering diagnostic and consulting services.

In Western Australia, the innovative learning centre 'Fun Track Learning' under the direction of Mandy Appleyard has made enormous progress in providing a complimentary service to parents and children with dyslexia. There are in fact many examples of this type of excellence in practice in schools and in learning centres in various countries.

Several independent schools dedicated to dyslexia are complementing the work being carried out by education authorities across the world. For example, Fraser Academy in Vancouver, Canada – a fully accredited day school for students with dyslexia and language-based learning difficulties; the Kenneth Gordon Maplewood School, also in Vancouver, whose school statement is 'they are bright, their potential is extraordinary, they simply learn differently'; the Red Rose School in Lancashire, UK, who received an 'outstanding' Ofsted report in 2009; the Center for Child Evaluation and Teaching (CCET) in Kuwait – a specialized Learning Disabilities Center developing innovative practices in assessment, teaching and training; and the Institute for Child Education and Psychology (ICEP) Europe – a source for online continuing education and professional development for educators and dyslexia course provision for teachers and parents.

These are just a few of the organizations that have done a great deal to develop excellence in meeting the educational and social needs of children with dyslexia. Interestingly, the *International Book of Dyslexia* (Smythe, Everatt and Salter 2004) features 53 countries, all showing a commitment to tackling dyslexia.

This new edition, therefore, is timely. The effect of the increase in recognition and training in dyslexia has resulted in classroom teachers and parents being much more aware of the learning difficulty. This book is therefore geared towards that end – that is, to provide classroom teachers with a range of strategies for identifying and teaching students with dyslexia.

The aim of this book is primarily to empower teachers to recognize that they have the skills to deal with dyslexia. What they need is the knowledge to develop an understanding of children with dyslexia: an understanding of their needs and their skills, as well as of the challenges they face in education and in the world at large. An understanding of children with dyslexia is at the heart of this book. It is hoped this will transmit into constructive and effective practice in schools, and allow all people with dyslexia to develop to their full potential, academically and socially, so that they can have a 'sense of belonging' in the community.

There is much still to be done, but one of the crucial areas – that of teacher awareness – has been a priority for education authorities in several countries, leading to, I hope, more opportunities and better teaching for children and young people around the world.

1

Dyslexia: Current Perspectives

The understanding, identification and intervention for dyslexia have been the subject of many government reports, research studies and practitioner initiatives and this has been ongoing particularly since the launch of the British Dyslexia Association's dyslexia-friendly campaign over 10 years ago. There is now a great deal of information on dyslexia and a wide range of resources that can impact on practice. At the same time the increase in this knowledge and resources can result in problems for teachers and parents. Researchers do not always agree and there are different angles on dyslexia and a range of suitable approaches that can be used – while this can provide choice it can also cause some confusion. It is important that teachers and parents have a straightforward account of dyslexia and know how to identify and intervene in the classroom. Additionally it is important that they are able to appreciate the impact of dyslexia on the child, the young person or adult, and others in the family.

It is the aim of this book to provide this straightforward response to clarify and enhance teachers understanding of dyslexia. The book provides pointers from research that can inform practice and offers strategies for identification and teaching. There is an emphasis on making the curriculum accessible for students with dyslexia within an inclusive educational setting, and information on the social and emotional needs of people with dyslexia. The book also covers issues relating to multilingualism and dyslexia, as well as the relationship with dyslexia to coexisting conditions, such as dyspraxia, dysgraphia, dyscalculia and ADHD. It is important for all professionals and parents to appreciate the overlap between the different learning difficulties.

In the US and Canada there has been a thrust towards evidence-based practice and proactive intervention. This is evident in the Response to Intervention (RTI) programmes. Evidence-based practice is taking hold in the UK and Europe, as well as in Australia and New Zealand and these initiatives will be discussed in this book.

Response to Intervention (RTI) is essentially an 'evidence-based' proactive model used mainly in the US that seeks to prevent academic failure through early intervention and frequent progress measurement. It attempts to avoid the 'wait-to-fail' method which is used in many areas in the assessment of children with dyslexia. The key objective in RTI is to select an instructional or behaviour-management strategy that matches a student's specific needs. The implication is that children with serious academic skill deficits will require very different intervention strategies. But it is appreciated that intervention strategies should be scientifically based and feasible to carry out with the resources available to the teaching staff. There is a considerable amount of ongoing research in the US debating RTI and the notion of scientifically-based approaches. On the positive side, however, theoretically at least, it should lead to early identification and can facilitate early intervention, but it may not distinguish between a child with dyslexia and some other learning difficulty.

Dyslexia is a global concern and having lectured on dyslexia in over 60 countries in every continent I have come to realize that the issues are similar irrespective of geographical location. This book will therefore be appropriate for teachers and parents in every country who require information and guidance on how best to understand and deal with dyslexia.

Defining Dyslexia

There is a range of descriptions that are currently used to describe dyslexia. Many of these have been converted into formal definitions. Most of the definitions, however, include the following aspects:

♦ the neurological and genetic causes of dyslexia
♦ the characteristic difficulties associated with dyslexia, such as phonological, visual and auditory processing difficulties
♦ the associated characteristics of dyslexia – difficulties relating to memory, time management, processing speed, organization, and sequencing and planning
♦ the need for over-learning and specialized and specific teaching approaches
♦ the overlap with other conditions such as dyspraxia, dyscalculia and ADHD.

For example, the British Dyslexia Association (BDA) definition includes the following. Dyslexia:

♦ is a *specific learning difficulty*
♦ mainly affects reading and spelling

Dyslexia

♦ is characterized by difficulties in processing *word-sounds*
♦ is a weakness in short-term *verbal memory*
♦ can be noted in spoken language as well as written language
♦ is linked to *genetic differences.*

Reid (2009) developed the following definition. Dyslexia is a *processing difference* characterized by difficulties in literacy and

♦ it can affect *cognition,* such as memory, speed of processing, time management, coordination and directional aspects
♦ it can involve visual and phonological difficulties
♦ there are usually *discrepancies* in performances
♦ it is important that the *individual differences* and learning styles are acknowledged
♦ the learning and work *context* must be acknowledged too.

This latter point is particularly important as it indicates that the learning environment and the nature of the task can have a major influence on the outcome for people with dyslexia.

Characteristics of Dyslexia

There are a number of core characteristics of dyslexia that are important for identification and assessment, including reading, writing and spelling difficulties. For example, quite often, poor reading (decoding) contrasted with good comprehension can be an indicator of dyslexia.

Point of caution
Children with dyslexia usually have good comprehension skills.
   This statement acts as a reminder of the importance of recognizing the individual differences among people with dyslexia and we have to be wary of not being too prescriptive or rigid in our characteristics and criteria of dyslexia. Some may well have excellent comprehension but others, perhaps due to their learning experiences, may not.

Barriers to Learning

It can be useful to view the difficulties associated with dyslexia as barriers to learning. This means that the barriers, whatever they may be – cognitive, educational or environmental – need to be considered in both an assessment and in intervention. When identifying the barriers to learning it is important to look at students' holistic needs. This would include: cognitive (learning skills), environmental (learning experience) and progress in basic attainments (literacy acquisition).

This highlights a number of key factors relating to the learner, the task and the learning experience, in particular the need not to solely focus on the student, and what he or she can or cannot do, but to look at the task that is being presented, the expectations being placed on the learner and the learner's readiness for the task. From that premise the first step is to identify those factors – cognitive, educational, environmental and social/emotional – that may be presenting barriers to the learner in acquiring competent literacy and other skills.

It is important to obtain an understanding of the type of difficulties experienced by learners with dyslexia and to identify how these difficulties can be recognized and dealt with. Some of the most common difficulties are discussed below.

Understanding the Task

It is important to appreciate that the learner with dyslexia may not actually understand the task. Tasks have to be made clear and explicit. If not, students with dyslexia may not be able to utilize their full abilities and will provide an incorrect response. Understanding the task therefore can be a barrier that confronts the student with dyslexia in many curriculum areas. They may well have the necessary cognitive skills to understand the task, but if it is not presented clearly the task can become challenging and it may overwhelm the student with dyslexia.

The Print Medium

Accessing the curriculum can be dependent on accessing print, and this is usually the most formidable barrier experienced by students with dyslexia. But it is also important to consider that materials can be accessed using other means. There is now a great deal of technology for use in schools and many programmes have been developed specifically for the learner with dyslexia. Additionally, the presentation, content and layout of worksheets can make a difference to the learning outcome. It is important, for example, to pay careful consideration to the use of visuals, space on the page, and font style and size, as well as ensuring the content is expressed clearly and that set tasks are achievable.

> The layout and presentation of worksheets are as important as the content and the tasks.

Curriculum Approaches

Many of the barriers to dyslexia can be overcome through particular approaches, such as differentiation, as well as through the use of specialized resources. There are some specific programmes for dyslexia (discussed later in this book), but the answer can also be found by considering the teaching and learning process. Differentiation is part of this process, as are interactive question-and-answer sessions, and the building of the students' confidence and self-esteem. Differentiation essentially represents good teaching and careful advanced planning. If the curriculum is effectively differentiated to take account of the task, the learner and the use of resources then it is likely that the needs of all students with dyslexia will be catered for in some way. Differentiation is about supporting the learner and guiding them from where they are now to where they should be. In other words, it is about helping to make all curricular materials accessible. Differentiation, therefore, needs to consider the learner, the task and the outcome as well as the resources.

Cultural Factors

When looking at the barriers to learning it is also important to consider cultural factors. These are important as they can influence the selection of books and whether some of the concepts in the text need to be singled out for additional and differentiated explanation. Cultural values are an important factor. It has been suggested that the 'big dip' in performance noted in some bilingual children in later primary school may be explained by a failure of professionals to understand and appreciate the cultural values, and the actual level of competence of the bilingual child, particularly in relation to conceptual development and competence in thinking skills. In order for a teaching approach with bilingual students to be fully effective, it has to be comprehensive, which means that it needs to incorporate the views of parents and the community. This requires considerable preparation and pre-planning, as well as consultation with parents and community organizations.

Self-Esteem

Self-esteem is an important area to consider for students with dyslexia. Positive self-esteem is crucial for learning as this can provide the learner with confidence and motivation enabling them to utilize different learning approaches and become more motivated to learn. A student with dyslexia with a low self-esteem will very likely have a cautious approach to learning and will have an over-reliance in the structure provided by the teacher. It is unlikely that such learners will develop a risk-taking approach to learning, as they will not have the confidence to take responsibility for their own learning. Yet it is important that students with dyslexia assume responsibility for their own learning and in time develop their own strategies and structures and eventually have the skills to assess their own competencies in tasks.

It is important that tasks, indeed all learning and learning experiences, are directed towards developing the student's self-esteem. In order to develop self-esteem the learner with dyslexia must have some perception of success. It is obvious that if a learner is continually in a failure situation this will in turn have some influence on the learner's self-esteem. It is crucial that tasks are developed to ensure that the learner will succeed. This will require tasks being broken down into manageable units for the learner. This will ensure that the child with dyslexia will achieve some early success when undertaking a task, which will provide motivation for subsequent learning.

Dyslexia Research

The dyslexia research field has many different dimensions. There are research activities in different aspects of neurology/brain structure; neurological processing; the cerebellum; the visual cortex; speech and language processing; and the processes involved in learning. Cognitive psychologists are involved in studies involving memory and dyslexia, as well as the role of processing speed and the cognitive routes to literacy acquisition. This can present a confusing picture for teachers who are seeking straightforward explanations of dyslexia and guidance for practice. It might therefore be useful to view dyslexia as a difference rather than as a deficit: that is, a difference in how the child processes information. The research perspectives and the current views on research in dyslexia are described in more detail in Chapter 2.

> Children with dyslexia can have a different and individual way of processing information. Difference does not mean deficit!

Dyslexia as a difference

Dyslexia can be described as a *difference* in the following ways:

♦ how information is processed
♦ the strategies that are needed to learn effectively

Dyslexia

♦ the speed of processing
♦ the style of processing.

Children with dyslexia usually have a visual, right-brained global processing style, so it is important to acknowledge the characteristics and the strengths of this style.

Identification and Intervention

When identifying dyslexia, it is preferable to have both a rationale and a strategy for the assessment. Often a suspicion of the presence of dyslexic difficulties can be identified through observation, or through the results of routine assessments. This information, however, needs to be contextualized, so that an overall picture of the child's profile can be seen and any evidence of dyslexia can be noted. It is important that the identification is linked to intervention. Some general aspects relating to the purpose of an assessment include the following.

Identification of the learner's general strengths and weaknesses

It is important to identify both the strengths as well as the areas of weakness of the person in question. This can be helpful in developing a programme and suggesting appropriate strategies. For example:

Strengths:

♦ good visual skills
♦ excellent expressive vocabulary
♦ good in team games
♦ good understanding of language.

Weaknesses:

♦ difficulty remembering spelling rules
♦ difficulty reading aloud
♦ slow reading speed
♦ difficulty organizing work.

A programme for a particular child could therefore ensure that he or she gets the opportunities to use visual skills and participate in team games. The strengths can be used to develop interest in a topic, as well as to develop skills in the weaker areas.

Indication of the learner's current level of performance

The child's performance level can easily be ascertained from standardized assessment. It is important to have this information as it can help to monitor progress, and can be used to note the discrepancy between the child's reading/spelling age and his or her chronological age. It is important not to rely too much on standardized data of this type, but they can provide a guide.

An explanation for the learner's lack of progress

This involves identifying aspects of the learner's performance in reading, writing and spelling that may typify a 'pattern of errors'. For example, reading the word 'useless' as 'unless' or vice versa can indicate some visual difficulties as these words are visually similar. Focus on the following:

♦ identify specific areas of competence
♦ understand the student's particular learning style
♦ recognize aspects of the curriculum that may interest and motivate the learner
♦ identify specific aspects of the curriculum that are challenging for the child.

Specific difficulty: reading

Difficulty recognizing and remembering word sounds
Some learners experience difficulty recognizing and remembering sounds in words. For instance, letter combinations that make sounds, such as 'ph' and 'th' found in a word like 'elephant', can be difficult for someone with dyslexia. Other confusions can be noted in words like 'necessity'. Consider the example of an 18-year-old with an IQ of 120 who still experiences these difficulties. His pattern of errors can be noted in the following words: *physicion, predujuce nessecity and comision.*

Substitution of words with similar meanings when reading aloud
This is called semantic confusion. Words that have similar meanings, such as 'bus' and 'car', can be confused when reading aloud. This, however, means that the reader does understand the text and is reading for meaning and context rather than focusing on reading accurately. Sometimes it can be difficult for the child with dyslexia to read for accuracy and meaning at the same time, and for some it may be more effective to focus on reading for meaning. This would mean

that language experience and pre-reading discussion are important to ensure that the reader has a good idea of what the text is about.

Difficulty with rhymes
Difficulty with rhyming, such as remembering nursery rhymes and the sequence of the rhyme, can be addressed in an early identification programme. Some children can become quite adept at joining in with nursery rhymes, but are not able to recite these on their own.

Children with dyslexia may not only forget the actual words in the rhyme, but also get some of the lines confused and out of sequence.

Reverses, omits and additions
These characteristics are quite characteristic of dyslexia, as they indicate that the child is reading or writing using context. Children who have difficulty decoding often compensate by over-depending on context.

Loses their place when reading
This is also very common and can indicate the presence of a visual difficulty. Sometimes complete lines can be omitted. A ruler that masks the line below can be used, but this can also restrict the opportunities and the flow necessary for reading in context. A good resource is the transparent ruler with a colour transparency.

Difficulty with the sequence of the alphabet
This can make using a dictionary very time-consuming and frustrating. There are some alphabet games that can be used to help with this. This colour-coding of groups of letters can also be helpful: the alphabet can be divided into seven sections, with a different colour for each section.

Difficulty pronouncing multi-syllabic words, even common ones
Words like 'preliminary', 'governmental' and 'necessity' can be easily mispronounced and misspelt by people with dyslexia. The use of colour-coding can also help with this.

Poor word attack skills
This can be a problem particularly when tackling new, unknown words. If the child has poor word attack skills then he or she is likely to read the word visually, and not break the word down into its constituent parts. This can be a difficulty when learning new vocabulary.

Slow reading speed with little expression
Some children exhibit a particularly slow verbal reading speed, sometimes with little or no expression. This happens because children with dyslexia spend a great deal of effort on reading accuracy, which can

result in a loss of emphasis on meaning and expression. It can also make reading speed quite slow, and a loss of reading fluency can therefore be evident. This is a major concern, as reading fluency can be linked to reading comprehension. It is important that comprehension is given a prominent position in a reading programme for children with dyslexia.

Reluctance to read for pleasure
With most skills, practice can develop competence. This is also the case with reading. It is important that reading takes place every day, even if it is only magazines. Reading for pleasure can result if reading is daily, and particularly if the reader chooses his or her own reading material.

Reading comprehension
Reading comprehension can often yield better results than single-word reading for many children with dyslexia. This is because they read for meaning and context. With single-word reading there are no contextual clues available. To ascertain the actual level of decoding, therefore, a single word test would be better than reading a passage. The use of non-words is also a good method of testing actual decoding skills.

Word confusion
Confusing words that have the same or similar sounds (such as 'their' and 'there', and 'access' and 'assess') is very common in children with dyslexia. This is why, when they are doing written work, time should be allocated for proofreading so that they can check these potential errors. The best way to remember these words is to use them – through usage, automaticity can occur. The more they are used, the more likely it is that the differences between these commonly confused words can be learnt and consolidated.

Specific difficulty: spelling

Examples include remembering spelling rules, making phonological errors in spelling (for example, 'f' for 'ph'), letters being out of sequence, inconsistent use of some letters with similar sounds such as 's' and 'z', difficulty with word endings (for example, using 'ie' for 'y'), confusion or omission of vowels, and difficulty with words with double consonants such as 'commission'.

These types of errors can be quite characteristic of dyslexia. One of the difficulties with spelling is that once a word has been habitually misspelt, it is difficult for the child to unlearn the error. This means that many of these errors can persist throughout all stages of school and beyond.

Specific difficulty: writing

This can often be noted in the inconsistent use of capital letters and small letters. Often these are used wrongly and there is little or no pattern to how they are used.

Figure 1.1 Spelling pattern of a dyslexic boy aged 10 with an IQ of 110

Slow writing speed and reluctance to write at length
This may be the result of not being able to generate sentence and grammatical structure very fluently, as well as a difficulty in finding the most appropriate words to explain things. Because this can take some time, the written piece can take longer than might be expected.

It is helpful to provide a framework for the written piece as well as the key words that are to be used. This can speed up the writing process.

Unusual writing grip or sitting position
This can often indicate a visual/perceptual difficulty, or dyspraxic-type difficulties that can affect hand–eye coordination. Special adapted pencils with rubber or spongy grips can help. It is also important to recognize the importance of good posture when writing and using a keyboard.

Specific difficulty: memory

Poor short-term and working memory intervention
This means that there can be difficulties in remembering lists of information, even short lists, or short instructions. It is important therefore

to provide one piece of information at a time, otherwise the child will become confused.

Poor long-term memory/organizational difficulties
These two factors can be linked. Long-term memory is to a certain extent dependent on good cognitive organization. That means being able to organize information at the point of learning. The use of strategies to categorize information will make recall easier and strengthen long-term memory. The use of personal memory strategies is therefore important for children with dyslexia. They may show poor organization of their timetable, materials, equipment and items needed for learning, such as having difficulty remembering and organizing their homework notebooks.

Specific difficulty: movement

There can be an overlap between dyslexia and dyspraxia (which is a difficulty with motor and movement control, such as difficulty with tasks like tying shoelaces, bumping into furniture, tripping and falling frequently). Some of the factors associated with coordination difficulties can provide clues in early identification of dyslexia. These factors can often be noted at the pre-school stage.

Specific difficulty: speech development

Examples of this include: confusing similar sounds; poor articulation; difficulty blending sounds into words; poor awareness of rhyme; poor syntactic structure and naming difficulties.

Speech difficulties in the early years can also be an indicator of dyslexia. Not all children with dyslexia will have speech difficulties but those who have will usually have the phonological difficulties associated with dyslexia.

It is important to recognize that many of these specific difficulties can be seen in a continuum from mild to severe, and the extent and severity of these difficulties will have an impact on the assessment results and the subsequent recommendations for support.

Information Processing

Dyslexia is a difference in how some children process information. Information processing describes the interaction between the learner and the task. The information processing cycle has three components. These are:

♦ *input* – auditory, visual, tactile, kinesthetic
♦ *cognition* – memory, understanding, organizing and making sense of information
♦ *output* – reading aloud, talking, discussing, drawing, seeing, experiencing.

Children with dyslexia can have difficulty at all three stages of this cycle. It is important therefore to draw on information that relate to these three stages. For example, one can ask whether the same difficulties are experienced if the material is presented visually as opposed to auditorily; or perhaps the individual can learn more effectively if he or she is able to experience the learning through the kinesthetic modality. Although related to teaching approaches, it is crucial that this is acknowledged in the identification and assessment process, as it is important that reasons for the difficulty are sought, and, further, that a clear link can be forged between assessment and teaching approaches.

Dyslexia: Some Key Points

Dyslexia is individual

This means that children with dyslexia may have slightly different characteristics from each other. These characteristics can have a varying impact on the child. In some children this may not be too noticeable, but in others it can be very obvious. Dyslexia therefore can be evident along a continuum, from mild to severe.

This of course means that what works for one dyslexic child may not work successfully for another.

Dyslexia relates to how information is processed

This means that dyslexia involves more than reading: it affects learning and how all information – and that includes oral instructions – is processed.

It is important to recognize that the cycle of learning called the 'information processing cycle' is important. It can help us to understand the difficulties experienced by children with dyslexia. This cycle applies to how we take information in, how we memorize it and how we display to others that we know the information.

Children with dyslexia can have difficulty displaying knowledge and understanding in written work

In schoolwork, children usually display what they know through the written mode. Yet this may be the dyslexic child's weakest way of presenting information. Writing can be laborious and tedious for the dyslexic child. However, it can be made easier and more enjoyable if he or she is provided with a structure for writing and perhaps even the key words. One of the important points to consider here is that we need to identify and acknowledge the specific strengths of each child with dyslexia.

Children with dyslexia can have difficulty learning through the auditory modality (i.e. through listening)

There are many ways of learning, particularly today with computer games and other electronic learning and leisure tools. Yet in many cases we still rely on what is called the auditory modality: that is, the person's ability to listen and understand through sound, rather than through pictures (visual) or through experience (kinesthetic). Most research indicates that children with dyslexia have a phonological difficulty – that is, they have difficulty with sounds, and remembering the sound combinations and sequence of sounds that make up a word. Listening may therefore not be the easiest means of acquiring information. Usually it is better if children with dyslexia can see the information to be learnt.

Children with dyslexia have difficulty remembering information

This can apply to short-term and working memory and means it can affect the remembering of oral instructions, especially if a list of items is presented. The short-term (or working) memory can only hold a limited amount of information at any one time, but children with dyslexia can have difficulty in remembering even a limited amount accurately, so it is best to provide only one instruction at any one time.

Children with dyslexia can have difficulty organizing information

Whether we are aware of it or not, we always make some attempt to organize new information. We might group new items to be remembered into one category, and when we are recalling information we generally do so in a fairly organized way, so that a listener can

17

understand. This can be especially important if we are recalling a sequence of events. Children with dyslexia can have some difficulty in organizing information, and this can affect both how efficiently information is remembered, and how they can present the information to others. This can affect their performance in examinations unless additional support is made available.

Children with dyslexia need more time to process information

This is very characteristic of dyslexia: usually children with dyslexia will take longer to process information because they may take an indirect route to arrive at an answer. This emphasizes the individuality of dyslexia and the right-hemisphere method of processing information that children with dyslexia often use.

Children with dyslexia usually have difficulty reading and spelling accurately and fluently

You will note that the word 'usually' is mentioned here. This is because not every child with dyslexia will have difficulty in reading and spelling. Some children can compensate for a reading difficulty by becoming very adept at using context, and tend to read for meaning. These children may still, however, show some of the other characteristics of dyslexia, particularly those aspects that relate to information processing, such as memory and organization.

Similarly, they may have difficulty in reading but not in spelling, or vice versa. This again emphasizes the individual nature of dyslexia, which means that each child can exhibit dyslexic characteristics to a different degree.

Although the degree of dyslexia can differ, the indicators are usually fairly constant; but these can also depend on the age of the child. It is possible to note some of the indicators of dyslexia before the child attends school, that is, before he or she starts to learn to read.

It is important to recognize that dyslexia occurs within a continuum and that there can be shared and overlapping characteristics between dyslexia and other specific learning difficulties.

In summary, this chapter

♦ provides a list of some of the characteristics associated with dyslexia

♦ presents some of the key factors in current research and current thinking on dyslexia
♦ suggests that differentiation and acknowledgement of learning styles can help access the curricular needs of students with dyslexia
♦ identifies the barriers and suggests that dyslexia should be seen as a difference rather than a deficit
♦ indicates the key factors in the identification of dyslexia
♦ provides a summary of the key points that need to be acknowledged if you are to have a clear understanding of dyslexia.

2

Research in Dyslexia

This chapter will provide some of the key points in current research in dyslexia. This will help to give you an understanding of the different perspectives on dyslexia and how these may relate to practice. There are three key areas that inform current research in dyslexia: the neurological, cognitive and educational areas. These are discussed below.

Neurological Research

There is now considerable evidence that there is a neurological basis to dyslexia. This means that the brain structure and the neural connections needed for processing information may develop differently in dyslexic children. This also means that dyslexic children and adults will learn differently and find processing some types of tasks, such as those involving print and language, more challenging than some other learners.

There are two hemispheres in the brain – the left and the right – and the roles of both hemispheres are important in relation to dyslexia research. Each hemisphere is more adept at processing certain types of information. Usually the left hemisphere processes language and the small details of information, such as print. This means that the left hemisphere is important for decoding tasks that are necessary for accurate reading.

The right hemisphere on the other hand tends to process information that incorporates a more holistic perspective. This involves processing pictures and other types of visual information. The right hemisphere also usually deals with comprehension and some aesthetic aspects, such as the appreciation of art and music. Some neuro-psychologists, such as Dirk Bakker in Holland, have related this to reading and have suggested that right-hemisphere readers can become 'sloppy' readers, but may have good comprehension (Robertson and Bakker 2002). Left-hemisphere readers on the other hand have the potential to become pedantic and precise readers, but may miss out on the comprehension aspect. Ideally, reading is a balance between left (accuracy) and right (comprehension) hemispheres.

While children with dyslexia can show abilities in right-hemisphere processing, they may have difficulty in processing information using the left hemisphere. The skills necessary for accurate reading tend to be left-hemisphere skills, such as, being able to discriminate different sounds in words. These skills are called phonological skills and they are essential for identifying the clusters of letters that make certain sounds, such as 'ough' as in 'tough' and 'ight' as in 'right'. It is now widely accepted that children with dyslexia have a weakness in phonological skills, and this affects their ability to read fluently, especially when they are young (Snowling 2005). There is, however, evidence that if intervention to teach phonological skills takes place at an early age, the acquisition of literacy can become easier. This is a very important point.

> *If intervention to teach phonological skills takes place at an early age, the acquisition of literacy can become easier and the impact of dyslexia can be minimized.*

Information transfer

Breznitz (2008) has coined the phrase the 'Asynchrony Phenomenon' to explain dyslexia. This implies that dyslexia is caused by the speed of processing gaps within and between the various components in the word decoding process. Breznitz and colleagues have devised a programme that attempts to train the brain to process information at a faster speed. Implementing this programme has resulted in a substantial improvement among dyslexic children regarding the speed at which they process information (Breznitz and Horowitz 2007).

Breznitz (2008) also claims that dyslexic learners exhibit difficulties when transferring information from one hemisphere to another. These differences in inter-hemisphere transfer among dyslexics may stem from information decay in the corpus collosum, or delay in inter-hemisphere transfer time. This may be the reason for the success of programmes such as Brain Gym (Dennison and Dennison 2001), which consist of a series of exercises to cross the midline. These exercises can enhance the development of the corpus collosum and foster the transfer of messages from hemisphere to hemisphere.

Visual deficits

Stein (2008) argues that there is genetic, sensory, motor and psychological evidence that dyslexia is a neurological syndrome affecting the development of the brain. He also provides evidence that the development of magnocellular neurons, which impact on the visual system, is impaired in children with dyslexia. Stein argues that the visual system provides the main input to both the lexical and the sub-lexical routes for reading and therefore vision should be seen as the most important sense for reading. He maintains that the quality of teaching is very important. The fashion, Stein argues, for abandoning phonics teaching in favour of real books and flash cards of whole words that took hold in the 1960s, may have done children without highly developed visual memories a profound disservice. Stein also strongly asserts that the evidence shows that dyslexia is more than just a problem with acquiring reading skills. He argues that dyslexia is associated with brain differences, which affect other areas as well as reading. This amounts to a neurological syndrome that is characterized by a very wide variety of symptoms involving impaired temporal processing, including: phonological difficulties, visuo-motor, speech, short-term memory, attention, coordination and general sequencing problems. This emphasizes the view that dyslexia is more than a reading difficulty. This is important for teachers to understand for while special programmes and specialized input can allow a child with dyslexia to make substantial progress, they are still dyslexic. This point can easily be misunderstood and it is important that additional considerations that are provided for children with dyslexia are not removed too soon or discontinued once improvement takes place.

Stein does place a heavy emphasis on visual processing and argues that the magnocellular system plays a very crucial role in stabilizing the eyes during reading. These fixations on each word only last about a quarter of a second, but it is only during these moments that the fine details of the letters in a word can be recognized. Stein argues that it is very important to keep the eyes stationary and the magnocellular system ensures this happens. Some children with dyslexia have a faulty magnocellular system and are not able to fixate on the features of the word efficiently. Children in this situation may find that the words become blurry, fuzzy or jump off the page, and some corrective treatment will be necessary. Stein (2008) argues that there is now a great deal of evidence that in many, but probably not all, dyslexics, development of their visual magnocellular system is mildly impaired.

Hereditary factors

There have been a considerable amount of studies that have confirmed the genetic links in dyslexia. Familial risk is in fact a useful indicator of dyslexia (Molfese *et al.* 2008). Advances during the last 20 years in the field of genetics research have brought the search for the underlying genetic basis of dyslexia to the forefront. This has been helped by advances in neuro-imaging techniques and this has helped neuro-scientists explore the structure and function of the brain more clearly.

The cerebellum

The cerebellum is the brain's autopilot mechanism responsible for coordinating the precise timing of muscle contractions as well as the planning of movement and coordination. Stein (2008) suggests the cerebellum very likely plays an important role in reading. The cerebellum is one of the first brain structures to begin to differentiate, yet it appears to be the last to achieve maturity as the cellular organization of the cerebellum continues to change for many months after birth. According to Fawcett and Nicolson (2008) there is now extensive evidence that the cerebellum is a brain structure particularly susceptible to injury, particularly in the case of premature birth, and that such damage can subsequently lead to a range of motor, language and cognitive problems. Fawcett and Nicolson (2008) argue that the cerebellar deficit hypothesis may provide close to a single coherent explanation of the three criterial difficulties in dyslexia – reading, writing and spelling. They also suggest the cerebellur deficit hypothesis provides an explanation for the overlapping factors between dyslexia and other developmental disorders.

One of the hypothesized functions of the cerebellum concerns the precise timing of procedures (e.g. several motor movements) that accomplish some sort of behavioural response or task performance. They argue that this timing may play a critical role in task accomplishment and making learnt skills automatic. This leads to automaticity, which is in fact a critical aspect of learning new skills. Automaticity means that the skill can be carried out without the individual giving it too much thought. For most adults and children, the ability to walk, talk and possibly read and write may be partially or completely automatic. Fawcett and Nicolson (2008) have put forward the hypothesis that dyslexic children experience difficulty automatizing any skill (cognitive or motor). They suggest that reading is subject to automaticity and since all dyslexia hypotheses predict poor reading as a factor in dyslexia, then the automatization deficit hypothesis would be valid in

Dyslexia

relation to dyslexia. Fawcett (1989) and Fawcett and Nicolson (1992) argue that there is clear support stemming from a set of experiments in which they asked dyslexic children to do two things at once. If a skill is automatic, then the children should be able to do two tasks at the same time. These findings strongly suggested that dyslexic children were not automatic, even at the fundamental skill of balance. For some reason, dyslexic children had difficulty automatizing skills, and had therefore to concentrate harder to achieve normal levels of performance. This has clear implications for teaching and learning in that there will be a significant need for over-learning to be utilized with children with dyslexia in the classroom.

Cognitive Research

Researchers/theorists who concentrate on the processes that go into reading and writing usually look at these from a cognitive perspective. Speed of processing can be seen as an aspect of cognition, as can memory and effective use of learning processes. These are considered to be key factors in relation to dyslexia and they are areas where there can be a clear link between research and classroom practices.

Phonological difficulties

The most dominant causal view on dyslexia is the phonological deficit hypothesis. This perspective has been derived from the substantial evidence that difficulties in phonological processing, particularly when related to phonological decoding, have been a major distinguishing factor between dyslexics and non-dyslexics from early literacy learning to adulthood. Children who find it difficult to distinguish sounds within verbally presented words would be predicted to have problems learning the alphabetic principle that letters represent sounds. These children are those who are most likely to be dyslexic based on the phonological deficit perspective. The most comprehensive data related to teaching literacy to children diagnosed with dyslexia, revolves around the benefits of phonological training methods, particularly if performed early in the literacy learning process. The phonological deficit hypothesis is compatible with the success of these methods. Teaching methods that develop skills in grapheme–phoneme translation, as well as providing a basis for building a sight vocabulary, may be successful because they overcome the problems associated with the phonological deficits. Reading programmes used for children with dyslexia would need to have a strong phonological element. This view is strongly supported by many because they believe that acquisition of phonological skills is in fact crucial for successful reading (Vellutino *et al.* 2004). Peer (2009) has developed a strong argument emphasizing the need to acknowledge glue ear syndrome as an influential causal factor in dyslexia. She suggests that hearing loss during the first two years of life may result in a delay in emerging receptive or expressive language or both. This further underlines the importance and the role of early identification and intervention. Peer suggests that some of the symptoms of glue ear include: early speech difficulties, language or communication difficulties, confusion of letters and/or words (especially when young), mishearing words in speech, difficulty in following a conversation when background noise is present, spelling difficulties – omission of letters/sounds or phonetically spelled, reading weaknesses with single word and pseudowords and difficulty in following instructions. Peer strongly supports the view that there is a need to identify and provide for children experiencing dyslexic-type difficulties as early as possible if they are to make the greatest progress in their language and learning, and that the same is necessary for those who have experienced glue ear. If glue ear is diagnosed or suspected, therefore, it is important that the child has a heavy input in the development of phonological skills, language and listening skills.

Educational Research

The educational perspective relates to the observed characteristics of dyslexia. That is how the child performs in the classroom within the different areas of the curriculum. This relates to reading, spelling writing and maths, but also in general how children cope with the pace and level of the curriculum presented. The implication is that there are two approaches that can be used.

Skill development approaches

These involve identifying the child's weak areas and remediating them through providing special programmes in reading, spelling or whatever area they are weak in.

Curriculum adaptation approaches

These use differentiation to ensure that the student is able to access the curriculum. Task presentation/environmental approaches follow on from curriculum adaptation approaches and involve preparing materials that are consistent with the learning needs and learning style of the person with dyslexia. The approaches known as 'dyslexia friendly' come into this category.

'Dyslexia Friendly'

It is important for teachers to incorporate dyslexia-friendly approaches into their teaching strategies and materials. There is evidence that making teaching dyslexia friendly can make a substantial difference. Coffield *et al.* (2008) show that the development of 'dyslexia-friendly standards' for all schools within a local authority provide a useful tool for developing effective in-class intervention.

In their study they found that, often, being dyslexia-friendly is not enough. Many students were still not receiving the right kind of dyslexia-friendly approaches. For example, they found in their study that over half the pupils with dyslexia (54 per cent) agreed with the statement 'I get lots of red marks in my exercise books'. This, they suggested, shows that there is still some way to go towards establishing sympathetic marking systems for pupils whose reading and spelling difficulties should perhaps be accommodated in a more positive way. A further 21 per cent of the dyslexic pupils said they did not have time to write their homework down and they were nearly twice as likely as their non-dyslexic peers to perceive teachers as being more likely to get cross if they brought the wrong equipment to lessons.

Those teachers who were using dyslexia-friendly approaches in their classrooms tended to focus more on making sure that tasks were introduced and explained clearly and on providing support materials to help pupils write their own answers rather than looking at ways to assist pupils with the writing process itself. This is illustrated by the fact that one of the least common activities for children with and without dyslexia was 'working with a partner who writes down my ideas for me'. They also found that 32 per cent of pupils with dyslexia said they did not have time to finish their written work in class.

These examples indicate that making accommodations in the classroom has become an effective remediation technique without necessarily resorting to specialized programmes. In the Coffield *et al.* (2008) study there appears to be some very positive outcomes from asking the students for their views. The majority of students were able to identify some aspects of classroom practice that they found beneficial. These included:

♦ teachers reading out information to the whole class
♦ the provision of cue cards and other support materials
♦ the use of readers and scribes in examinations
♦ the possibility of working with a partner.

Riddick (2006) points out that to sustain the dyslexia-friendly schools movement it is necessary to have strong leadership from school governors, the head teacher and senior management team, supported by local authority services. It is important that dyslexia-friendly policy is fully understood and translated into practice that can be established and maintained.

Environmental Factors

The learning environment is an influential factor in the success or otherwise of all children. This is particularly relevant for children with dyslexia. This implies that social and emotional factors can impact on the outcomes of the learners' experience and have an impact on eventual success or failure. The environment includes the classroom and the school and these factors influence learning and teaching. Much attention has been placed on teaching and how we should teach children with dyslexia. It is important, however, to also consider learning and particularly the child's individual learning styles. Learning styles will be discussed in more detail later in this book but at this point it is important to acknowledge that recognizing different learning styles can have an important influence on the outcome of the learning process for children with dyslexia.

Labeling, Advocacy and Identity

Before we leave this brief overview of research it is important to consider the issue of labeling and the impact this can have on the individual. Often a label can be helpful as it provides an explanation for the person, the teacher and the parents. At the same time it can be counter-productive and promote a sense of helplessness in some students, particularly if there is no constructive support available. Ideally it is helpful if the dyslexic person is given positive messages about being dyslexic. The word 'cure' should never enter the conversation – it is a 'no-go' area because dyslexia is not a disease and we are not looking for a cure. What the dyslexic person needs is support and understanding. Cooper (2009) provides interesting insights into what it is like to be dyslexic, which can be summed up in the comment: 'take away the dyslexia and it would no longer be me'. The implication of this is that dyslexic identity is important and that, for many people, dyslexia is a way of life. Support and empathy are the answer and along with this goes the need to help the dyslexic person develop self-advocacy skills. It is important therefore, despite all the research and the accompanying innovations in practice, to consider individuals with dyslexia – their needs – and to listen to what they have to say. They are the ones who can point practitioners in the right direction.

In summary, this chapter has:

♦ looked at a number of key research areas from neurological, cognitive and educational perspectives
♦ acknowledged that every child and adult with dyslexia will process information in a different way and may tend to utilize right-hemisphere strategies in developing literacy skills
♦ looked at inter-hemispheric transfer of information and the time delay in processing information
♦ discussed visual difficulties in dyslexia and the role of the magnocellular system
♦ acknowledged the role of hereditary factors and the importance of early identification
♦ appreciated the new research relating to the role of the cerebellum in integration of processing activities
♦ considered the importance of developing and using identification and intervention strategies that focus on phonological difficulties, as this is usually the main source of dyslexia
♦ identified the role of new research looking at the impact of glue ear in relation to dyslexia
♦ acknowledged that educational research and work relating to teaching and learning strategies, as well as the learning environment, can make a significant difference
♦ recognized the recent work on developing dyslexia-friendly schools and providing strategies that can be readily accessed by teachers
♦ described the importance of promoting and developing advocacy skills for young people with dyslexia to provide them with an awareness of their challenges and how to deal with them.

3

Identification and Assessment

Dyslexia assessment is a specialized undertaking – but that does not mean that the teacher does not play a key role in the process. The teacher is usually the first person to identify that the child is not performing as he/she should. The teacher can often note discrepancies in the child's performances, particularly between oral and written.

Informal Assessment

Informal assessment involves the use of checklists or headings that the teacher can use with a child. The results of these can lead the teacher to suspect that a child is not performing as he/she should. This type of assessment can often be the first step in a diagnosis of dyslexia.

In many ways an informal assessment can yield more useful, and more detailed, information than formal standardized assessment. A diagnosis of dyslexia often rests on the results of standardized assessment. Yet one can often obtain a lot of information about children, their learning habits and preferences, from informal assessment, and some of this information may not be as easily obtained from formal, standardized assessment.

One of the powerful points in favour of informal assessment is that it can be seen as dynamic. That is, it does not only measure the 'here and now' as formal assessments do, but informal assessments can be used over time and adapted to suit different situations. While formal assessment is static and measures the performance at the time the actual test is conducted, dynamic assessment is flexible and can report and collect information on children's behaviours over time. The flexibility and the adaptability of observation in particular is a significant strength of informal assessment. Moreover, informal assessment is based on the actual learning situation and reports on the pupil's actual learning experiences (see Came and Reid 2007). For resources for an informal test, go to: www.learning-works.org.uk.

Early Screening

Informal assessment can be useful for early identification. It is best to observe at-risk children as early as possible. This increases the chances of success with intervention. In the UK the *No To Failure* project (2008) initially took the form of an empirical study to demonstrate the educational importance of screening for dyslexia and to understand how dyslexia, if ignored, could lead to educational failure. The project also evaluated the impact of specialist teaching on the literacy skills and educational development of pupils found to be at risk of dyslexia.

In the screening phase of the study, a total of 1,341 pupils were screened in Years 3 and 7 in 20 schools across three different local authorities in England. The results showed that, overall, 55 per cent of all pupils who failed to reach expected levels for national Standard Assessment Tests (SATs) were found to be at risk of dyslexia/SpLD. This indicated that unidentified dyslexia can be seen as a major cause of educational failure. The report also suggests that, with appropriate screening and intervention, this failure can be remedied but at present this is largely ignored. This is important information that further highlights the need for all teachers to be made aware of dyslexia and to have some skills in identifying children who may be at risk of dyslexia.

Crombie (2002) suggests that screening should mainly focus on the following areas of learning:

♦ Emotional, personal and social development. Home life and culture are likely to have a strong influence.
♦ Communication and language. Children with poor phonological skills and a lack of awareness of rhyme and rhythm may experience difficulties learning to read and write.
♦ Listening. Difficulty listening to stories may indicate later attention problems.
♦ Memory in language and communication skills. For example, remembering a sequence of events in a story or repeating syllables that make up words.
♦ Speech. Ensuring the child has sufficient control of the tongue and lips to reproduce sounds in the desired way. This can be assessed when the child is telling or retelling a story.
♦ Nonsense words can be repeated as part of a game. Often children who have dyslexia have difficulty repeating nonsense words.
♦ Skills used in some activities, such as categorization, naming, ordering and sequencing, can be problematic for children at risk of dyslexia.
♦ Physical development and movement. Movement can be assessed by the teacher as part of the routine observations made within the

classroom situation. Being able to distinguish left and right is an important factor.
♦ Coordination and balancing skills. This can be done by asking the child to balance on one foot while at the same time reciting a rhyme or carrying out an activity.

Processes and Strategies

The above guidelines make it clear that dyslexia should not *only* be identified through the use of a test. Rather, assessment for dyslexia is a process that involves much more than testing. The assessment needs to consider classroom and curriculum factors and the learning preferences of the child, as well as his or her specific difficulties and strengths. Observational and informal assessment can also be used in this way.

Specifically, assessment should consider three aspects: difficulties, discrepancies and differences, and these should relate to the classroom environment and the curriculum.

> Assessment for dyslexia is a process that involves more than a test.

Difficulties

The main problem for children with dyslexia usually relates to the decoding or the encoding of print. This may be due to difficulties with

♦ acquiring phonological awareness
♦ memory
♦ organization and sequencing
♦ movement and coordination
♦ language problems
♦ visual/auditory perception.

Discrepancies

The discrepancies may be apparent

♦ in comparing decoding skills with reading/listening comprehension
♦ between oral and written skills
♦ in performance within the different subject areas of the curriculum.

Differences

It is also important to acknowledge the differences between individual children with dyslexia. The identification process should therefore also consider

♦ learning styles
♦ environmental preferences for learning
♦ learning strategies.

> Assessment should inform teaching.

Informal assessment can also be used all the way through the school. For example, at the secondary level in history the teacher can note the difficulty a student has in recognizing the importance and relevance of certain pieces of information and ideas. Any difficulty in sorting and arranging historical information can also be noted, as can difficulty distinguishing between general and particular pieces of evidence and judging their relative importance. Students with dyslexia can have difficulty with these aspects.

Diagnostic Assessment

Diagnostic assessment can be a misleading term as you are not necessarily looking for a label, but focusing on the kind of difficulties the child is displaying and what this might mean in practice. You are therefore looking at the implications of the students' difficulties for learning and teaching. One way of doing this is to identify learning and teaching priorities. For example, a number of priorities were identified from the assessment of the student below:

> **Areas of Priority for Darius**
> Spelling in context
> Language concepts
> Reading comprehension
> Writing skills
> Following instructions and directions
> Focusing on text and working independently

These six points were identified as significant difficulties in the assessment for Darius. The task now is to translate this information into suggestions for practice and to become aware of the challenges that Darius faces because of these difficulties. These are shown below in an extract from a report on the assessment.

Spelling in context

Darius will require extended support in spelling. This can be in the form of spelling practice with individual words, or by providing passages with blanks in some words so he has to insert the missing letters.

It is important to introduce 'multiple spelling choices' as this will help him visually remember the spelling that fits into the context. Darius will benefit from practice in spelling and this can be done by using key words and visuals to reinforce spelling rules. Mnemonics and kinesthetic clues can also be used, as Darius does have good visual abilities so he should be able to relate well to visual strategies. Mnemonics and kinesthetic clues will help with retention and recall.

Language concepts

It is important to focus on Darius's language concepts. This is his weakest area. He needs to be questioned and given an opportunity for discussion during and following reading as this will make the text more meaningful and help him to bridge the new learning with his previous learning. This is how concepts develop. There are a number of strategies for developing language concepts, as outlined below.

Using graphs or webs to highlight key points and to group similar items together
Spend time discussing the comprehension of the ideas and concepts in a piece of writing rather than writing a paragraph about the text.

Games and activities such as role-play can reinforce concepts
Drama is good as the active participation can help to develop ideas and concepts. Drama uses the experiential and kinesthetic modality, which can be good for keeping Darius on task.

Encouraging reflection is an effective strategy.
Ask questions that will encourage Darius to think about his previous learning and to link it to what is currently being learned. This encourages transfer of knowledge and can help concept development.

Discussion is crucial for developing concepts
Darius should respond to this quite well. Discussion is an active form of learning and can help keep Darius on task.

Collaboration can be an effective method of developing concepts
It is important that Darius is given a designated role in a group situation as this will also help to keep him focused.

Metacognition means thinking about thinking and this is important for the development of concepts
This puts the emphasis on the learner to reflect on his learning. Darius may have difficulty with this so will need a structure and guidance to do this. He will need to be provided with questions, such as those below.

♦ Questioning – 'Why/what/where/how?'
♦ Clarifying – 'I see, but what about this?'
♦ Understanding – 'Right, I get it now'
♦ Connecting – 'I did something like this last week'
♦ Directing – 'Okay, I know what to do now'
♦ Monitoring – 'Maybe I should do this now – that does not seem to be correct'
♦ Assessing – 'So far so good; I think I am on the right track'

This type of process can keep Darius on track and at the same time help to begin to give him responsibility for his own learning.

Reading comprehension/critical literacy

There are a number of strategies for developing reading comprehension, such as discussion of the text and encouraging self-questioning of the text. Questions like: What is the book about? Who are the main characters? What is the plot and how might it end? These are all crucial questions that can help to develop comprehension in reading. The term critical literacy is now used to refer to higher levels of comprehension, such as the use of inferences and prediction and the author's motives and background and how this can impact on the text. These are all areas that are important for developing concepts and comprehension and also for acquiring motivation and learning skills.

Critical literacy can be placed at the highest stage of the literacy hierarchy. It involves constructing meaning from text and these meanings are achieved during interaction with the text, during discussion of text and when listening and responding to others. Critical literacy requires investigation, questioning and challenging the assumptions of the text. These are areas that Darius is weak in as he does not seem to get involved in the text. Encouraging critical literacy is a way of doing this.

Some questions for critical literacy:

♦ Where did the book take place?
♦ What is the author's background?
♦ Why did the author write this book?
♦ What is the key message of the book?
♦ Is there a hidden message in the book?
♦ Why is the book popular?
♦ Did it serve its purpose?
♦ Did the book change the way you think about anything?
♦ What wasn't said about the topic? Why?

Writing skills

There is a lot of scope for developing Darius's writing skills. He is not using his full understanding and his vocabulary. Some strategies for developing writing skills include: using themes related to Darius's particular interest; working with him to examine the purpose of writing and to suggest aims for the writing piece; trying to encourage him to write in different genres, such as poetry, drama and script-writing.

Another strategy involves getting Darius to list his ten favourite things. Then ask him to number the list from 1 to 10 with number 1 being his absolute favourite. Ask him to draw a cloud in the centre of the page and inside write 'My Favourite Things'. Next ask him to write his top three favourite things coming out of the web and then sketch a small drawing of those three things.

The next step is getting him to expand on each of his favourite things with details and descriptive words; this will be the 'what' and 'why' of his favourite things. He should also continue with visuals, adding little drawings that represent what he is writing. Adding colour will help with the detail and the description when he moves to the paragraph writing stage.

Some other suggestions include:

♦ brainstorming – ideas, themes, topics
♦ using background knowledge
♦ researching – get him to find out about things and make notes
♦ mind map – construct a mind map of the story.

Following instructions and directions

It is important to provide short instructions and to ensure Darius has understood these. He should repeat them before he carries out the activity to ensure he has retained the instructions.

It will also be helpful if he writes down in number form the directions he has been given for work. This will help him to decide what to do first, second and so on. It is important that he refers to this and ticks each item off as he carries it out.

Focusing on text and working independently

Some of the above suggestions can help with independent working. It is important that Darius does not become dependent on adults for directions and instructions. Eventually he needs to be able to:

♦ Self-question – ask himself questions about the text or task
♦ Self-clarify – by thinking about the topic and using previous knowledge he can develop his own clarification and understanding of the topic
♦ Self-monitor – be able to keep on track and realize when he has gone off track
♦ Self-assess – be able to work out if he has done well and why.
♦ This is what we need to try to get Darius to aspire to – this will take time but it should be one of his key learning targets.
♦ The comments above in relation to the assessment of Darius is an example of linking the assessment with teaching. This is one of the key purposes of an assessment.

Miscue Analysis During Oral Reading

The strategy known as miscue analysis is an example of a diagnostic assessment, which also can link to practice. It is based on the 'top-down' approach to reading, which suggests that, when reading, the reader has to make predictions as to the most likely meaning of the text. Such predictions are based on how the reader perceives the graphic, syntactic and semantic information contained in the text.

Miscue analysis is the process that occurs when a teacher listens to a child read, and notes the mistakes or 'miscues'. Miscues can arise from symbolic, syntactic or semantic errors.

Symbolic errors

Symbolic errors occur when the child has misread the actual letter(s), and this can be a result of a visual difficulty.

Syntactic errors

Syntactic errors occur if, for example, the child reads a word as 'of' instead of 'for'. This indicates that the child does not have the grammatical structures of sentences but can make a fairly good stab at the symbolic features of the word – even though it is still wrong.

Semantic errors

Semantic errors are quite common among children with dyslexia, as they indicate that the reader is relying heavily on context. An example of a semantic error would be reading the word 'bus' instead of 'car'.

Miscue analysis can provide impetus to a more diagnostic approach to the assessment of reading. This approach was further emphasized by Marie Clay in the Reading Recovery Programme (Clay 1985), which also uses miscue analysis as one of the fundamental approaches to diagnosing a child's reading level.

One of the important aspects about miscue analysis is that it can help the teacher make deductions about the reader's understanding of the text. For example, if the child read 'the poor horse bolted his food' instead of the 'the scared horse bolted fast', this would indicate that he or she has little real understanding of the text apart from the fact that it concerns a horse. This would most likely indicate a difficulty with the semantics of the text, since the guess does not properly fit the context. The syntactic flow of the sentence appears to be okay, and there is some attempt to represent the symbols. Other types of errors are often noted in miscue analysis and the significance of these are discussed below.

Omissions

These may occur if the child is reading for meaning rather than the actual printed words. He or she may omit small words that do not add anything significant to the meaning of the passage.

Additions

These may reflect superficial reading, with perhaps an over-dependence on context clues.

Substitutions

These can be visual or semantic substitutions, and they may reflect an over-dependence on context clues.

Repetitions

These may indicate poor directional attack, especially if the child repeats the same line. They may also indicate some hesitancy on the part of the child, perhaps because he or she is unable to read the next word in the line.

Reversals

These may reflect the lack of left-to-right orientation. They may also indicate some visual difficulty, and perhaps a lack of reading for meaning.

Hesitations

These can occur when the reader is unsure of the text and perhaps lacking in confidence in reading. For the same reason that repetitions may occur, the reader may also be anticipating a difficult word later in the sentence.

Self-corrections

These occur when the reader becomes more aware of meaning and less dependent on simple word recognition.

It is important to recognize the extent of self-corrections, as this can indicate whether or not the child has an understanding of the passage.

Children with dyslexia can experience most of the miscues noted above, especially as they often read for meaning and therefore additions and substitutions can be quite common.

Assessment should be diagnostic so that the information can support the selection of teaching approaches.

Phonological Assessment

To a great extent, phonological assessment can be carried out by the teacher using adapted materials, or by observation of the child's reading pattern. Phonological assessment covers the following areas:

♦ non-word reading
♦ sound recognition
♦ syllable segmentation
♦ recognition of prefixes, suffixes and syllables
♦ rhyme recognition and production
♦ phoneme segmentation (such as blending, recognition of initial and final phonemes).

There are standardized phonological assessments available and recommended for use in an assessment for dyslexia. One such assessment available in the UK is the *Phonological Assessment Battery (PHAB)*. This consists of five measures:

♦ alliteration test
♦ rhyming test
♦ naming speed test
♦ fluency test
♦ spoonerism test.

This technique is very suitable for assessing dyslexic difficulties. There is good evidence that dyslexic children have difficulty with rhyme and alliteration, and some researchers have indicated that naming speed is in itself a significant feature of dyslexic difficulties (Wolf and O'Brien 2001; Fawcett and Nicolson 2001).

The Phonological Assessment Battery (Frederickson, Frith and Reason 1997) can be accessed by all teachers and is available from www.gl-assessment.co.uk.

In the US, Canada and the UK, the Comprehensive test of Phonological Processing (CTOPP) (Wagner, Torgesen, and Rashotte 1999) is used for this purpose. This test assesses phonological awareness, phonological memory and rapid naming.

Persons with one or more of these phonological processing deficits may have more difficulty learning to read than those who do not, so this can be an important test – particularly for younger children.

Screening/Baseline Assessment

There are some issues that can be raised in relation to screening and baseline assessment:

♦ What is the most desirable age (or ages) for children to be screened?
♦ What skills, abilities and attainments in performances should children be screened for?
♦ How should the results of any screening procedures be used?

It is important that the results of screening and baseline assessments are used diagnostically, and not to label children prematurely. There are some screening tests that have been developed specifically to identify the possibility of dyslexia. These can yield very useful information but should be used in conjunction with other data, obtained from observations made by the teacher of the child's work, and of progress in class and in different areas of the curriculum. Some examples of these are shown in Appendix 2.

Checklists

There are many variations in checklists for identifying dyslexia (which in itself highlights the need to treat them with considerable caution). Checklists are not, in any form, definitive tools for diagnosis of dyslexia, but can be used as a preliminary screening to justify a more detailed assessment. Some checklists (such as those shown below) can provide a range of information that may produce a picture of the child's strengths and weaknesses. Even these, however, are still very limited, and are no substitution for a comprehensive and contextual assessment.

Checklist: Reading

	Comments
Sight vocabulary	
Sound blending	
Use of contextual clues	
Attempting unknown vocabulary	
Eye tracking	

Difficulty keeping place	
Speech development	
Motivation in relation to reading material	
Word naming difficulty	
Omitting words	
Omitting phrases	
Omitting whole lines	

Checklist: Writing

	Comments
Directional difficulty	
Difficulty associating visual symbol with verbal sound	
Liability to sub-vocalize sounds before writing	
Unusual spelling pattern	
Handwriting difficulty	
Difficulty with cursive writing	
Using capitals and lower case interchangeably and inconsistently	
Poor organization of work on page	

This form of assessment can provide some general data on the broad areas of difficulty experienced by the child – for example, the teacher may decide the child has a pronounced difficulty in the use of contextual cues; but this does not provide information as to why this difficulty persists and the kind of difficulties the pupil experiences with contextual cues. Does the child use contextual cues on some occasions, and under certain conditions? The teacher must carry out further investigations to obtain further explanations of the difficulty.

Dyslexia

Checklists/screening can be good starting points but they have limitations.

Discrepancies

An approach to assessment that can be readily carried out by the teacher involves noting discrepancies between different components of reading. This kind of assessment can include:

♦ decoding tests (non-words reading test)
♦ word-reading tests
♦ phonological awareness tests
♦ listening comprehension tests
♦ reading comprehension tests.

The information gleaned from this type of assessment strategy can be used to note any obvious discrepancies between achievements in the different tests. For example, a child with dyslexia may have a low score on a decoding test, particularly one that involves non-words, while scoring considerably higher in the listening comprehension test.

Differences

It is important to obtain information on the differences as well as the difficulties and the discrepancies. The interactive observational style index shown below can provide some pointers on the kind of information that can be useful.

Interactive observational style index (adapted from Given & Reid 1999; Reid 2005a)
Emotional
MOTIVATION
♦ What topics, tasks and activities interest the child?
♦ What topics does the child speak about confidently?
♦ What kinds of prompting and cueing are necessary to increase motivation?
♦ What type of incentives motivate the child – leadership opportunities, working with others, gold star, free time, physical activity, etc.?
♦ Does the child seem to work because of interest in learning or to please others – parents, teachers, friends?

PERSISTENCE
- ♦ Does the child stick with a task until completion without breaks?
- ♦ Are frequent breaks necessary when working on difficult tasks?
- ♦ What is the quality of the child's work with and without breaks?

RESPONSIBILITY
- ♦ To what extent does the child take responsibility for his or her own learning?
- ♦ Does the child attribute his or her successes and failures to self or others?
- ♦ Does the child grasp the relationship between effort expended and results achieved?
- ♦ Does the child conform to classroom routines or consistently respond with non-conformity?

STRUCTURE
- ♦ Are the child's personal effects (desk, clothing, materials) well organized or cluttered?
- ♦ How does the child respond to someone imposing organizational structure on him or her?
- ♦ When provided with specific, detailed guidelines for task completion, does the child faithfully follow them, or work around them?

Social
INTERACTION
- ♦ Is there a noticeable difference between the child's positivity and interactions when working alone, one-to-one, in a small group, or with the whole class?
- ♦ When is the child's best work accomplished – when working alone, with one other child or in a small group?
- ♦ Does the child ask for approval or to have work checked frequently?

COMMUNICATION
- ♦ Is the child's language spontaneous, or does he or she need prompting?
- ♦ Does the child like to tell stories with considerable detail?
- ♦ Does the child give the main events and gloss over details?
- ♦ Does the child listen to others when they talk, or is he or she constantly interrupting?

43

Dyslexia

Cognitive
MODALITY PREFERENCE
♦ What type of instructions does the child most easily understand (written, oral, visual)?
♦ Does the child respond more quickly and easily to questions about stories heard, or read?
♦ Does the child's oral communication include appropriate variations in pitch, intonation and volume?
♦ In his or her spare time, does the child draw, build things, write, play sports or listen to music?
♦ When working on the computer for pleasure, does the child play games, search for information, or practise academic skill development?
♦ Does the child take notes, write a word to recall how it is spelt, or draw maps when giving directions?
♦ Given an array of options and asked to demonstrate his or her knowledge of a topic by drawing, writing, giving an oral report, or demonstrating/acting, what would the child choose?
♦ Under what specific areas of learning (reading, maths, sports, etc.) is tension evident, such as nail-biting, misbehaviour, distressed facial expressions, limited eye contact, etc.?

SEQUENTIAL OR SIMULTANEOUS LEARNING
♦ Does the child begin with step 1 and proceed in an orderly fashion, or have difficulty following sequential information?
♦ Does the child jump from one task to another and back again, or stay focused on one topic?
♦ Is there a logical sequence to the child's explanations, or do his or her thoughts 'bounce around' from one idea to another?
♦ When telling a story, does the child begin at the beginning and give a blow-by-blow sequence of events, or does he or she skip around, share the highlights, or speak mostly in terms of how the movie *felt*?
♦ When asked to write a report, does the child seek detailed directions or want only the topic?
♦ What types of tasks are likely to be tackled with confidence?

IMPULSIVE OR REFLECTIVE
♦ Are the child's responses rapid and spontaneous, or delayed and reflective?
♦ Does the child return to a topic or behaviour long after others have ceased talking about it?

♦ Does the child seem to consider past events before taking action?

Physical
MOBILITY
♦ Does the child move around the class frequently or fidget when seated?
♦ While learning, does the child like to stand or walk?
♦ While working, does the child slump, or sit up?
♦ Does the child jiggle his or her foot a lot?
♦ Does the child become entangled in his or her chair when working quietly?

FOOD INTAKE
♦ When working, does the child snack, chew on a pencil or bite on a finger?
♦ Does the child seek water frequently?
♦ Does the child chew on his or her hair, collar, etc. while working?

TIME OF DAY
♦ At what time of day is the child most alert?
♦ Is there a noticeable difference between morning work as compared to afternoon work?

Environment
SOUND
♦ Under what conditions is the child relaxed but alert when learning – noisy or quiet?
♦ Does the child seek out places to work that are particularly quiet?

LIGHT
♦ Does the child squint in 'normal' lighting?
♦ Is there a tendency for the child to put his or her head down in brightly-lit classrooms?
♦ Does the child like to work in dimly-lit areas, or say that the light is too bright?

Dyslexia

TEMPERATURE
- Does the child leave his or her coat on when others seem warm?
- Does the child appear comfortable in rooms below 68° Fahrenheit?

FURNITURE DESIGN
- When given a choice, does the child sit on the floor, lie down or sit in a straight chair to read?
- When given free time, does the child choose an activity requiring formal posture or informal posture?
- Metacognition
  - Is the child aware of his or her learning style strengths?
  - Does the child analyze the environment in regard to his or her learning with questions such as:
    - Is the light level right for me?
    - Am I able to focus with this level of sound?
    - Is the furniture comfortable for me?
    - Am I comfortable with the temperature?
- Does the child demonstrate internal assessment of self by asking questions, such as:
  - Have I done this before?
  - How did I tackle it?
  - What did I find easy?
  - What was difficult?
  - Why did I find it easy or difficult?
  - What did I learn?
  - What do I have to do to accomplish this task?
  - How should I tackle it?
  - Should I tackle it the same way as before?

PREDICTION
- Does the child make plans and work towards goals, or let things happen as they will?
- Is the child willing to take academic risks, or does he or she play it safe by responding only when called upon?
- Does the child demonstrate enthusiasm about gaining new knowledge and skills, or does he or she hesitate?
- Is there a relationship between the child's 'misbehaviour' and difficult tasks?

FEEDBACK
♦ How does the child respond to different types of feedback: non-verbal (smile), check mark, oral praise, a detailed explanation, pat on the shoulder, comparison of scores with previous scores earned, comparison of scores with classmates' performance, and so forth?
♦ How much external prompting is needed before the child can access previous knowledge?

This type of information can help to inform teaching and can be used before embarking on the developing of differentiated materials. It should be recognized that not all learners with dyslexia will have the same learning behaviours. It therefore follows that the type of intervention and the presentation of materials will differ. For that reason it is important to obtain as much information as possible on the learner's preferences.

The Principles of Assessment

Some general principles can be noted in the carrying out and interpretation of an assessment:

♦ The lack of availability of a test must not prevent a child's dyslexic difficulties from being recognized – many of the characteristics can be quite obvious in the classroom situation.
♦ Teachers must have an understanding of dyslexia so that these characteristics can be recognized.
♦ Appropriate materials and teaching programmes need to be developed that are based on the results of the assessment.
♦ It is important to look at assessment diagnostically whether formal or informal tests are used.
♦ It is important to link assessment with teaching.

To summarize this chapter:

♦ Assessment of dyslexia is a process that involves more than simply using a test.
♦ The assessment process needs to consider the difficulties, the discrepancies and the differences.
♦ Teachers can develop a diagnostic phonological assessment that is contextualized for the classroom.
♦ Assessment of reading, spelling and expressive writing should be diagnostic.

Dyslexia

♦ The differences and the child's preferences in learning styles need to be taken into account.
♦ Assessment must have a clear link to intervention.

4

Teaching Approaches

This chapter will describe some appropriate teaching approaches for use with children with dyslexia. There are many excellent commercial and established teaching programmes available. Many of these utilize similar principles and strategies. These will be discussed in this chapter and some examples of programmes will also be shown to highlight these principles and strategies. The chapter divides teaching approaches into three broad areas: individualized approaches, curriculum approaches and whole-school approaches.

In determining the most appropriate approaches for children with dyslexia, a number of factors must be considered. These include:

- ◆ The context – this includes the provision, the type of school, class size and the training of the staff as well as the age and stage of the learner.
- ◆ The assessment – this provides an indication of the strengths and the difficulties experienced by the learner. This type of profile is important initial information needed to develop an appropriate programme.
- ◆ The curriculum – what are the expectations being placed on the learner? To what extent is the curriculum accessible and differentiated?
- ◆ The learner – what motivates the learner? What do we know about his or her learning style? How can we use this information to develop a programme?

> Programmes and strategies need to be individualized for the child with dyslexia to take into account the learning context and the learner's strengths and weaknesses.

It is interesting to note the comments made in the independent report from Sir Jim Rose to the Secretary of State for Children, Schools and Families June 2009 – 'Identifying and Teaching Children and Young People with Dyslexia and Literacy Difficulties'. The report suggested that there is a well-established evidence-base showing that intervention programmes which systematically prioritize phonological skills for reading and writing are effective for teaching reading to children with dyslexia.

This report recognizes that children with dyslexic difficulties benefit from teaching that adheres to the following principles:

♦ highly structured
♦ systematic
♦ 'little and often'
♦ uses graphic representation
♦ allows time for reinforcement
♦ encourages generalization.

It also suggests that intervention sessions for dyslexia need to have a strong, systematic phonic structure and be sufficiently frequent to secure children's progress and consolidate learning. We will in fact note throughout this chapter that many of the programmes and particularly the individualized ones do consider these factors. It is significant, however, that they have been highlighted in a government report.

Developing Reading Skills

There is a range of views on what constitutes the essential skills for accurate and fluent reading. Some of the important factors include: word attack skills (such as letter recognition, segmentation, blending, phonemic awareness, analogy strategies and grapheme–phoneme correspondence) and word recognition skills (such as recognition of word patterns and the use of visual memory skills). There is also substantial evidence that phonological awareness is crucial to the acquisition of print (Vellutino *et al.* 2004, Mahfoudi and Haynes 2009). Phonological awareness is an umbrella term that includes awareness and manipulation of speech at the word, syllable and phoneme levels. Mahfoudhi and Haynes (2009) quoting the National Reading Panel (2000) in the US argues that explicit, structured phonics instruction – teaching of rules that link speech information with letters and letter patterns – improves word recognition skills and contributes to spelling, decoding fluency and reading comprehension in typically developing children as well as children with dyslexia and related language-learning difficulties (National Reading Panel 2000).

Programmes and Strategies

The various types of programmes and strategies that can be used are outlined below.

Individualized programmes

These programmes are usually:

♦ highly structured
♦ essentially free-standing
♦ one to one
♦ a main element of the overall strategy for teaching children with dyslexia.

Curriculum strategies

These usually:

♦ utilize the same principles as some of the individual programmes
♦ can be used more selectively by the teacher
♦ can be integrated within the normal activities of the curriculum.

Whole-school approaches

These approaches:

♦ recognize that dyslexia is a whole-school concern and not only the responsibility of individual teachers
♦ focus on consultancy, whole-school screening, and monitoring of children's progress.

Early identification is a key aspect of a whole-school approach.

Individualized Programmes

Most individualized programmes incorporate some, or all, of the following principles:

Multisensory

'Multisensory' means utilizing visual, auditory, tactile and kinesthetic modalities. Multisensory methods utilize all available senses simultaneously. This can be summed up in the phrase 'hear it, say it, see it and

51

write it'. These methods have been used for many years and are a key component in the Orton-Gillingham (OG) programme and in most other phonic programmes.

Over-learning

They ensure that *over-learning* is present, as this is necessary to achieve automaticity. Over-learning is deemed necessary for children with dyslexic difficulties. The short- and long-term memory difficulties experienced by dyslexic children mean that considerable reinforcement and repetition is necessary.

Structured

They are highly *structured* and usually phonically based, and are *sequential and cumulative* (see below) – which means that progression can be easily noted.

The structured approaches evident in programmes of work for dyslexic children usually provide a linear progression, thus enabling the learner to complete and master a particular skill in the reading or learning process before advancing to a subsequent skill. This implies that learning occurs in a linear developmental manner.

Sequential

There is usually a progression in a sequential approach. It is necessary for children with dyslexia to master sub-skills before moving to more advanced materials. Hence, a sequential and cumulative approach may not only provide a structure to their learning, but help to make learning more meaningful and effective.

Key components of a teaching programme

The following are some of the key components of a reading programme for children with dyslexia:

♦ bottom-up emphasis on phonics
♦ emphasis on listening skills
♦ opportunities for oral work
♦ recognizes the importance of discussion
♦ phonic skills a key focus
♦ whole-word recognition skills
♦ develops sentence awareness
♦ includes comprehension-building activities

- looks at reading and spelling connections
- develops skills in creative writing
- provides opportunities to develop imagination and creativity
- ensures practice in the use of syntactic and semantic cues
- places emphasis on learning the 44 phonemes of the English language, and a knowledge of the 17 vowel sounds and the 27 consonant sounds
- includes development of pre-reading skills such as visual and auditory perception
- provides opportunities to practise visual and auditory discrimination
- facilitates practice in fine motor skills
- ensures knowledge of spatial relationships
- ensures a knowledge of colour, number and directions
- includes game activities
- develops syllable segmentation
- develops rhyme judgement and rhyme production
- alliteration, onset and rime, and phoneme segmentation.

IDA matrix of programmes

The International Dyslexia Association (IDA) have produced a short matrix of multisensory structured language programmes indicating the type of programme, delivery, the level of phonic instruction, how each programme deals with fluency, comprehension, written expression and text construction, and the level of training needed for the programme. The programmes included in the matrix are OG (www. OrtonAcademy. org), Alphabetic Phonics (www.ALTAread.org), Association Method (www.usm.edu/dubard), Language! (www.SoprisWest.com), Lexia-Herman Method (www.Hermanmethod.com), Lindamood–Bell (www. Lindamoodbell.com), Project Read (www.Projectread.com), Slingerland (www.Slingerland.org), Sonday System (www.sondayreadingcenter. org), Sounds in Syllables, Spalding Method, (www.Spalding.org), Starting Over, Wilson Fundations and Wilson Reading (www.wilson-language.com). (Source: IDA, www.interdys.org)

Materials

Some supplementary materials that can be used in association with teaching reading include:

- wall friezes
- code cards and flashcards
- word books, copymasters and workbooks

♦ cassettes and songbooks
♦ games and software
♦ videos and interactive CDs/DVDs
♦ interactive whiteboards.

Examples of programmes

Orton-Gillingham
Programmes based on this approach have become a central focus for multisensory teaching for children with dyslexia. The programmes offer a structured, sequential, phonic-based approach that incorporates the total language experience and focuses on letter sounds, the blending of these sounds into syllables and words, reading, spelling rules and syllabication. The approach rests heavily on the interaction of visual, auditory and kinesthetic aspects of language. Orton-Gillingham lessons are success-oriented with the goal of the student becoming a self-correcting, independent learner (Green 2006).

Orton-Gillingham lessons, according to Henry (1996, 2003; see also Green 2006), can incorporate spelling and reading and usually include activities such as:

♦ card drills – these involve the use of commercial or teacher-made cards containing the common letter patterns to strengthen the visual modality: phonemes (sounds) for auditory and kinesthetic reinforcement, and syllables and whole words to help develop blending skills
♦ word lists and phrases
♦ spelling of phonograms in isolation, as well as of phonetic and non-phonetic words
♦ handwriting – with attention to pencil grip, writing posture and letter formation. This also includes tracing, copying and practice, and making phonetically correct cursive connections, such as 'br' and 'bl'.
♦ composition – encouragement to write sentences, paragraphs and short stories.

Henry (2003) also maintains that lessons take place as a 'dynamic discussion session with the teacher acting as facilitator as well as instructor'.

The process
1. To begin with, ten letters are taught – two vowels (a, i) and eight consonants (f, l, b, j, h, m, p, t).
2. Each of the letters is introduced with a key word.

3. Once the child has mastered the letter name and sound, the programme then introduces the blending of letters and sounds.

Green (2006) suggests that blending can begin as soon as the child knows two letters that can be blended together.

For example, after learning the short vowel 'a' as in apple, and 'm' as in mitten, the child can blend to read 'am'. The task is to teach children to smoothly blend sounds together and to hear the word. Therefore, it is not acceptable to hear 'a-m'. The child must hold the vowel to the consonant and hear 'am'.

There are two important factors in teaching blending. First, it is important to begin blending with phonograms that can hold their sound continually, such as 'mmmmmmmmmmmmmmm', as opposed to a stop consonant such as 't'. The following sounds are continuous: m, s, n, f, h, l, v, z; their sound can be held. Blending will start with vowel (v)– consonant (c), and then cv grows to cvc, ccvc and ccvcc, until finally reaching polysyllabic words. Second, blending sounds together should only be done with phonetically correct phonograms.

To help a child achieve proficiency with blending it is helpful to have him or her practise with drills before reading actual words. Torpedo drills are easy to prepare and use all the modalities. An example of a torpedo drill is shown below. Note, there are only continuous consonants in the first column, and all sounds should be known to the child. Using a crayon to torpedo phonograms together, the child should be saying the sounds aloud while blending them and then producing the word they have made. The words a child makes from this blending exercise can be nonsense or Martian words.

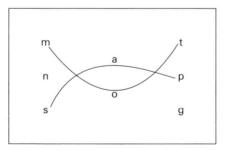

Figure 4.1 Torpedo drill

4. The visual-kinesthetic and auditory-kinesthetic associations are formed by the child tracing, saying, copying and writing each

phonogram. Children are taught phonograms, spelling concepts and rules so they can read and spell unknown words that follow the same spelling pattern.

5. Reading of text begins after the child has mastered the consonant–vowel–consonant words to a higher automatic level, i.e. when he or she can recognize and use these words.

The programme is more suited to one-to-one teaching, but the key principles of over-learning, automaticity and multisensory approaches are very apparent in Orton-Gillingham, and these principles can be utilized within the classroom curriculum.

There is also considerable scope in this programme for building metacognitive skills and developing comprehension-building exercises (Green 2006).

Hickey Multisensory Language Course
The Hickey Multisensory Language Course (Augur and Briggs 1992) recognizes the importance of the need to learn the letters of the alphabet sequentially. The dyslexic child will usually have some difficulty in learning and remembering the names and sequence of the alphabetic letters, as well as understanding that the letters represent speech sounds which make up words.

The process
The programme is based on multisensory principles and the alphabet is introduced using wooden or plastic letters; the child can look at the letter, pick it up, feel it with eyes open or closed and say its sound. Therefore, the visual, auditory and tactile-kinesthetic channels of learning are all being utilized with a common goal.

The programme also suggests some activities to help the child become familiar with the alphabet. These include:

♦ learning the letters sequentially
♦ learning the positioning of each letter of the alphabet
♦ naming and recognizing the shape of the letters.

These programmes involve games and the use of dictionaries to help the child become familiar with the order of the letters and the direction to go: for example, he or she needs to know that 'i' comes before 'k', and the letters in the first half of the alphabet and those letters in the second half. The alphabet can be further divided into sections, which makes it easier for the child to remember the section of the alphabet in which a letter appears, for example:

A B C D
E F G H I J K L M
N O P Q R
S T U V W X Y Z

The Hickey Multisensory Language Course includes activities related to sorting and matching the capital, lower-case, printed and written forms of the letters; practising sequencing skills with cut-out letters and shapes; and practising positioning of each letter in the alphabet in relation to the other letters (this involves finding missing letters and going backwards and forwards in the alphabet).

The course also indicates the importance of recognizing where the accent falls in a word, since this clearly affects the spelling and rhythm. Rhyming games can be developed to encourage the use of accents by placing the accent on different letters of the alphabet. This helps to train children's hearing to recognize when a letter has an accent or is stressed in a word.

The course includes reading and spelling packs that focus on securing a relationship between sounds and symbols. This process begins with single letters, and progresses to consonant blends, vowel continuations and then to complex letter groupings.

The reading packs consist of a set of cards; on one side the lower-case letter is displayed in bold, with the upper-case (capital) letter shown on the bottom right-hand corner, in order to establish the link between the two letters. The reverse side of the card indicates a key word, which contains the sound of the letter, with the actual sound combination in brackets. Rather than providing a visual image of the key word, a space is left for the child to draw the image. This helps to make the image more meaningful to the child and also utilizes and reinforces visual and kinesthetic skills.

The spelling pack is similar in structure to the reading pack. On the front of the card the sound made by the letter is displayed in brackets, while the back contains both the sound and the actual letter(s). Sounds for which there is a choice of spellings will in time show all the possible ways in which the sound can be made. Cue words are also given on the back as a prompt, in case the child forgets one of the choices.

Spelling is seen as being of prime importance by the authors of the programme, since they view it as an 'all-round perceptual experience'. The multisensory method involves the following process. The child

♦ repeats the sound heard
♦ feels the shape the sound makes in the mouth
♦ makes the sound and listens
♦ writes the letter(s).

Dyslexia

This process involves over-learning and multisensory strategies.

Alphabetic Phonics

The key principles found in the majority of individualized programmes for dyslexic children – multisensory techniques, automaticity and over-learning – are all found in the Alphabetic Phonics programme. Additionally, the programme also recognizes the importance of discovery learning, with opportunities for this throughout the highly structured programme.

The programme, which stems from the Orton-Gillingham multisensory approach, was developed in Dallas, Texas, by Aylett Cox. She has described Alphabetic Phonics as a structured system of teaching students the coding patterns of the English language (Cox 1985).

Cox asserts that such a phonic-based programme is necessary because around 85 per cent of the 30,000 most commonly used English words can be considered phonetically regular and therefore predictable. Thus learning phonetic rules can allow the child access to the majority of the commonly used words.

The process

Alphabetic Phonics provides training in the development of automaticity through the use of flashcards, and over-learning through repetitive practice in reading and spelling until 95 per cent mastery is achieved.

1. An alphabetic activity, which emphasizes sequence and directionality.
2. Introduction of a new element or concept, which begins with discovery and is reinforced with multisensory techniques.
3. Training in automatic recognition of letter names, through flashcard presentation (Reading Decks).
4. Training in recognition of letter sounds, by having students pronounce the sounds for a letter or letters presented on flashcards (Spelling Decks) and then naming and writing the letter or letters.
5. Practice in reading and spelling (10 minutes allotted for each). Each task is continued until student reaches 95 per cent mastery, as measured by the Bench Mark measures.
6. Handwriting practice.
7. Practice in verbal expression, first oral and later written, focusing on various skills (e.g. sequencing ideas, creative expression, vocabulary, syntax).
8. Listening to good literature and building comprehension skills, while reading instruction focuses on decoding skills.

The programme also incorporates opportunities to develop creativity in expression and in the sequencing of ideas.

The programme is highly structured, with daily lessons of around one hour. Lessons incorporate a variety of tasks, which helps to keep the child's attention directed to the activities and prevents boredom.

In this programme, reading comprehension instruction does not begin until the student has reached a minimal level of accuracy in relation to decoding skills. Cox, however, does recognize that children will learn and retain new vocabulary more effectively and efficiently through experiential learning, and that this is particularly applicable to dyslexic children.

The principles and practices of this programme, such as structure, multisensory technique, emphasis on automaticity, emphasis on building comprehension skills, experiential learning and listening skills, and in particular recognition of letter sounds, can have desirable outcomes. These can readily be adapted and implemented into teaching programmes devised for different needs and contexts.

Synthetic Phonics
A number of studies (Johnston *et al.* 1995) have indicated the merits of synthetic phonics. The Rose Review into the teaching of reading in the UK (DfES 2005) also indicated the merits of this approach. The report discusses the differences between synthetic phonics and analytic phonics.

The process
Synthetic phonics refers to an approach to the teaching of reading in which the phonemes (sounds) associated with particular graphemes (letters) are pronounced in isolation and blended together (synthesized). For example, children are taught to take a single-syllable word, such as 'cat' apart into its three letters, pronounce a phoneme for each letter in turn – /k, æ, t/ – and blend the phonemes together to form a word. Synthetic phonics for writing reverses the sequence: children are taught to say the word they wish to write, segment it into its phonemes and say them in turn, for example /d, g/, and write a grapheme for each phoneme in turn to produce the written word 'dog'.

Analytic phonics on the other hand refers to an approach to the teaching of reading in which the phonemes associated with particular graphemes are not pronounced in isolation. Children identify (analyze) the common phoneme in a set of words in which each word contains the phoneme under study. For example, teacher and pupils discuss how the following words are alike: 'pat', 'park', 'push' and 'pen'.

Studies suggest that the synthetic phonics programme is an effective method of teaching reading. Many of the approaches suggested for teaching reading to children with dyslexia utilize a synthetic phonics approach. One such programme is discussed below.

THRASS

THRASS is an acronym for Teaching Handwriting Reading And Spelling Skills. It is a whole-school phonics programme for teaching learners, of any age, about the building blocks of reading and spelling: that is, the 44 phonemes (speech sounds) of spoken English and the graphemes (spelling choices) of written English.

The process

The programme teaches learners that, basically, when spelling we change phonemes to graphemes, and when reading we change graphemes to phonemes.

The programme is very comprehensive and has an excellent user-friendly website (www.thrass.com) with free downloads. The components include speaking and listening skills, phonemes and key graphemes and letter names, and it is suitable for all ages.

The THRASS pack consists of four resources for teaching essential speaking, listening, reading and spelling skills. The THRASS Picture Book, THRASS Picture Cards, THRASS Workbook and THRASS Spelling Tiles can be used in classes by teachers and assistants. The resources can also be used by parents, at home, to support the introduction, revision and assessment of the THRASS keywords and basewords.

If when using the Workbook and Spelling Tiles additional help is required in identifying the phonemes (speech sounds) of English, then the first section of the THRASS Phoneme Machine, the 'Phoneme Grid', can be used. It is downloadable, without charge, from the THRASS website. This is an excellent resource that enables the user to produce the sounds of each phoneme simply by clicking on the lips of the symbol.

The Slingerland Programme

The Slingerland Programme is an adaptation of the Orton-Gillingham Programme. Essentially, the programme was developed as a screening approach to help minimize the difficulties experienced by children in language and literacy. The Slingerland Screening Tests accompany the programme and are usually administered in the early stages of education.

The programme shares similar features with other programmes. Multisensory teaching permeates the programme, which begins by introducing letters of the alphabet.

The process
WRITING
This is the first step and usually uses the following order:

♦ tracing
♦ copying
♦ writing in the air
♦ simultaneously writing from memory and saying the letter.

LETTER SOUNDS
This involves naming the letter, then the key word associated with the letter, and then the letter sound.

BLENDING
This is introduced with oral activities and may involve repetitive use, and blends with kinesthetic support to reinforce the material being learnt.

DECODING
In decoding, students begin with three letters c–v–c, for example words such as 'bay' and 'way'. They are required to:

♦ pronounce the initial consonant
♦ then pronounce the vowel
♦ then blend the two
♦ then pronounce the final consonant
♦ and lastly say the whole word.

Vowel digraphs and vc digraphs are taught as units, although Slingerland maintains that consonant blends are usually learnt more easily.

Sound Linkage
Sound Linkage (Hatcher 1994, 2004) is an integrated phonological programme for overcoming reading difficulties. In addition to a section on assessment it contains ten sections on teaching, each dealing with a specific aspect of phonological processing. For example, Section 3 deals with phoneme blending, Section 5 deals with identification and discrimination of phonemes, and some other sections deal with phoneme segmentation, deletion, substitution and phoneme transposition.

The process
Although Sound Linkage can be used as an individually structured programme, each section contains a series of activities that can be used to support mainstream curriculum work with dyslexic children.

Dyslexia

The activities are clearly presented and no complex instructions are necessary. Many of the activities are, however, not new, and many teachers will be aware of the importance of them. To have all these activities in a methodical package, linked to assessment, with a clear overall rationale is an appealing feature, and provides a good example of a programme that can be used within the curriculum.

Reading Recovery

Reading Recovery is an early reading and writing intervention programme, developed by Marie Clay, which focuses on children who after one year at school have lagged significantly behind their peers in reading and writing (Clay 1985). Clay originally introduced the programme in New Zealand, but it has now been shown that the programme can be successfully transferred to other countries and contexts.

The programme aims to boost the reading attainments of the selected children over a relatively short period (around 12 to 20 weeks), with specially trained teachers carrying out the programme, seeing children on an individual basis for 30 minutes every day.

The process

The programme centres around the individual child's strengths and weaknesses as assessed by the actual reading programme. It is not, therefore, structured around a set of principles and practices to which the child has to be accommodated, but rather the programme adapts itself to the child's specific requirements and needs. It utilizes both bottom-up and top-down reading approaches and therefore encourages the use of decoding strategies through the use of phonics, and awareness of meaning through an awareness of the context and language of the text.

The programme aims to produce 'independent readers whose reading improves whenever they read' (Clay 1985). There is an emphasis, therefore, on strategies that the reader can apply to other texts and situations, and there is evidence that gains made in the Reading Recovery programme are maintained over time.

For some children the Reading Recovery programme may need to be supplemented by additional sessions, which could include:

♦ re-reading familiar books
♦ taking a running record (see 'Identification' opposite)
♦ reinforcing letter identification
♦ writing a story, thus learning sounds in words
♦ comprehension of story
♦ introducing a new book.

It is also important that the child is helped to develop a self-improving system. This encourages the child to:

♦ be aware of his or her own learning
♦ take control and responsibility for this learning.

The goal of teaching reading is to assist the child to produce effective strategies for working on text, and according to Clay this can be done through focusing on the practices of self-correcting and self-monitoring.

The process
The main components of the programme include:

♦ learning about direction
♦ locating and focusing on aspects of print
♦ spatial layout of books
♦ writing stories
♦ learning sounds in words
♦ comprehension and cut-up stories
♦ reading books
♦ using print as a cue
♦ sound and letter sequence
♦ word analysis
♦ fluency.

A typical Reading Recovery lesson would include an analysis of the child's decoding strategies, the encouragement of fluent reading through the provision of opportunities to link sounds and letters, the reading of familiar texts, and the introduction of new books.

Identification
Since the programme provides intensive input to those children lagging in reading, it is vitally important that the identification procedures are sound in order to ensure that the children who receive the benefits of the programme are those who would not otherwise make satisfactory progress.

The lowest-achieving children in a class group, after a year at school, are admitted into the programme at around six years of age. Clay believes that by the end of the first year at primary school it is possible to identify children who are failing. She suggests that this can be achieved through systematic observation of children's learning behaviour, together with a diagnostic survey.

The systematic observation takes the form of noting precisely what children are saying and doing in relation to reading, so the focus is on reading tasks rather than specific sub-skills, such as visual perception or auditory dissemination. In order to identify the child's reading behaviour Clay has developed a diagnostic survey, which involves taking a 'running record' of the child's reading ability. This type of analysis can provide clues as to the child's strengths and weaknesses in this area.

The diagnostic survey includes directional movement (which looks at general directional concepts, including motor coordination, impulsivity and hesitancy), error behaviour (focusing on oral language skills, speed of responding and the use of semantic and syntactic context), the use of visual and memory cues, the rate of self-correction, and the child's preferred mode of identifying letters (alphabetic, sound or cueing from words). The survey also includes details of the child's writing skills. This is particularly important since it may provide some indication of any reading problems as well as language level and message quality.

> It may be necessary to use a combination of approaches: no single approach will be successful for all children with dyslexia. It is important to obtain a comprehensive assessment in order to help in the selection of approaches.

Curriculum Approaches

In addition to the impressive number of individualized programmes available for children with dyslexia, there is also an abundance of support materials that can be utilized by teachers to complement teaching programmes within the curriculum. Conceptually, most of the individualized programmes have much in common, emphasizing areas such as structure, multisensory aspects, over-learning and automaticity. Curriculum approaches do not necessarily provide an individual one-to-one programme, but can be used by the teacher to help the child develop competencies to facilitate access to the full range of curriculum activities.

Some of these curriculum approaches are discussed below.

Phonological Approaches

There is strong evidence to suggest that phonological factors are of considerable importance in reading (Stanovich 1991; Snowling 2000, 2005). Children with decoding difficulties are considerably restricted in reading because they are unable to generalize from one word to another. This means that every word they read is unique, indicating that there is a difficulty in learning and applying phonological rules in reading. This emphasizes the importance of teaching sounds (phonemes) and ensuring that the child has an awareness of the sound/letter correspondence. Learning words by sight can enable some children to reach a certain standard in reading, but prevents them from adequately tackling new words and extending their vocabulary.

> Children with dyslexia need a phonic programme to give them the basic foundations of literacy.

If children have a phonological awareness difficulty they are more likely to guess the word from the first letter cue and not the first *sound*; that is, the word 'kite' will be tackled from the starting point of the letter 'k' and not the sound 'ki', so the dyslexic reader may well read something like 'kept'. It is important, therefore, that beginning readers receive some structured training in the grapheme/phoneme correspondence; this is particularly necessary for dyslexic children who would not automatically, or readily, appreciate the importance of phonic rules in reading.

Creativity and the 'gifted' dyslexic student

One of the pitfalls about teaching a structured reading programme to dyslexic children is that the programme can often be so structured that it stifles creativity and indeed comprehension. It is important that teachers are aware of this and establish teaching procedures that can accommodate the 'gifted' dyslexic to ensure that a preoccupation with decoding does not result in a lack of development of thinking and comprehension skills.

Silverman (personal correspondence 2005) suggested, following a presentation on developing learning skills with dyslexia children given by the author (Reid 2005a), that these approaches are very similar to those she recommends for gifted children. Silverman has produced a number of books on visual/spatial processing and creativity for learners who have a different way of learning. It is important that these types of approaches and the different way of learning that underlies them are accepted by all. Further, Silverman's approach also accommodates the needs of the whole child, looking at the importance of positive relationships with peers, coping with their differences and making appropriate career choices. Silverman's websites are www.gifteddevelopment.com and www.visualspatial.org.

The area of giftedness focusing on the learning needs of children

65

with dyslexia is very much the focus of the work of Yoshimoto (2005), who has developed programmes and strategies for the gifted dyslexic following the Orton-Gillingham programme. This ensures that crucial thinking and learning skills are developed alongside the basic decoding skills needed by all dyslexic children, and essential for reading fluency. Yoshimoto suggests that gifted dyslexic learners can have:

◆ expansive vocabulary
◆ superior listening skills
◆ excellent general knowledge
◆ good abstract reasoning skills
◆ unusual capacity for processing information
◆ good problem-solving skills
◆ the skills to be creative, original thinkers
◆ artistic or musical talents.

At the same time, Yoshimoto claims that they also have a:

◆ low self-concept
◆ propensity to use humour to divert attention away from perceived failure
◆ low frustration tolerance
◆ tendency to react poorly to criticism
◆ increased likelihood of refusing to perform tasks in order to avoid failure.

An example of a model for gifted dyslexic students is shown below.

> It is important to extend the thinking skills of learners with dyslexia. This should not be restricted on account of their reading difficulties.

Counselling Approaches

Hales (2001) suggests that considerable scope exists for personal counselling of the dyslexic individual. This would allow people with dyslexia the opportunity to talk through their fears, and some attempts could be made to help to match 'self-image' with reality, since dyslexic children often have a self-image that presents a distorted and unrealistic picture of themselves. Hales points out that while there is no specific personality disorder that affects dyslexic children independently of other factors, there is still a strong case for closely considering the

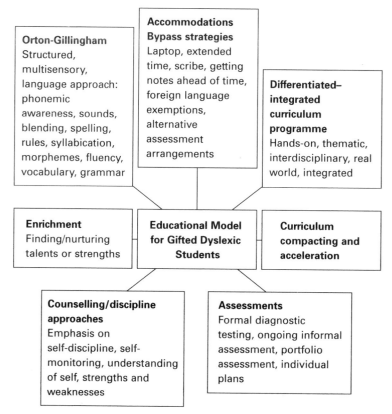

Figure 4.2 A model for gifted dyslexic children
From Yoshimoto (2005)

individual and personal aspects of children and adults with dyslexia. Indeed, he argues that it may be important to consider counselling and social support of the 'dyslexic person' before dealing with the 'dyslexic difficulty'.

Effective provision for dyslexic employees can also reduce potential stress in the workplace, and help a large number of competent and experienced individuals to work up to their full potential.

Some strategies to help facilitate the emotional development of the young person with dyslexia include:

♦ ensuring that the child's difficulties are accurately described in order to remove doubts, anxieties or prejudices

Dyslexia

♦ ensuring agreement between the significant adults in the child's life, such as parents and teachers
♦ ensuring the child has a voice, is understood and has a trusting relationship with those adults.

The case for an approach to the teaching of reading that incorporates counselling is very strong. Counselling can perform a dual role: it can be utilized to help with interaction with dyslexic children, in order to foster skills in learning, and can also be seen as integral to the implementation of a teaching programme and conducted simultaneously with teaching.

There are some excellent self-esteem programmes available that can be successfully utilized for dyslexic children. These include the Mosley (1996) 'circle time' activities.

> Self-esteem can be the most crucial predictor of success in reading.

The use of visualization

Bell (1991b, 2005) suggests that one has to be wary of the 'cognitive cost' of some analytic phonic programmes – a cost that is reflected in a weakening of the gestalt (right) hemispheric skills. The gestalt hemisphere is usually associated with visual imagery, creativity and comprehension.

The stress and effort that is necessary for children with dyslexia to fully engage their cognitive resources and to develop phonological skills is so great, according to Bell, that a weakening of the gestalt hemisphere results as resources are diverted from the right-hemispheric functions to concentrate on the left-hemispheric skills of decoding and phonological processing. This results not only in a restriction in the use of visual imagery, but also in a stifling of the development of skills in comprehension, and perhaps in creativity.

Bell's well-known programme 'Visualizing and Verbalizing for Language Comprehension and Thinking' deals with this aspect. This programme provides a comprehensive procedure for the use of visualizing to promote and enhance reading and comprehension. The stages outlined by Bell include picture imagery, word imagery, single sentence, multiple sentence, whole paragraph and whole page. Additionally, the programme provides an understanding of the functions of the gestalt hemisphere and useful strategies for classroom teaching.

Paired Reading

Paired Reading is a well-established and successful method that can be utilized by learners with dyslexia and their parents or carers. There are a number of reasons why paired reading is successful, such as the fact that failure is not a factor, because if the child 'sticks' at a word, the adult says the word almost immediately. Children are provided with an example of how to pronounce difficult words and can simultaneously relate the auditory sound of the word to the visual appearance of that word. Children can then derive understanding from the text because words are given expression and meaning by the adult, and discussion about the text follows at periodic intervals.

The experience of gaining enjoyment from the language of the text also helps reading become pleasurable and increases the desire to read.

Paired Reading can be useful as:

♦ a strategy to develop motivation and confidence in reading
♦ an aid to the development of fluency and expression in reading
♦ a technique that can also enhance comprehension on the part of the reader.

The process

Paired Reading involves the adult (tutor) and the child (tutee) reading aloud at the same time. It is, however, a specific structured technique. Both adult and child read all the words out together, with the tutor modulating his or her speed to match that of the child, while giving a good model of competent reading. The child must read every word, and when the child says a word incorrectly, the tutor just tells the child the correct way to say the word. The child then repeats the word correctly, and the pair carry on. Saying 'no' and giving phonic and other prompts is forbidden. However, tutors do not jump in and correct the child straight away. The rule is that the tutors pause and give the children four or five seconds to see if they will put it right by themselves (see Figure 4.3).

It is intended only for use with individually chosen, highly motivating non-fiction or fiction books, which are *above* the independent reading level of the tutee. Topping suggests, however, that the name has been a problem: the phrase 'Paired Reading' has such a warm, comfortable feel to it that some people have loosely applied it to almost anything that two people do together with a book. One of the important aspects of Paired Reading, and indeed any reading activities, is praise: the adult should look pleased when the child succeeds using this technique.

Figure 4.3 Paired Reading

Whole-School Practice and Policy

What is meant by whole-school policies? Clearly they embrace an acceptance to meet the needs of all children in the school. Further, the term indicates an acceptance that the responsibility for certain pupils does not reside exclusively with trained specialists, but rather with all staff under the direction of a school management team.

The implications of this are twofold. First, identification and assessment procedures need to be established and monitored to ensure that children who may present with specific learning difficulties, even in a mild form, are identified at an early stage.

Second, the school needs to be resourced in terms of teaching materials and training of staff to ensure that the educational needs of children with all specific learning difficulties are effectively met.

As these children progress through the school it is important that each new teacher they meet has at least some training and understanding of specific learning difficulties/dyslexia. Additionally, the school will need to possess a teacher with a high degree of specialist training to complement the class teacher input and to provide consultancy and training to staff and management.

A thinking skills programme is an example of a type of programme that can be undertaken from a whole-school perspective, irrespective of a child's particular skills or abilities. Many of these programmes involve children in decision-making and problem-solving activities without having to read long instructions. This ensures that the dyslexic child can participate virtually on the same terms as other children in the class.

There are many examples of thinking skills programmes – one of the most well known is CORT, developed by Edward De Bono. De Bono's views are expressed in his book *Six Thinking Hats* (De Bono 1986), which aims to allow students to, for example, separate emotion from logic and creativity from information. Essentially De Bono defines and describes the nature and contribution of different types of thinking. Different-coloured hats are used to describe these different types of thinking. For example, white hat thinking relates to facts and figures. The red hat to emotions and feelings; the black hat relates to negative assessment; the yellow hat to speculative and positive thinking; the green hat to creative and lateral thinking and the blue hat to focused and controlling thinking.

Paired Thinking

Thinking skills should be embedded into the teaching of reading because reading is a vehicle that can achieve deep processing. The method called 'Paired Thinking' is essentially a framework for pairs working together. Some difference in reading ability is needed in each pair. The pairs can be peers of the same or different ages, parents working with children at home, teaching assistants working with children in school, or volunteer adults working with children in school.

Paired Thinking is very active, interactive, socially inclusive and flexible. It integrates thinking skills with reading skills, particularly upon the specific structured method of 'Paired Reading' and promotes paired reading into higher-order reading skills and beyond. Thinking skills can have a spin-off effect for reading skills and particularly higher-order reading skills.

Guidance for Teachers

Some suggestions that can complement the approaches discussed in this chapter are shown below.

Small steps

It is important, especially since children with dyslexia may have short-term memory difficulties, to present tasks in small steps. In fact, one task at a time is probably sufficient. If multiple tasks are specified then a checklist might be a useful way for the child to note and self-monitor his/her progress.

Group work

It is important to plan for group work. The dynamics of the group are crucial, and dyslexic children need to be in a group where at least one person in the group is able to impose some form of structure to the group tasks. This can act as a modelling experience for dyslexic children – it is also important that those in the group do not overpower the dyslexic child – so someone with the ability to facilitate the dyslexic child's contribution to the group is also important. This would make the dyslexic child feel they are contributing to the group. Even though they may not have the reading ability of the others in the group, they will almost certainly have the comprehension ability, so will be able to contribute if provided with opportunities.

Use of coloured paper

There is some evidence that different colours of background and font can enhance some children's reading and attention

Layout

The page layout is very important and this should be visual but not overcrowded. Coloured background is also usually preferable. Font size can also be a key factor and this should not be too small. In relation to the actual font itself it has been suggested that Sasoon, Comic Sans and Times New Roman are the most dyslexia-friendly fonts.

Allow additional time

Some dyslexic children will require a substantial amount of additional time, particularly for tasks like copying from the board and writing exercises.

Checklist

Produce a checklist to ensure instructions have been understood, including such questions as: What is actually being said/asked? What is required of me? How will I know if I am right?

Allow sufficient time

Often dyslexic children do not get the answer right because they have not fully understood the task. Take time to ensure the task is fully understood before allowing the child to work independently.

Headings

Put different types of information under different headings. This can help with long-term memory and the organization of information.

Key words

Provide key words. This is crucial as dyslexic children often have difficulty in identifying key words. They may go for the irrelevant aspects of a passage or provide too much information because they have this difficulty in identifying the key points.

Multisensory techniques

Use multisensory techniques – visual, auditory, kinesthetic and tactile. This is important as it ensures that at least some of the activities will be tapping into the child's strong modality.

Mnemonics

Use mnemonics to boost memory. This can be fun as well as an effective means of learning. It is best to personalize the mnemonic, so encourage the child to develop his/her own mnemonic.

ICT

Use of ICT will help with processing speed and learner independence. There are a vast number of excellent ICT programmes that can boost all aspects of learning (see Appendix). Computer programmes can also help with learner autonomy.

Group dynamics

Make sure group dynamics are right and constructive for the dyslexic student. This is important as group work can be very rewarding but only if the dyslexic child is in a constructive group. Try to ensure the group does not have too many children who do a lot of talking – groups need listeners too.

Enquiry approaches

Use enquiry approaches to promote thinking skills. Problem-solving activities can be useful as there is often not too much reading required before the problem can be tackled. Similarly with fact-finding tasks – these can also be motivating but ensure there is clear guidance on how to find the information. A child with dyslexia can waste a lot of time looking for information on the internet or in the library and may gather irrelevant information. It is important therefore to provide a clear structure for this.

Record their voices

Use tape recorders to allow them to record their thoughts. This can be good for helping with metacognition (being aware of how one learns). By recording their thoughts on a tape it promotes self-awareness. They need to be aware of how they are actually tackling a task in order to record their thoughts and this process helps with metacognitive awareness.

Self-esteem

Look for ways of boosting the learner's *self-esteem*. It is important that children's self-esteem is continually being boosted as it will encourage them to take risks with learning where otherwise they may have given up. It is crucial therefore that tasks are designed to ensure the child will experience some success. It is through success that self-esteem is boosted and success comes if the presented task is achievable. That is why it is so important that the planning of tasks is given a high priority.

Develop questioning ability

It is important if the child understands the task if they know the right kind of questions to ask. This can be quite difficult and it is important that this is practiced through pre-task discussion.

Printed material

Highlight photocopied text and use a dyslexia-friendly typeface. There are a number of different typefaces that can be seen as dyslexia-friendly. Comic Sans is one such font, but it may not be best for all dyslexic children so it is best to try a few different fonts and let the child decide what is the best.

Concise instructions

Ensure instructions are short and clear. It is best to provide a series of short tasks rather than one long one. This also makes it easier for the child to monitor their own progress.

Games

Use games to consolidate vocabulary – game activities can be excellent for motivating students with dyslexia. Crossbow Education has an excellent range of games (www.crossboweducation.com). These include digital phonics, spingoes phonics activities, magic e spin it, knockout, and vowel digraph triplets.

Develop creativity

Try to develop creativity and problem-solving skills. This is vitally important and is an area that is often overlooked when teaching dyslexic children, because there is inclined to be a preoccupation with teaching literacy skills. It is crucial that the higher-order thinking skills are not overlooked and these need to be given a high priority.

Subject glossary

It is a good idea to incorporate a subject glossary into your dyslexia-friendly approaches. This can consist of challenging words or concepts in different subjects and you can encourage students to develop their own glossary of terms and this can be added to from time to time and also illustrated to make it easier for them to understand and retain.

In this chapter we have addressed the following:

♦ There is a vast range of different types of teaching approaches that can be used with dyslexic children.
♦ It is fair to say that no one single approach holds the key to completely dealing with dyslexic difficulties.
♦ Many of the programmes and strategies described in this chapter can be used together and can be complementary to other teaching and curriculum approaches.
♦ Irrespective of the type of provision used for dyslexic children, it is important that at all times every opportunity is taken to help them access the full curriculum. This can present real

difficulties for some dyslexic children, but the challenge can be met through careful planning, utilizing the skills of teachers and being aware of the abundance of approaches and strategies available.

♦ It is important to recognize the abilities and the creativity of children with dyslexia. It can be too easy to restrict their creative process and progress through a preoccupation with improving attainments in literacy.

♦ It is also important to consider the teaching and development of spelling and writing in addition to reading.

5

Spelling

Many of the skills needed for accurate and consistent spelling can be difficult to acquire for dyslexic children. It is not unusual for children with dyslexia to be more advanced in reading than in spelling. Spelling can require an understanding of the context, the need to be familiar with phonological representations and the correspondence between phoneme and grapheme, it can place demands on the memory and because it is a written activity it can also place demands on mental operations involved in the kinesthetic processing.

Snowling (1994) highlighted the nature of dyslexic children's spelling errors and showed that there was a significant difference in the nature of the spelling errors in dyslexic children compared with a control group. The dyslexic children showed more 'phonetically unacceptable' errors than the control group. That is, the errors of the dyslexic group may have made the words in question unrecognizable because of a lack of phonetic similarity. This implies that the group of dyslexic children did not have developed phonological representation, but were using letter-naming strategies to spell phonologically regular words. Liberman and Shankweiler (1985) have also shown that a clear difference exists in the performance of phonological tasks between good and poor spellers. This implies that successful spelling is related to children's awareness of the underlying phonological structure of words. This is supported by Rohl and Tunmer (1988), who found that good spellers were better at phonemic segmentation tasks than older children matched for spelling age.

Further, Bradley and Bryant (1991) showed that measures of rhyme judgement and letter knowledge in pre-school children were good predictors of subsequent performance in spelling. Thus, children who can recognize words that sound and look alike tend to have a good memory for spelling patterns. Indeed, Bradley and Huxford (1994) show that sound categorization in particular plays an important role in developing memory patterns for spelling. Bradley (1989, 1990) has shown that rhyming is a particularly useful form of categorization for developing spelling skills, and that practice in sound categorization through nursery rhymes and rhyming word games in early language play helps spelling. This can be noted in the simultaneous oral spelling technique developed by Bradley (see below).

Many children have problems remembering 'chunks', such as 'igh' in 'sight' and 'fight'. If children cannot do this, then every word will be unique. Phonological aspects are important in the development of reading and spelling skills. This seems to have considerable importance, particularly for dyslexic children, who do not automatically relate the sounds to the visual images of print. Exercises in phonological awareness are therefore of great importance, not just to assist with reading but also to help with spelling, by allowing children to learn and understand sound patterns and to recognize how these are transposed into print.

Spelling Skills

Chall and Popp (1996) suggest that children who are good in phonics are usually good in spelling, and those who are good in phonics and spelling are usually good in word recognition, oral reading accuracy and silent reading comprehension.

Achievement in spelling and phonics is therefore closely associated, particularly in the early years. This underlines why spelling is important in the acquisition of literacy.

Blending spoken words into sounds is also associated with spelling. This emphasizes the need for children to experiment with writing at an early stage as this provides practice in sounding out words as they write them and blending the sounds into words before moving on to making representations of the phonic structures in writing the beginning of words. This can be done visually as well as auditorily and underlines the importance of multisensory principles, particularly in the early stages. All the skills in this initial stage of learning to spell – which all involve some competence in the early acquisition of phonological skills – are challenging for dyslexic children.

In order to spell correctly, children also need to recognize the individual sounds and regular word patterns, which would involve knowledge of consonant and vowel digraphs and consonant blends. Children with dyslexia can find this challenging because of the difficulty with the sound–symbol correspondence. Additionally, however, they find irregular words particularly challenging as these often have to be learnt visually and may not conform to the rules they are learning for conventional spellings.

Bradley and Bryant (1991), Snowling (2000), and Joshi and Carreker (2009) explain that measures of rhyme judgement and letter knowledge

in pre-school children are a good predictor of subsequent performance in spelling. This means that children who can recognize words
that sound and look alike tend to have a good memory for spelling
patterns.

Spelling Strategies

Simultaneous oral spelling (Bradley 1990)

1. Read the correctly written word.
2. Say the word.
3. Write the word, using cursive script, spelling out each letter as it
   is written.
4. Check to see if the word is correct.
5. Cover up the word and repeat the process.
6. The child needs to:
   - see each letter
   - hear its name
   - receive kinesthetic feedback through the movement of the
     arm and throat muscles.
7. Continue to practise the word in this way, three times a day, for
   one week. By this time the word should be committed to memory.
   However, only one word will have been learnt.
8. Group the word with other words that sound and look alike. So if
   the word that has been learned is 'round', the child is then shown
   that he or she can also spell 'ground', 'pound', 'found', 'mound',
   'sound', 'around', 'bound', grounded', 'pounding', etc. Therefore,
   he or she has learned six, eight or more words for the effort of
   one.

A strategy that can be helpful for spelling suggested by Lee Pascal is
shown below:

♦ Spell the word aloud as you write it down.
♦ Look at the word.
♦ Cover the word with a piece of paper.
♦ Try to see the word on the paper.
♦ Copy the word as you see it.
♦ Check to see if you have spelt the word correctly.
♦ Have a 10-minute break, then repeat the exercise above.
♦ A few hours later repeat again.
♦ Repeat at various times over the next few days.
♦ Add a new word to the list each week and repeat the sequence.

Word Lists

The use of word lists can be a successful strategy. A word list can be composed from words commonly used by children at certain ages. It may also be useful to construct word lists of subject-specific words and those that have similar sounds, or look similar. In regard to biology, Howlett (2001) suggests it can be useful to compile an alphabetically arranged biology spelling book for each year group. She suggests that such a checklist can include other useful information, such as definitions. Additionally, the spelling book can also contain a table showing singular and plural endings such as 'vertebra' and 'vertebrae' and irregular ending such as 'stoma' and 'stomata' – these can be problematic for dyslexic children.

There are many different strategies that can be used to help with spelling, but ideally one needs to draw from a range of methods, as the same approach may not be effective for all. The general principles, however, of good teaching – that is, multisensory strategies, such as visual, auditory, kinesthetic and tactile – should not be overlooked as these help with over-learning and automaticity. The most effective way to achieve automaticity is through using the word that is being learnt in as many different forms as possible, in different subjects and different contexts.

Visual Strategies

There are a number of visual strategies that can be applied in spelling. In fact, Peters (1970; 1975) suggests that spelling is essentially a visual–motor activity. One of the predominant visual approaches is described below.

Look, Cover, Write, Check

This is a well-established strategy for spelling, and was the outcome of longitudinal research conducted by Peters (1985). The stages include:

Look
This involves the writer looking closely at the word with the intention of reproducing it. Finger-tracing the word at this stage, which utilizes kinesthetic memory, can result in a stronger memory trace and enhance the chances of the child with specific difficulties remembering the visual features of the word. Bradley (1990) suggests in her 'simultaneous oral spelling' strategy that saying the letters at this initial stage can also help to reinforce the memory trace for the word. It is also important that

the 'look' stage is not skipped or rushed through before the child has had an opportunity to develop visual strategies to help memorize the visual features. Such strategies can include making visual analogies of the word by recognizing the visual features and similarities of the letters and the word to other words, or acknowledging the distinctive features. For example, in the word 'window' there are a number of visual aspects that could help with memory, such as the first and last letter being the same and the distinctiveness of the letter 'w'. At this stage it is also possible to draw attention to words within words such as the word 'tent' in 'attention' and 'ask' in 'basket'.

Cover
This involves visual memory and takes practice. Some children can adapt to this better than others. This type of activity lends itself very well to a game, which can be motivating for children. Visual memory can of course be practised with a range of games and activities involving visual discrimination.

For example, Crossbow Educational (www.crossboweducation.com) produce a wide range of games, such as 'Rummyword', 'Breakdown' and 'Funfish', all of which can help provide practice in visual activities that can have a spin-off for spelling. Additionally, mnemonics as well as game-type activities can be used as an aid for visual memory.

Write
This is an important stage as it provides the kinesthetic practice. Many practitioners suggest that at this stage cursive handwriting should be encouraged. In fact, Peters (1985) suggests that there is a link between clear cursive writing and good spelling.

Check
This provides the learner with some responsibility for his or her own spelling. It is important to reduce dependency on the teacher as soon as possible and to promote the activity of self-correction. While 'look, cover, write, check' as a strategy can be very successful for many children, it does place demands on memory and particularly visual memory. It is important therefore to ensure that it is suitable for the individual child and that other strategies are also considered.

Language Experience Approaches

There is a great deal of scope for encouraging expressive writing using an 'adult helper' to facilitate the development of language experience and spelling. It can be suggested that writing for communication and spelling need to be kept separate otherwise the expressive output of the writing may become inhibited through constantly checking and correcting the spelling. Topping (1992, 2001a, 2001b) suggests actually drawing a line through the misspelling as it helps to visually reinforce the wrong spelling. Although children can make progress with practice, this can only really effectively occur in spelling if the child has the opportunity to correct and note the correct spelling before proceeding with further work, otherwise the spelling error pattern is reinforced. It therefore requires a degree of judgement by the teacher to help the child self-correct, indicate spelling errors not noted by the child and to motivate the child to write freely irrespective of the errors.

Cued Spelling

The Cued Spelling technique shares the same principles as paired reading. The technique comprises ten steps for learning and spelling, four points to remember and two reviews. The points to remember help to consolidate the learning and the two reviews involve a daily and a weekly review. In the daily review the speller writes all the words for the day and checks them – the wrong words are then noted and the learner goes through the ten steps again for these words.

The speller adopts the same procedure for the weekly review and identifies the wrong words. Discussion would then take place on the best approach for the learner to tackle the incorrectly spelt words. If the learner writes a word inaccurately he or she is encouraged to delete the word from memory by erasing it or boldly scoring it out. This can be particularly useful if the learner has a strong visual memory and the image of the incorrect word may remain and be recalled at some future point. The cued spelling technique is highly interactive, but aims to encourage 'self-managed' learning. The technique attempts to eliminate fear of failure through the use of prompt correction procedures. As in paired reading, modelling and praise are integral to the application of Cued Spelling. The Cued Spelling technique is relatively simple to apply and the pack includes a demonstration video.

Games for Spelling

Smith (1997) provides a range of different types of games for different stages of spelling. In the early stages of spelling this includes rhyming games, such as: 'objects that rhyme' featuring tangible objects whose names have the same sound; 'rhyming snap' using cards containing familiar pictures; and the 'rhyming lotto' board game. Memory games can also be used to help with spelling. This can involve picture and sound memory games. Word searches can also help with the visual pattern of words as can providing a number of alternative spellings of a word in a sentence and asking the child to identify the correct one. Older children should be encouraged to engage in proofreading activities as this can also help with the visual identification of the word in context.

Models and Stages of Spelling

There are a number of different spelling models and these have an impact on the approaches used in teaching spelling. An example of this is displayed below.

♦ Stage one – recognition of rhymes and rhyming words; blending spoken word into sounds; making some representations of phonic structures in writing words
♦ Stage two – writing single sounds and some common harder words such as 'have' and 'went'
♦ Stage three – using consonant digraphs (ch, sh, th), consonant blends (sl, fr, sk, nd), vowel digraphs (ea, au, ow) and magic e (came, mine)
♦ Stage four – able to spell most words and able to use dictionary.

This is perhaps a simplified form of the spelling stages and not everyone is in agreement on the stage theory of spelling. For example Treiman (1993) suggests that children at the very outset rely heavily on phonology but also suggests that children are aware of orthographic conventions even at an early stage and they seem to be aware of any two letters that are always grouped together – for example, 'ed' at the end of a word. It might be suggested that this view conflicts with the stage model of spelling, which suggests that the orthographic rules are not acquired until a later stage.

Joshi and Carreker (2009) in fact note a number of models showing stages of spelling. They suggest that the transition stage – the stage when children move from the reliance on phonemes to a recognition of the importance of graphemic (visual) patterns – can be challenging for children with dyslexia. At this stage the spelling errors of children are often through the misuse of phonic equivalents – for example, they may put 'gait' for 'gate' because they have attempted to learn the vowel sound 'ai'. According to Smith, Hinson and Smith (1998), at the transitional stage the teacher should prioritize work on silent letters, suffixes and prefixes, and activities to encourage visual skills such as looking for small words within longer words and variations of the 'look, say, cover, write and check' method.

Ehri (2002) outlined four distinct levels that capture the essences of the different models for spelling. These can explain the progression in which spelling skills are acquired, these are: pre-alphabetic, partial alphabetic, full alphabetic and consolidated alphabetic. The first three levels of this model suggest, as other models do, that children's spellings become more informed as the children's alphabetic knowledge increases. In the final level, children become aware of units for spelling – syllables, prefixes and suffixes – and are better able to spell or invent multisyllabic words.

It is important to consider the caution noted by Ehri and reported by Joshi and Carreker that there is variability in spelling development among children. It is unlikely that children will move through the stages in a distinct progression. Ehri cautions that stages are not tied to a maturation timetable but are inextricably tied to instruction.

In this respect it is important to consider the comment by Moats (2005) that, 'rather than a developmental progression characterized by distinct stages, learning to spell is more accurately described as a continual amalgamation of phonological, morphological, and orthographic knowledge' (p. 14).

Spelling Materials

The ACE Spelling Dictionary (Moseley and Nicol 1995)

This dictionary is specifically aimed at dyslexic children and can provide them with an easy and independent means of finding words at speed. There are also activities that accompany the dictionary, *ACE Spelling Activities*. These consist of photocopiable worksheets with spelling activities based on the use of syllables, discriminating between different parts of speech and other activities linked to the *ACE Spelling Dictionary*. It also includes advice on the use of common word lists.

Catchwords

This set of books can be useful for observing the progression from the semi-phonetic to phonetic to the transition stage in spelling. The first book provides examples of rhyming activities, and subsequent books in the series highlight word-building and common letter patterns. The series also contains suggestions for developing a whole-school spelling policy, a comprehensive word bank and guidance for involving parents.

Photocopiable resources

There are a number of photocopiable resources for spelling, usually in ring-bound files, which can be easily accessed by the teacher:

♦ Exercise Your Spelling (Hodder & Stoughton).
♦ Early Steps to Literacy (Kickstart Publications).
♦ Folens Spelling File (Folens).
♦ High Frequency Spelling Fun (Timesavers).
♦ Limericks, Laughs and Vowel Digraphs (Crossbow Educational).
♦ Rime Time (Crossbow Educational).
♦ Sound Beginnings (LDA).
♦ Spell It Out (Hilda King Educational Services).
♦ Spelling Rules OK (Chalkface Publications).
♦ Thrass Spelling Book (Collins Educational).
♦ Wordsnakes (Crossbow Educational).
♦ Crackerspell (Jordanhill Publications).

These photocopiable activities are useful for children with dyslexia as they can be used and developed in a multisensory way. Additionally, because they are photocopiable, they can be used repetitively and interspersed with other activities. This can promote over-learning and, as will be addressed in some of the following chapters, over-learning is essential for students with dyslexia.

Although spelling can be problematic for children with dyslexia, it is important that this should not restrict their expressive writing in any way. Do not use a red pen or crosses to correct spelling; doing so will discourage and dishearten the learner.

This chapter has indicated:

♦ That there are a number of important prerequisite skills needed for spelling, including auditory skills, visual skills, language skills, memory skills and an understanding of the text.
♦ While spelling can be learnt in isolation, it is often more effective to practise spelling in context.
♦ Multisensory approaches should be used when teaching spelling.
♦ Game activities can be useful in spelling to help children strengthen auditory and visual associations with different objects and words.
♦ There are a number of commercially available spelling materials but it is also possible to develop your own.
♦ Encouraging word lists and specific lists for different subject areas in secondary school can be useful.

6

Supporting the Writing Process

Expressive and informative writing is an important aspect of literacy. It can promote higher-order thinking skills, reflection and can have a transfer effect on other language and literacy skills. There is also evidence of a relationship between writing and spelling and that lack of confidence in spelling can have a considerable detrimental effect on children's written expression.

A number of cognitive skills are associated with writing, such as: organization, including the logical connections among ideas, planning, sequencing, identifying key points, relevance, elaboration, imagination, grammar/syntax and memory. While some of these skills can be readily accessed by students with dyslexia, they may find others challenging. One of the ways of supporting writing is to integrate the activity into the curriculum. Moats (2005) has been very influential in this respect. She argues that reading comprehension is enhanced when students write a response to their reading. She suggests that writing facilitates phonological awareness, spelling knowledge, vocabulary, a familiarity with language structures, and, very importantly, with thinking itself. She believes that writing is a difficult skill to master for students with dyslexia. It takes longer to write proficiently because writing uses the four processors essential for word recognition – phonological, orthographic, meaning and context – but also draws on other skills, such as language skills, motor, memory, attention and cognitive functions, such as organization and sustained attention. She argues that it is dependent on high and low levels of cognitive skills. According to Moats (2005), high-level skills are logical connections, connecting ideas, maintaining a writing goal and taking the reader's perspective. Lower-level skills are letter formation, sound/spelling links, recall of sight words and use of punctuation.

She suggests that writing involves three distinct subprocesses. These are: generating ideas, setting goals and organizing information. These factors need to be discussed and dealt with at the planning stage of writing and this is particularly important for children with dyslexia.

Relationship Between Writing and Spelling

According to Chall and Popp (1996) the practice of writing and sounding out words that have been written is excellent preparation for learning conventional spelling and phonics. Additionally, they suggest that early writing also illustrates the important principle that learning is cumulative – which means that children need to know the alphabet letters in order to use them in writing. This in turn helps to provide children with the opportunity to practise using these letters in writing, together with the sounds of the letters.

Additionally, being aware of a spelling difficulty can restrict a child's enthusiasm for writing. For that reason it is preferable to insist that spelling will not be taken into account in a written piece. It is important to grade a piece of work purely on content. Berninger and Wolf (2009) argue that children with spelling problems write fewer words than children who do not have such a problem. They also present a view that handwriting and spelling account for 66 per cent of the variance in primary-grade writing fluency. This highlights the point that the student should be aware that spelling will not impact on the overall grade, but it also highlights the need to encourage students with dyslexia to use a word processor as early as possible in the writing process.

Expressive writing: the process

There are many stages involved in the writing process. Writing relies on prior experiences and ideas. Reading and language experience can therefore be beneficial for writing. Some of the skills associated with writing can include:

Organizing
- organizing information
- making logical connections between ideas
- pre-planning and structuring written work

Sequencing
- following a plan
- ordering events
- structuring written work

Identifying key points
- ensuring the writing is relevant
- making sure the important points are considered
- highlighting the points that are important by giving them prominence

Story development
♦ encouraging imagination
♦ ensuring vocabulary can be accessed
♦ logical storyline
♦ beginning, main part and end of story should all be identifiable

Creativity
♦ using imagination
♦ engaging in pre-writing discussion
♦ assisting in the development of ideas

Grammar/syntax
♦ reading the piece aloud to identify grammatical errors
♦ using word processing programmes, such as Text help©, to help with syntax, organization and spelling

Memory
♦ recalling information by discussing key points and ideas
♦ providing key words.

Paired Writing

Writing is a complex task. In a further elaboration of the paired approach to literacy development, Keith Topping has piloted a 'Paired Writing' technique using the same principles of 'training' parents/tutors in its use (Topping 2001b). For example, he advocates using the technique as frequently as possible after the initial training session in order to reinforce and promote fluency in its use. He recommends drawing up an informal contract to establish minimum usage and suggests Paired Writing for three sessions of 20 minutes per week for six weeks. PW works within clear behaviourist principles of constant in-built feedback and cross-checking, both to ensure that what is written makes sense to both partners and to address the issue of the fear of failure and anxiety about spelling or punctuation. Again, Topping (2001b) suggests that

Paired Writing is a framework for a pair working together to generate a piece of writing for any purpose they wish. Paired Writing usually operates with a more able writer (the Helper) and a less able one (the Writer), but can work with a pair of equal ability so long as they edit carefully and use a dictionary to check spellings. The structure of the system consists of six steps, ten questions (for Ideas), five stages (for Drafting) and four levels (for Editing).

Step 1 is Ideas Generation. The Helper stimulates ideas by using given Questions and inventing other relevant ones, making one-word notes on the Writer's responses.

Step 2 is Drafting. The notes then form the basis for Drafting, which ignores spelling and punctuation. Lined paper and double-spaced writing is recommended. The Writer dictates the text and scribing occurs in whichever of the five Stages of Support has been chosen by the pair. If there is a hitch, the Helper gives more support.

In step 3 the pair look at the text together while the Helper reads the Draft out loud with expression. The Writer then reads the text out loud, with the Helper correcting any reading errors.

Figure 6.1 Paired writing

Step 4 is Editing. First the Writer considers where he/she thinks improvements are necessary, marking this with a coloured pen, pencil or highlighter. The most important improvement is where the meaning is unclear. The second most important is to do with the organization of ideas or the order in which meanings are presented. The next consideration is whether spellings are correct and the last whether punctuation is helpful and correct. The Helper praises the Writer then marks points the Writer has 'missed'. The pair then discuss and agree improvements.

During step 5 the Writer (usually) copies out a 'neat' or 'best' version. Sometimes the Helper may write or type or word-process it, however. Making the final copy is the least important step.

Dyslexia

Step 6 is Evaluate. The pair should self-assess their own best copy, but peer assessment by another pair is also very useful. The criteria in the Edit levels provide a checklist for this.

Learning to write clearly and effectively has proven to be particularly problematic for students who experience difficulties in literacy development. Writing problems may, in large part, be the result of three factors:

♦ lack of proficiency in text production skills, i.e. frequent errors in spelling, the use of upper-and lower-case, and punctuation. The amount of attention that has to be expended on lower-level skills is thought to interfere with higher-order skills of planning and the generation of content
♦ lack of knowledge relating to the subject content of the script to be written, and/or of the conventions and characteristics of different writing genres
♦ ineffective strategies in planning or revising text.

Wray (2009) advocates that teachers need to ensure that children are given adequate opportunities to acquire the requisite knowledge about themselves as writers, about the writing process and about the demands of particular writing tasks, including textual structures. They also need to ensure that this knowledge develops beyond simply knowing that certain things can be done in writing to knowing how they can be done, and why they should be done. Therefore, the focus is on the process involved in the emerging and finished product rather than on the product itself.

Some strategies to help integrate metacognitive skills in the writing process include thinking aloud while writing and critically examining and revising writing decisions – for example, asking themselves: 'why did I write this?'; or 'why did I explain it in this manner?'

According to Wray, writers also need to anticipate potential difficulties, and make judgments and reconciliations between competing ideas, as well as show an alertness to the needs of their potential and actual readership.

Writing Frames

A writing frame consists of a skeleton outline given to students to scaffold their non-fiction writing. This is essentially a framework that consists of a number of different key words or phrases and can form a template for the piece of writing. This is important for students with dyslexia as often they have the ideas but have difficulty putting them into a logical sequence and sometimes even generating the information in the first place. Writing frames can act as a cue or prompt to help generate the argument, particularly in non-fiction writing.

Extending Literacy through Writing

Wray (2009) provides a convincing argument for extending literacy by extending writing skills. He suggests this can involve looking at print and finding out information from a variety of sources. One method of doing this is the KWL grid. KWL stands for: what do I *know* already, what do I *want* to know and what did I *learn*.

The KWL grid was developed as a teaching method in the US and is a simple and effective strategy that takes children through the steps of the research process involved in writing, and also records and monitors their learning. It gives students a logical structure for tackling research tasks as a prerequisite for creative writing. It involves a combination of a simple, but logical, support scaffolding – that is: 'what do I know already', 'what do I want to know' and 'what have I learnt'. The information that stems from this process can be recorded by the student in three columns representing each of these three areas.

Writing – 6+1 Traits

The above approach represents one of the most significant breakthroughs in developing writing skills for all learners in the US. Culham (2003) has illustrated this model in practitioner-friendly texts that highlight the importance of developing ideas, organization, using the writer's 'voice', word choice, attending to sentence fluency and writing conventions, as well as presentation. This represents a powerful and successful model for developing writing skills. One of the bases of this model is to identify the writer's strengths and build on that – it is therefore about growth rather than remediation. The structure within this model is well tailored for children with dyslexia and it focuses particularly on helping the student take control over the writing process. There are a number of excellent resources developed around the Trait model.

The Importance of Writing

Writing can influence thinking skills and the development of language ideas and concepts. Often children with dyslexia avoid writing because it can be challenging, yet writing like any other learning task can be made dyslexia-friendly. There are many strategies that can help to make writing more meaningful and fulfilling for the dyslexic child. These include:

- the use of themes related to the particular interest of the dyslexic child
- examining the purpose of writing
- using writing to experience poetry, drama and script-writing
- linking the writing task to the interests of the child.

Reid and Green (2007) suggest that writing can be embellished through the use of themes. They suggest that themes can be based on a student's 'favourite things' to help to motivate the student to write. Students with dyslexia will, however, still need a structure and often the key words presented to act as a prompt during the writing exercise.

Helping to Motivate Children to Write

Motivation is an important factor in writing. It is important that the child has a sense of purpose (Reid 2007). For many children with dyslexia the thought of writing tasks can be sufficient to demotivate them. It is important, therefore, that when the writing task is set it is seen as an achievable task by the student. This, in fact, can be the first major barrier that has to be overcome in order to maintain motivation. Some learners with dyslexia, if they have experienced repeated failure, will become totally demotivated and will not want to engage in writing in any way at all. It is important that children can experience success before this happens.

It is for this reason that great care must be taken to ensure writing tasks are motivating and that the learner believes the task is achievable. It is important that the writing task is broken down into small chunks and that every one represents an achievable outcome for the learner. It is important therefore to see writing as a series of steps.

Planning

Planning is important for writing. Aspects such as: the generation of ideas, context – i.e. where the story is taking place, the audience – who it is to be written for, the organization (what should come first, how much detail will be provided by the opening paragraph and what each paragraph will cover are all crucial aspects and are important if effective planning is to take place).

It is important to view the writing process for children with dyslexia as being of paramount importance. Spelling, handwriting and vocabulary have all been made more easily accessible with word processing and the appropriate software.

In summary:

♦ Successful writing can lead to positive self-esteem and this can influence other areas of learning.

♦ Children with dyslexia require a structure to lead them into the writing process. They should not necessarily start with a blank sheet of paper.

♦ The use of visuals as cues can be helpful, and structure words can provide the essential vocabulary components as well as acting as a trigger to extend writing.

♦ Pre-task discussion can facilitate reflection on the part of the student and allow him/her to think through the various paragraphs and the purposes of the piece of writing.

♦ Planning is important and time needs to be taken to deal with this aspect.

♦ The link between spelling and writing needs to be considered, but it is important that difficulties with spelling do not inhibit the writing process.

7

Learning Differences

It is important to recognize the distinction between 'learning differences' and 'learning disabilities'. The label 'learning disabilities' carries with it the notion that such children need remediation. In some way this is correct but it also suggests that the children in question are lacking some necessary skill which is required to learn effectively. What this notion overlooks is that children with dyslexia can have considerable skills but need consideration, adaptation and support in order to access these skills. It is therefore more constructive and more feasible to use the term 'learning differences' and the term 'support' rather than 'remediation'.

In an ideal world, children with dyslexia need

- ♦ a sympathetic mix of one-on-one specialist intervention focusing on the components of reading, writing and spelling
- ♦ curriculum support to ensure they can access the materials and the tasks presented
- ♦ help to develop the skills to make learning more effective for them – this will enable them to become independent learners, which is important for learning beyond school.

It is the role and the responsibility of the education system, the school, and the individual teacher to ensure that these differences are catered for within the system. This can be an ambitious objective and perhaps an idealistic one, and it can represent an attitude shift in how schools perceive children who are experiencing difficulties. Yet such a shift is necessary if teachers are to be able to accommodate the range of differences within classrooms today.

The Challenges

Many of the challenges experienced by children with dyslexia arise from difficulties with information-processing. This includes reading, spelling, writing, language-processing, organization and speed of processing. There is no shortage of programmes to deal with these difficulties (see the previous chapter and Reid 2009) but one of the drawbacks is that, by necessity, they often single out, or even isolate, children from others in the class. This may have a negative effect on the child's self-esteem, and further, it may result in the child missing out on some aspects of the mainstream curriculum.

It is appreciated, however, that some children with significant difficulties in literacy will benefit from some type of specialized input. There are many tutorial and extended teaching and learning centres in most countries that provide this (for details, see Appendices), but good examples of how it can work in practice can be seen in the work of the Red Rose School in England (www.redroseschool.co.uk), Fraser Academy in Vancouver, Canada (www.fraseracademy.ca), and Fun Track Learning in Perth, Australia (www.funtrack.com.au).

> Specialized provision can complement, and help the child access, the mainstream curriculum. There needs to be a balance between curriculum adaptation and specialized individual input.

For the main part, however, the onus is on the teacher to prepare and present the curriculum in a dyslexia-friendly manner. This will require effective differentiation in the preparation of materials. These need to consider classroom and environmental factors, such as learning styles and classroom layout, as well as content of materials.

> It is important that interventions take a curricular and classroom perspective and focus not only on the child, but on the learning and teaching context.

Interventions and Dyslexia

The debate

There is an ongoing debate regarding the 'special' type of teaching that is required for children with dyslexia. This is encapsulated in the views presented by Norwich and Lewis (2001). In their paper they question the claims that differential teaching is required for children with special educational needs, including dyslexia. They observe that the 'unique differences position' (p. 313) has little supportive empirical evidence, and suggest that the approaches for children with dyslexia are in fact adaptations of common teaching approaches. Conner (1994) argues that specialist teaching approaches for dyslexia are little different from teaching literacy to any pupil, although arguably there seems to be more of a preference for bottom-up approaches relating to phonological awareness, as well as for structure and over-learning.

Norwich (2009) also suggests that although the concept of dyslexia-friendly schools (see later in this chapter) is a commendable concept, it does represent a sectional interest and may for that reason not be accommodated within the wider-reaching concept of inclusion and that 'dyslexia-friendly' is too narrow a movement for enhancing school provision.

Reason *et al.* (1988) also questions the differences in approaches, indicating that individual differences between dyslexic students is the most crucial reason for utilizing specific teaching approaches.

Given this controversy and debate, it may be more productive to identify specific approaches by examining the barriers to learning experienced by the child. This would imply that each child is individual and the specific barriers may be different for different children. This can have implications for staff development as often these barriers can be seen as whole-school barriers, for example: the pace of the curriculum, the environment, the curriculum content and the resources and materials available.

Norwich (2009) points out that the debate about dyslexia was further fuelled following the screening of a high-profile television documentary in the UK (Elliott 2005). Elliott questioned whether clear distinctions can be made between dyslexic and non-dyslexic groups and whether identification of dyslexia had implications for appropriate interventions. He also raised the question of whether identification of dyslexia should result in additional resourcing. Elliot did not deny that some children have difficulties in literacy but questioned whether these difficulties can be identified as qualitatively different from other literacy difficulties. Elliot suggests what is needed is a description of individual needs as he says the label dyslexia can be misleading.

One way of dealing with this uncertainty and ambiguity is through the use of the term 'barriers to learning' and utilizing the principles and practices of Individual Education Plans. These can identify the barriers, highlight strategies that can be used, and identify specific teaching approaches that may help to overcome these barriers.

At the same time, it needs to be recognized that in practice many children do not qualify for an IEP unless they have been diagnosed with a label such as dyslexia. Identification is therefore necessary, but identification and the label 'dyslexia' should be regarded as the beginning and not the end!

Individual Education Plans – implications for children with dyslexia

Individual Education Plans (IEPs) can provide a means of ensuring the needs of children are met within the educational setting. The principles used in an IEP can be applicable to all education systems in all countries.

In order for an IEP to be used appropriately it should, as a minimum, contain details of:

♦ the nature of the child's learning difficulties
♦ the special educational provision to be made
♦ strategies to be used
♦ specific programmes, activities, materials
♦ any specialized equipment
♦ targets to be achieved
♦ the timeframe for any specified targets
♦ monitoring and assessment arrangements
♦ review arrangements (with dates).

Planning for Learning

In some schools the class teacher may be supported by specialist teachers, such as resource teachers, learning support staff and special needs coordinators (the titles vary from country to country but often the demands on this group are the same). Nevertheless, the responsibility for planning and preparing class work usually rests with the class teacher. It is important, therefore, that class teachers have some awareness of dyslexia, but equally it is important that consideration is given to the role of planning and preparation in meeting the needs of dyslexic children, within the class and curriculum context.

Dealing with dyslexia is a whole-school concern and not the responsibility of any one person.

Planning

Planning for learning should include

♦ consultation
♦ deciding how the information is to be presented
♦ deciding how materials and tasks are to be developed.

Dyslexia

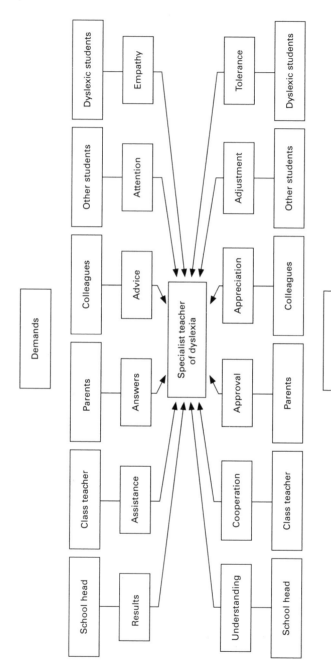

Figure 7.1 Demands on and support for specialist teachers

There are many fundamental factors that can be incorporated into the planning and presentation of curricular materials and tasks. Some of these are discussed below.

Knowledge of the child's strengths and difficulties
This is essential, especially since not all children with dyslexia will display the same profile. It is therefore the best starting point, as often strengths can be used to help deal with weaknesses.

For example, dyslexic children often have a preference for visual and kinesthetic learning, and a difficulty with auditory learning. So, phonics, which relies heavily on sounds and is therefore an auditory modality, needs to be introduced together with visual and experiential form of learning. The tactile modality involving touch and feeling the shape of letters that make specific sounds should also be utilized, as well as the visual symbols of these letters and letter/sound combinations.

Consultation
The responsibility for dealing with children with dyslexia within the classroom should not solely rest with the class teacher. Ideally it should be seen as a whole-school responsibility. This means that consultation with school management and other colleagues is important, and it is equally important that time is allocated for this. Information from previous teachers, support staff, school management and parents is necessary, and such joint liaison can help to ensure the necessary collaboration to provide support for the class teacher. Importantly, this should be built into the school procedures and not be a reaction to a problem that has occurred. Such collaboration can therefore be seen as preventative and proactive.

Knowledge of the curriculum content
It is understood that the teacher will have a sound awareness of the content of the curriculum, which the child needs to know. Anticipating those areas for the different aspects of the curriculum that may present a difficulty for dyslexic children may, however, be a bit more tricky. Yet it is important that the teacher can do so.

Such areas can include information that contains lists or dates, for example in history. Learning the sequence of dates can be as difficult as remembering the dates themselves. It is crucial, therefore, that such information is presented in a dyslexia-friendly manner.

Current level of literacy acquisition
An accurate and full assessment of the child's current level of attainments is necessary in order to effectively plan a programme of learning. The assessment should include listening comprehension as well as

reading accuracy and fluency. Listening comprehension can often be a more accurate guide to the abilities and understanding of dyslexic children than reading and spelling accuracy. Indeed, it is often the discrepancy between listening comprehension and reading accuracy that can be a key factor in identifying dyslexia. Information on the level of attainments is an instrumental factor in planning for differentiation.

Cultural factors
Background knowledge, particularly of cultural factors, is important, as this can influence the selection of books and whether some of the concepts in the text need to be singled out for additional and differentiated explanation. Cultural values are an important factor. It has been suggested that the 'big dip' in performance noted in some bilingual children in later primary school may be explained by a failure of professionals to understand and appreciate the cultural values, and the actual level of competence, of the bilingual child, particularly in relation to conceptual development and competence in thinking skills. It is possible for teachers to misinterpret bilingual children's development of good phonic skills in the early stages of literacy development in English and to fail to note the difficulties that these children might be having with comprehension. When the difficulties later emerge, these children can be grouped inappropriately with native speakers of English who have the more conventional problems with phonic awareness, or else their difficulties are assumed to derive from specific perceptual problems rather than from the cultural unfamiliarity of the text.

In order for a teaching approach with bilingual students to be fully effective it has to be comprehensive, which means that it needs to incorporate the views of parents and the community. This requires considerable preparation and pre-planning, as well as consultation with parents and community organizations.

Berryman and Wearmouth (2009) describe the benefits to literacy learning that result when schools work to address issues of cultural understanding between themselves and their home communities. They suggest that literacy values and practices, which are evident in different cultural communities, need to be respected by schools, and that collaboration on literacy tasks between home communities and schools do result in improvements in students' literacy achievements.

Teachers' expectations can also be noted in cultural variations within a community. Rubie-Davies, Hattie and Hamilton (2006) noted, in their study involving primary school teachers at 12 Auckland schools in New Zealand, that teachers' expectations for Māori students were lower than their expectations for Pacific, Asian and New Zealand European students. Not only were teacher expectations lower for Māori, these were significantly lower than the actual achievement of Māori students during the period of the study.

> Knowledge of the child and the prevailing culture are crucial when planning a learning programme. This should take a holistic perspective, looking at social, emotional, cultural and educational factors, as well as cognitive factors.

Dyslexia-Friendly

Riddick (2009) suggests that the dyslexia-friendly schools pack in the UK, which represents a set of detailed guidelines for mainstream schools on the best way to support and educate dyslexic children, were influenced to an extent by the students themselves. She suggests that their perspectives played an important part in shaping the guidelines. The dyslexia-friendly guidelines recommend a range of approaches and adaptations that teachers can readily make in their classrooms and in their teaching practices. These include not asking children to read out loud in front of the class unless they wish to do so and marking separately for content and presentation of work. A number of the approaches mentioned in the guidelines are discussed in this chapter.

Presentation

Small steps
It is important, especially since children with dyslexia may have short-term memory difficulties, to present tasks in small steps. In fact, one task at a time is probably sufficient. If multiple tasks are specified then a checklist might be a useful way for the child to note and self-monitor his or her progress (Reid and Green 2007).

Group work
It is important to plan for group work. The dynamic of the group is crucial, and dyslexic children need to be in a group where at least one person in the group is able to impose some form of structure on tasks. This can act as a modeling experience for dyslexic children. It is also important that those in the group do not overpower the dyslexic child, so someone with the ability to facilitate the dyslexic child's contribution to the group is also important. This will ensure the dyslexic child feels he or she is contributing to the group. Even though dyslexic children may not have the reading ability of the others in the group, they will almost

certainly have the comprehension ability, so will be able to contribute if provided with opportunities.

Dyslexia-friendly approaches are discussed by Reid and Green (2007) and some of these are listed below.

- ♦ multisensory teaching
- ♦ differentiated pace of work
- ♦ ensuring the learning outcomes are varied and that a range of approaches are used to assess these outcomes.
- ♦ utilizing learning styles when presenting information to children (see next section of this chapter)
- ♦ ensuring worksheets are in large type and that sentences are well spaced, using short sentences and clear visuals
- ♦ using pastel-colour paper rather than white
- ♦ considering classroom layout, such as the position of desks (see below on learning styles)
- ♦ providing short tasks rather than one long one
- ♦ keeping oral instructions short.

Learning Styles

This is one of the key aspects in understanding the importance of the presentation of materials and how the learning situation can be manipulated to promote more effective learning. It is important to recognize that different children have their own preferred learning style, and this includes dyslexic children. This means that there may be a great many similarities in how children with dyslexia learn and process information, but there will also be individual differences and these need to be taken into account in the planning and presentation of learning.

As suggested earlier, multisensory strategies are used widely in the teaching of dyslexic children. The evidence suggests that the effectiveness of these strategies is based largely on the provision of at least one mode of learning with which the learner feels comfortable. Thus, if the learner has difficulty dealing with information by way of the auditory channel, this could perhaps be compensated for through the use of the visual mode. The use of such compensatory strategies is well documented in the literature and is a feature of teaching programmes for dyslexic children. It is logical, therefore, that consideration of the learner as an individual should be extended to a holistic appreciation of the learner's individual style. Factors such as affective (emotional) and physiological characteristics will have some bearing on how the dyslexic child responds to the learning situation, and a holistic perspective should therefore be applied in both the assessment and the teaching of dyslexic children.

One of the most useful learning styles models is that developed by Dunn, Dunn and Price (1975–89). This model identifies five principal domains and 21 elements, all of which affect student learning. It is suggested that all of these elements have to be considered during the assessment process and in the subsequent planning of teaching. The domains and the elements across those domains are:

♦ environmental (sound, light, temperature, design)
♦ emotional (motivation, persistence, responsibility, structure)
♦ sociological (learning by self, pairs, peers, team, with an adult)
♦ physiological (perceptual preference, food and drink intake, time of day, mobility)
♦ psychological (global or analytic preferences, impulsive, reflective).

On examining this learning style model, one can recognize how the identified elements can influence the performances of dyslexic learners. It must be appreciated that dyslexic learners are first and foremost learners, and like any other learners will be influenced by different learning conditions. Some dyslexic students therefore will prefer a 'silent' environment for concentration, while others may need some auditory stimuli, perhaps even music, in order to maximize concentration and performance. Similarly, as regards light, individual preferences, such as dim light or bright light, should be recognized.

In relation to emotional variables, two of the elements, responsibility and structure, should certainly be addressed. It has been well documented that dyslexic learners benefit from imposed structure. Most of the teaching programmes recognize this and follow a highly structured formula. At the same time, however, taking responsibility for one's own learning can be highly motivating and generate success. Dyslexic learners, therefore, should not be deprived of the opportunity to take responsibility, as some may possess a natural preference for responsibility and structure.

It is possible to obtain some idea of the child's learning style from observation, and knowledge of how the child tackles tasks in the classroom.

Learning styles: some tips

Every effort should be made to organize the classroom environment in a manner that can be adapted to suit a range of styles. In classrooms where there are a number of dyslexic learners, the environment should be global, which means lighting, design and indeed the whole learning atmosphere need to be considered.

It is also important that the teacher has an awareness of what is meant by learning styles and how to identify different styles in children. Although there are many different instruments that can be used, teacher observations and discussion with students while they are engaged on a task can be extremely beneficial.

The different stages of the information-processing cycle – input, cognition and output – should be considered in relation to how children learn and how this can be used within a learning-styles structure. The experience of learning may be more important to children with dyslexia than the actual finished product.

It is important that children with dyslexia become aware of their own learning styles. This is the first and most important step to achieving a degree of self-sufficiency in learning. Acknowledging learning styles can help to promote skills that extend beyond school. Knowledge of learning styles can equip students, and particularly students with dyslexia, for lifelong learning.

Information-processing

Learning depends on how efficiently and effectively children process information. It is important therefore to recognize the key stages of information-processing (input, cognition and output) and how these may present potential difficulties for learners with dyslexia. Some of these difficulties are discussed in Chapter 1, but it is important to recognize how these potential difficulties can be overcome with forward planning and recognition of these in teaching. Some suggestions for this are as follows:

Input
Identify the student's preferred *learning style*, particularly visual, auditory, kinesthetic or tactile preferences, as these can be crucial in how information is presented. It is important to present new information to the learner's preferred modality.

Present new information in *small steps*. This will ensure that the short-term memory does not become overloaded with information before it is fully consolidated.

New material will need to be repeatedly presented through *overlearning*. This does not mean that the repetition should be in the same form – rather, it is important that it should be varied using as wide a range of materials and strategies as possible.

It is a good idea to present the *key points* at the initial stage of learning new material. This helps to provide a framework for the new material and can help to relate new information to previous knowledge.

Cognition

Information should be related to previous knowledge. This ensures that concepts are developed and the information can be placed into a learning framework, or schema, by the learner. Successful learning is often the result of efficient organization of information. It is important, therefore, to group information together and to show the connections between related information. For example, if the topic to be covered is the Harry Potter series of books, then concepts such as witchcraft and magic, and the words associated with these, would need to be explained and some of the related ideas discussed. This should be done before reading the text.

Some specific memory strategies, such as Mind Mapping and mnemonics, can be used to help the learner remember some of the key words or more challenging ideas.

Output

Often children with dyslexia have difficulty identifying the key points in new learning or in a text. This can be overcome by providing the child with these key points or words at the beginning stage of learning the new material. Additionally, the learner can acquire skills in this by practising using summaries: each period of new learning should be summarized by the learner – this in itself helps to identify the key points.

It may also be beneficial to measure progress orally rather than through writing, particularly in-class continuous assessment. It is not unusual for children with dyslexia to be much more proficient orally than in written form. Oral presentation of information can therefore help to instil confidence. By contrast, often a written exercise can be damaging in terms of confidence, unless considerable preparation and planning have helped to ensure that some of the points indicated above are put in to place.

Some Tips for Supporting Learning

Materials

Use colour

There is evidence that different colours for background (paper) and font can enhance some children's reading and attention.

Layout

The page layout should be visual but not overcrowded and font size should not be too small. Sassoon, Comic Sans and Times New Roman are the most dyslexia-friendly fonts.

Tasks

Provide a checklist
This can help keep the child with dyslexia on track. It will also help him or her to monitor progress.

Break tasks into manageable chunks
This can provide an opportunity for the learner to experience a regular sense of achievement.

Oral feedback
It is often a good idea to get dyslexic children to provide oral feedback on the task they have to do. This ensures they have understood the task. At the same time, it is important that the teacher provides oral feedback to dyslexic children on how they have managed the task. Oral feedback can be more effective than written comments.

> Do not use red ink when writing on pupils' workbooks!

Planning

Provide a sequence to help with planning
Dyslexic children often have difficulty developing and following an appropriate sequence. It can be useful to provide a structure that helps to sequence learning of new material. In the example that follows, the child is required to provide a summary of the key points in the passage. This, however, can be too demanding a task for the dyslexic learner unless the task is broken down into manageable chunks. For example:

♦ First underline the important words in the passage.
♦ Next write them out on a separate page.
♦ Then write the meaning of each word next to it.
♦ Take one word at a time and indicate why it is important for the passage.
♦ Once you have completed this, decide which word is the most important and say why.
♦ Lastly, give a summary of the key points in the passage.

Help the learner to prioritize his or her work
Often, dyslexic students have difficulty prioritizing their work. This can lead to them spending a lot of time on unimportant areas of the task.

It can be a good idea to indicate what aspects of the task are 'very important', 'quite important' and 'less important'.

Computers and technology

There is a wealth of information on the pros and cons of the extensive use of ICT in schools. See teacher net information on ICT in schools (www.teachernet.gov.uk) and also the book by Jane Healy (1998) *Failure to Connect: How Computers Affect Our Children's Minds and What We Can Do About It*.

There is, however, strong evidence from classroom practice that computers and the ICT can be extremely beneficial for students with dyslexia (Lannen 1990). As a result there are many programmes specifically designed for children and adults with dyslexia and many helpful websites. Some examples are shown below.

The website www.dyslexic.com/readingpen has a range of resources for ICT in the classroom specifically designed for dyslexic learners. These include:

The Reading Pen
This scans, displays, reads aloud and defines words. Designed specifically for people with dyslexia who require support with reading, the Reading Pen is an ideal tool to help with reading.

AcceleRead AcceleWrite CD-Rom with cards
This is a teaching guide to using speech technology to improve literacy skills. The detailed electronic manual explains how reading and writing can be improved dramatically using computer text-to-speech software plus a clear explanation of the theory behind the approach. The comprehensive package also includes perforated, colour-coded flash cards and photocopiable record sheets, along with blank flash cards for you to print off with your own sentences. It requires a computer with a sound card, and a talking word processor or text-to-speech programme.

Read & Write Standard
Read and Write offers speech feedback and word prediction for practically any Windows program. Read and Write has been specifically designed for users with dyslexia and provides many tools to help access and compose written material. Features include high-quality speech feedback, phonetic spellchecker, word prediction, dictionary and talking calculator.

The Teacher's Toolkit enables teachers, administrators or parents to customize Read and Write to meet the requirements of the individual; including turning functions on or off (such as the spellchecker during

Dyslexia

exams) and monitoring spelling mistakes and usage logs.

The style of the toolbar can be customized to be appropriate to the age of the user. Users can choose whether they want basic or advanced word lists and definitions in the dictionary, word prediction list and homophone checker.

This includes:

◆ synchronised speech with text highlighted
◆ screen-reading options, which enable speech from icons, menus, help files and menus
◆ spellchecking as you type. (The spellchecker includes medical and scientific words as well as town and city names.)
◆ phonetic spellchecker, which gives Spelt Alike and Sounds Alike suggestions
◆ word suggestion and completion for slow typists based on sentence context and specialist dictionaries
◆ spoken selection lists for spelling, prediction and dictionary
◆ abbreviation, expansion and automatic word endings

The following software is also available from www.dyslexic.com:

Assessment Software
Produce software such as Lexion and the Lucid range for the purpose of assessing verbal and non-verbal skills and indicating the likelihood of dyslexia. They also produce programs to simulate the experience of being dyslexic and to detect disabilities within a group of employees.

Cross-curricular Software
Dyslexia-friendly software for use across the curriculum.

General and Student Software
Standard office and productivity applications as well as more advanced graphic design and multimedia software, including student editions.

Numeracy Software
Basic maths, fractions, telling the time or calculating money, including the popular Numbershark.

Organizational Software
Concept-mapping and mind-mapping software to help you get ideas down and organize them, useful for those with dyslexia.

Reading and Literacy Software and Tools
A range of tools and software to help overcome literacy problems, such as dyslexia, and visual impairment. This includes text-to-speech tools and also scanning and OCR software, in order to produce electronic versions of paper documents.

Speech-recognition Software
Assistive technology (including market-leader Dragon) that displays dictation on screen and saves it in an electronic format. Spellcheck and editing facilities offer full control over the text. Maths and science versions are also available.

Spelling and Writing Software
Software to help with everything from spelling, grammar, punctuation and typing to actually shaping and producing written work.

Other suppliers

www.cricksoft.com/uk/ has created many high-quality resources for use with Clicker 5. The Clicker Writer is a talking word processor – you can write by using the keyboard, or by selecting letters, words or phrases in the Clicker Grid.

http://xavier.bangor.ac.uk/xavier/sounds_rhymes.shtml has a very comprehensive range of software for dyslexic pupils, such as Sounds & Rhymes.

There is always a constant stream of new software programs and it is important to try demo copies before committing to a purchase.

There are a number of companies that specialize in software for learners with dyslexia, such as iANSYST Ltd (www.dyslexic.com). They provide a full range of text-to-speech software using the more advanced RealSpeak® voices, which are a significant improvement on previous versions and have a much more human-sounding voice. Such software can be very helpful for proofreading, as it is easier to hear mistakes than to see them and it can help to identify if any words are in the wrong place.

The TextHelp® range is also highly recommended. TextHelp Type and Touch 4.0 has integrated speech output for PC or Mac, and includes the TextHelp spellchecker, which has been specifically developed for use by learners with dyslexia.

There are also a number of typing tuition programs that can assist with the development of touch-typing. These include the KAZ typing tutor, which has an age range of 7 to adults, and First Keys to Literacy, which has a recommended age range of 5–9 years. Some of the keyboarding activities include word lists, individual

Dyslexia

letter recognition, digraphs and rhymes, and picture, letter and word prompts.

There is also a program called Magictype, which is a fun interactive program for the 6–11 age range.

There is also a wide range of software on study skills and memory training. Two such programs developed by Jane Mitchell include Mastering Memory and Time 2 Revise/Timely Reminders (www.calsc. co.uk/). Mastering Memory helps to improve short-term memory, enhances the learner's capacity to transfer new information to other areas of learning, and improves long-term retention. Time 2 Revise/ Timely Reminders are packages that can help to structure the revision process, and utilize mind maps, index cards and revision notes. The emphasis is on encouraging the student to use the facts rather than to learn them by rote. This active learning has been shown to be significantly more successful for retention and recall, as well as in enhancing understanding.

There are also other popular programs that help to organize information, such as Kidspiration for the 5–11 age range, and Inspiration, which is also suitable for adults. These help to develop ideas and concepts with examples of concept maps and templates that incorporate a range of subject areas such as languages, arts, science and social studies.

Dimitriadi (2000) suggests that computer technology can facilitate access to the curriculum for bilingual children. She suggests that equipment and programmes can support simultaneous input from different languages in oral, written or visual format and provide bilingual learners with the opportunity to enrich the curriculum with their diverse cultural experiences. Dimitriadi suggests that technology can help to reinforce alphabet skills by establishing correspondence between phonemes and graphemes in one language, and making the necessary connections between the way in which apparently similar graphemes have different sounds in other languages. A talking word processor provides the learners with immediate aural feedback through typing of individual graphemes.

She also puts forward the idea that a voice recognition system programmed to understand regional accents and problematic utterance will encourage the input of speech for translating into script. This can help with spelling, and allow the opportunity to self-check and to construct simple sentences. Spellcheckers with phonically constructed wordbanks facilitate the writing process by generating lists of possible alternatives. It is possible, therefore, according to Dimitriadi, to simultaneously include an oral and a written translation of the word rule into another language. Talking word-processors with pre-recorded word banks can provide immediate aural feedback to the users by repeating each word or sentence typed, and the learner is prompted to self-correct the sentence they typed by seeing their spelling mistakes in the form of highlighted words.

Dimitriadi suggests that computers can help with some of the difficulties related to the directional flow of the learner's written language structure, such as in Cantonese Chinese or in Arabic scripts, where the characters follow a different course to that of European languages. She suggests a multimedia computer allows learners to record their voices instead of typing the information, so they temporarily overcome the burden a new script might pose.

> Technology and other resources can be very useful but there is no substitute for teaching skills and teacher–student interaction.

> Using examples of famous and successful dyslexics can help children with dyslexia to believe in their abilities, but take time to discuss their hopes and concerns with them.

In summary, in this chapter we have addressed the following:

- ◆ Do not only focus on the difficulties and try to use word support rather than remediation.
- ◆ Identify the strengths and take the opportunity to discuss these strengths with the child.
- ◆ Ensure it is possible for the child to achieve some success when tackling set tasks.
- ◆ Get the environment right – try out different types of learning environments.
- ◆ Acknowledge learning styles and learning differences.
- ◆ Provide short tasks.
- ◆ Use colour-coding and encourage the child to use his or her own strategies using colour for remembering information and for separating different pieces of information.
- ◆ Acknowledge that over-learning is necessary – this means repeating instructions and reinforcing the answer through other tasks or through oral discussion.
- ◆ Minimize the need for the child with dyslexia to read aloud.
- ◆ Help children develop strategies to identify the key words. This can be through the use of colour-coding or by underlining the main words.
- ◆ Take the time to ensure that the child has understood the task.

This might mean going over some basic information.

♦ Do not limit the demands of the task because of the child's low level of literacy. Try strategies such as taped books, voice-activated software, or working in groups.

♦ Children with dyslexia need over-learning but they also need time to complete tasks. They may need more time than other children.

♦ Discuss dyslexia with the children so they have an understanding of the differences in how they learn.

♦ Encourage independent learning – give the children the scope to make decisions and help them to have some control over their learning.

♦ Encourage the child to have high expectations. This is important in relation to career and subject choice.

♦ Help children monitor their own progress. This also allows them to provide a degree of control over their own learning.

♦ Give an overview of new learning first before asking them to tackle the individual aspects of it.

♦ Do not hand back marked work without going over it with the child first.

♦ In the class situation, do not obviously single children out because of their dyslexia.

♦ Acknowledge that performances may have an element of inconsistency and vary from day to day. Also remember that children with dyslexia will take longer to achieve automaticity. It is important therefore to provide opportunities for over-learning.

♦ Try to make the learning experience as stress-free as possible for the child with dyslexia.

♦ Above all, learning should be fun! It is important that the child with dyslexia is self-motivated to learn. This can only come about through an understanding of his or her difficulties, and through success.

8

Making Learning Effective

Students with dyslexia need additional support to help them with the reading and writing process. They also need support to help with developing effective skills in learning. This latter aspect is often overlooked as so much of the attention and resources is focused on developing basic literacy skills. It is a mistake, however, to focus on these basic skills at the expense of developing skills that can be used in the wider area of learning. There is a great risk that students with dyslexia can become dependent on teachers to help them structure their work and to organize their study patterns. This means that they often do not develop the potential for independent learning. The consequence of this is that when they leave school or transfer to college they have difficulty in knowing how to learn effectively and identifying the information to remember. One of the main difficulties students at college experience is with organization. This can result in hours of fruitless study and demoralizing results. Learning skills and developing effective learning should be given a high priority in schools, particularly for students with dyslexia. It is important that this is not seen as a priority only for those students in the secondary sector. Primary-aged children need programmes in effective learning just as much as those approaching major examinations.

Effective Learning

Effective learning involves a number of interactive cognitive processes. These cognitive processes include attention, memory, understanding and utilizing prior knowledge. It is also important that the learner knows the type of questions to ask of him/herself when tackling new material. The learner can control these cognitive processes to make learning efficient and effective. To enable this to happen, the skills associated with learning need to be developed from an early age, yet surprisingly these skills are not given the attention they warrant within the school curriculum. Study skills, for example, which can provide the learner with an opportunity to practise and experiment with learning to find the most efficient methods, are often not a curriculum priority; yet this type of programme can help to develop retention of information, comprehension, recall and language concepts. It is vitally important, therefore, that learning skills are addressed at an early stage in education.

> Study skills should be taught at an early age.

Learning Skills and Dyslexia

It is very important that children with dyslexia develop learning skills. One of the difficulties associated with dyslexia is in identifying key points and using efficient learning strategies. People with dyslexia may use many different steps to get an answer to a question, compared to someone who can achieve the answer using a more direct process. In some mathematical problems children with dyslexia may take twice the number of steps to get to the correct response compared with other children (Chinn 2002). This means that they may lose track of the actual problem, and certainly the additional time needed to solve problems in this tangential manner can be to their disadvantage. This emphasizes the importance of developing effective learning skills and strategies at an early age. This can be achieved through:

♦ the use of study skills
♦ discussion of how the child is learning
♦ using strategies such as scaffolding that can help to develop concepts and schemata
♦ comprehension-building exercises
♦ the use of learning styles.

The Process of Learning

The model of social constructivism proposed by Vygotsky (1986a) has been applied to many areas of assessment and learning. It essentially states that one needs to look at how the child's understanding of language and learning is mediated by the learning context and the classroom environment. Burden (2002) suggests that the cultural and social context within which learning takes place is crucial in mediating how a child learns. This implies that learning involves more than just presentation of information: it embraces factors relating to the whole child, and particularly the child's previous cultural and learning experiences. Previous experiences and learning can make new learning meaningful. It is important to establish this before or when new learning is being presented. This process has been termed 'reciprocal teaching' (Palincsar and Brown 1984). This is where the interaction between learner and teacher can establish a scaffold to help the child bridge his or her existing knowledge and experiences with the new material.

Essentially this is achieved through effective question-and-answer interaction between teacher and child. This interaction should build on the child's responses in order to extend his or her thinking.

Nicolson and Fawcett (2008) suggest that for a sensitive analysis of the learning skills of children with dyslexia it is important to follow a child's performance over a period of time, while he or she acquires a skill. This type of 'skills analysis' can reveal the nature of the hurdles experienced by children with dyslexia in relation to learning. They argue that one of the most severe limitations in analyzing learning skills is that often the investigations involve a 'snapshot' of the abilities of various groups of children at one point in time. Fawcett and Nicolson have shown that it is important to avoid this snapshot approach in order to obtain the type of data that can be used to inform more effective learning. They suggest that what is needed is a 'toolbox' of techniques for identifying problems in the various forms and stages of learning, and linking these problems to specific brain regions and appropriate interventions. The key point in this work is that it appears that it is necessary to focus on the development of learning skills as much as it is on literacy skills. Indeed these two sets of skills can be linked so this means that effective learners can learn to read more effectively.

Reciprocal teaching and scaffolding

Reciprocal teaching refers to a procedure that both monitors and enhances comprehension by focusing on processes relating to questioning, clarifying, summarizing and predicting (Palincsar and Brown 1984). This is an interactive process:

♦ the teacher leads the discussion by asking questions
♦ this generates additional questions from participants
♦ the questions are then clarified by the teacher and participants together
♦ the discussion is then summarized by the teacher or participants
♦ then a new 'teacher' is selected by the participants to
♦ lead the discussion on the next section of the text.

Zone of Proximal Development

Reciprocal teaching stems from what Vygotsky (1996b) describes as the 'Zone of Proximal Development'. This refers to the interaction between the teacher and the child, and how much of the learning can be independently accessed by the child and how much requires the teacher to mediate in order for the child to access full understanding and develop further additional related concepts.

Burden (2002) describes the Zone of Proximal Development as the zone where learning can be scaffolded by others. Then, when independent cognitive activity takes place, the scaffolding is gradually removed at appropriate moments. This can be seen as active rather than passive learning as it is a dynamic process and the child can actually determine the nature and extent of the learning experience. This has considerable implications for children and adults with dyslexia as they benefit from active learning, and the scaffolding experience can also help to clarify and establish concepts before the child moves on to further learning. An example is shown below.

Skill to be acquired
♦ Learning to ride a bicycle

Zone of Proximal Development (skills already achieved)
♦ Able to balance
♦ Able to pedal
♦ Has control over the handlebars
♦ Knows how to use the brakes

Scaffolds (supports needed to acquire the skill)
♦ Stabilizers on the bicycle – then removed
♦ Someone holding the seat of the bicycle – then removed

The scaffolds are therefore the link that can help to take the learner out of his or her comfort zone and into a new learning zone and skill.

Scaffolds for reading

Poor readers can find it difficult to make the transfer from book language to their own writing. As a result of this, their writing quite often lacks the precise vocabulary that was perhaps evident during reading. To overcome this difficulty, Cudd and Roberts (1994) introduced a scaffolding technique to develop both sentence sense and vocabulary. They focused on sentence expansion by using vocabulary from the children's readers, and used these as sentence stems to encourage sentence expansion. Thus, the procedure involved:

♦ selecting vocabulary from the basal reader
♦ embedding this vocabulary into sentence stems
♦ selecting particular syntactic structures to introduce the stem
♦ embedding the targeted vocabulary into sentence stems to produce complex sentences
♦ discussing the sentence stems, including the concepts involved
♦ completing a sentence using the stems
♦ repeating the completed sentence, providing oral reinforcement of both the vocabulary and the sentence structure
♦ encouraging the illustration of some of their sentences, helping to give the sentence a specific meaning.

Cudd and Roberts found that this sentence expansion technique provided a 'scaffold' for children to help develop their sentence structure and vocabulary. The children, including those with reading and writing difficulties, were seen to achieve better control over the writing process and gained confidence from using their own ideas and personal experiences.

> It is important that people with dyslexia gain some control over their own learning process.

Transfer of skills

Transfer of skills can best be achieved when emphasis is firmly placed on the *process* of learning, and not on the product. This encourages children to reflect on learning, and to interact with other learners and with the teacher. In this way effective study skills can help to activate learning and provide the child with a structured framework for effective learning.

This involves preparation, planning and reflection.

Preparation looks at the goals of the current work and how these goals relate to previous work. *Planning* looks at the skills and information necessary in order to achieve these goals. *Reflection* assesses the quality of the final piece of work, asking such questions as: 'What did the children learn from the exercise?' and 'To what extent could the

117

skills gained be transferred to other areas?'

This example displays a structure from which it is possible to plan and implement a study skills programme and at the same time evaluate its effectiveness in relation to the extent of transfer of knowledge and skills to other curricular areas.

It is important that children with dyslexia are able to reflect on how they learn, and discuss this.

Metacognitive strategies

Reid (2009) decribes metacognition as thinking about thinking and suggests that it plays an important role in how children learn. He also suggests that this can be vital to help dyslexic children clarify concepts, ideas and situations and therefore make reading more meaningful. Metacognitive strategies can also help in the transfer of learning from one situation to another. Flavell (1979) greatly influenced the field of metacognition and its applications to the classroom, and since then metacognition has been given considerable prominence in schools and in assessment and curriculum activities.

There have been a number of models implemented in relation to metacognition. One that is well established and relevant to the learning of dyslexic children is that proposed by Brown, Armbruster and Baker (1986). This model contains four main variables relevant to learning:

♦ text – the material to be learnt
♦ task – the purpose of reading
♦ strategies – how the learner understands and remembers information
♦ characteristics of the learner – prior experience, background knowledge, interests and motivation.

Children's knowledge of their metacognitive activities can be achieved through:

♦ Thinking aloud as they perform particular tasks.
♦ The encouragement of conscious awareness using self-questioning. For example, asking questions such as: Have I done this before? How did I do it? Is this the best way to tackle this problem?
♦ The encouragement of controlled over-learning. To develop particular strategies for dealing with a task, whether it be reading, spelling or creative writing and to encourage independent learning.

♦ Comprehension-monitoring. For example, the generation of questions while reading and re-reading to comprehend.
♦ Use of discussion to help to activate prior knowledge.
♦ Visual imagery to obtain the main ideas from text, develop concepts through mind maps or webbing and self-questioning, which attempts to relate previous knowledge with the new material to be learned.
♦ Meaningful experiences, which implies that metacognition should be an integral part of the learning process, and embedded within the curriculum and within curricular activities.

Metacognitive approaches can be vital in helping dyslexic children clarify concepts and ideas, and can make reading and learning more meaningful. They can help the child to consider:

♦ *text* – i.e. the material to be learnt
♦ *task* – the purpose of reading or the exercise
♦ *strategies* – how he or she understands and remembers information
♦ *characteristics of the learner* – his or her prior experience, background knowledge, interests and motivation.

It is important for children to be aware of how they learn and for teachers to get some insights into this.

> Try to get children to think about how they are learning or have learnt something. Get them to think aloud.

Assessing metacognitive awareness

This can be achieved by asking yourself if, when tackling a new task, the child demonstrates self-assessment by asking questions such as:

♦ Have I done this before?
♦ How did I tackle it?
♦ What did I find easy?
♦ What was difficult?
♦ Why did I find it easy or difficult?
♦ What did I learn?
♦ What do I have to do to accomplish this task?
♦ How should I tackle it?
♦ Should I tackle it the same way as before?

Dyslexia

This information can inform both the teacher and the child on how the child learns – that is, the processes involved in learning. Using metacognitive strategies is important, because they can help the learner to develop reading comprehension and expressive writing skills. Metacognitive strategies include:

♦ visual imagery – discussing and sketching images from text
♦ summary sentences – identifying the main ideas in text
♦ webbing – the use of concept maps of ideas from a text
♦ self-interrogation – asking questions about what learners already know about a topic and what they may be expected to learn from the new passage.

Healy Eames and Hannafin (2005) have acknowledged many of the points above in their study skills text *Switching on for Learning* (www.fheLearning.com). They emphasize that the learner needs to take responsibility to find out what his or her preferred learning conditions are. This encourages learners to reflect on the learning environment and the optimum environment for them. Healy Eames and Hannafin suggest that learners should reflect on their attitude to learning, as well as the social aspects of learning and the psychology of learning. This ensures that they are ready for the task and have self-knowledge of the best way to tackle it.

> Try to enable learners to monitor their own performances throughout the learning process.

Assessment through retelling

Ulmer and Timothy (2001) developed an alternative assessment framework based on retelling as an instructional and assessment tool. This indicated that informative assessment of a child's comprehension could take place by using criteria relating to how the child retells a story. Ulmer and Timothy suggested the following criteria:

♦ textual – what the child remembered
♦ cognitive – how the child processed the information
♦ affective – how the child felt about the text.

Their two-year study indicated that of the teachers in the study assessed for textual information, only 31 per cent looked for cognitive indicators, and 25 per cent for affective.

Yet the teachers who did go beyond the textual found rich information. Some examples of information provided by the teachers indicated that assessing beyond the textual level in relation to the use of the retelling method of assessment could provide evidence of the child's 'creative side', and they discovered that children could go 'beyond the expectations when given the opportunity'. This is a good example of how looking for alternative means of assessing can link with the child's understandings of text and promote and develop thinking.

It can be suggested that assessment instruments are often based on restrictive criteria, often examining at a textual level what the child may be expected to know but ignoring other rich sources of information that can inform about the child's thinking, both cognitive and affective, and therefore provide suggestions for teaching. Metacognitive assessment strategies go beyond the basic textual level and look at how the child actually relates to the information to be learnt. This is important for children with dyslexia as often they may not grasp the basic point but are able to consider more elaborate and higher-order thoughts. Tom West (1997), in his book *In the Mind's Eye*, highlights this well when he said that for learners with dyslexia, 'the easy is hard and the hard is easy'.

Assessment – dynamic and metacognitive

Traditional forms of assessment, such as standardized assessment can provide information on the child's level of attainments, but usually they do not provide information about the process of thinking utilized by the child. Metacognitive aspects that focus on this process can be extremely valuable and can identify the strategies being used by the child, and they can also be useful teaching tools, through the development of concepts and ideas through teacher–student interaction.

> Assessment should identify the learning strategies used by the student.

> **Reflective exercise**
> How did you learn to ride a bike? How did you learn to swim?
> How did you learn the times tables?
> How do you make sure you added a column of figures correctly with a calculator?
> How do you revise for exams? How do you remember birthdays?
> How do you remember telephone numbers?
> How do you remember people's names?

Dyslexia

The exercise above can help people work out the most effective way of learning for them. Some will have well-established strategies and be able to recollect these easily. For others, it might be the first time they have actually thought about how they did something. It is important to reflect on learning, as it can help to identify the most effective way for the individual to learn.

Multiple intelligences

Since Howard Gardner wrote *Frames of Mind* (1983), the concept of intelligence and its applicability to education has been re-examined. Before then, there was a commonly held view of intelligence as a unitary concept, although that was constantly being re-examined during the second half of the twentieth century. Gardner suggests that when Binet attempted to measure intelligence in the early part of the twentieth century there was indeed an assumption that intelligence was a single entity, and that this could be measured by a single paper-and-pencil instrument (Gardner 1999). This of course had considerable implications for how children were assessed and taught during the mid-twentieth century, and was particularly influential in streaming and in deciding the most appropriate education provision for children. Gardner acknowledges, however, that there has been considerable movement away from this view and application of intelligence, and attempts to highlight the need to 'pluralize the notion of intelligence and to demonstrate that intelligences cannot be adequately measured by short answer paper and pencil tests' (1999, vii).

Gardner also acknowledges that his conceptualization of intelligence is part of a larger effort to examine and define the concept and pluralization of intelligence. At present the multiple intelligence concept developed originally by Gardner involves eight intelligences (see Lazear 1999, p. 131).

Gardner himself therefore has developed his concept of multiple intelligence since the publication of *Frames of Mind*, and accepts that now he does not see intelligence as a set of human potentials but sees it rather 'in terms of the particular social and cultural context in which the individual lives'. According to Gardner, this means that a significant part of an individual's intelligence exists outside his or her head, and this therefore broadens the notion of assessing intelligence to involve many different aspects of a person's skills, thoughts and preferences. The notion of multiple intelligence therefore sits well with this contextualization view of intelligence, and because of this can be more comfortably applied to educational settings. Gardner accepts that intelligences do not work in isolation but usually interact and combine with other intelligences, and where one differs from another is in that combination and how that combination works for the learner. Gardner suggests that all of us possess these eight intelligences in some combination and all have the potential to use them productively. This has clear implications for the classroom and indeed for children with dyslexia, as they will possess these intelligences, perhaps in a different combination from some others, but with the same potential to develop in classroom activities. It is important, therefore, that the notion of multiple intelligence is incorporated not only into assessment but also into the teaching and learning process in schools.

Logical/Mathematical Albert Einstein	**Bodily/Kinesthetic** Sir Jackie Stewart Sir Steve Redgrave
Visual/Spatial Walt Disney Lord Richard Rogers Guy Ritchie	**Intrapersonal** John Irving Agatha Christie
Musical/Rhythmic Cher Noel Gallagher	**Interpersonal** Richard Branson Peter Stringfellow
Verbal/Linguistic Sir Winston Churchill W.B. Yeats	**Naturalistic** Jack Homer

Figure 8.1 Famous dyslexics within the multiple intelligence framework

Lazear (1999) has made considerable efforts to incorporate Gardner's model of intelligence into both assessment and teaching. Each of the eight intelligences can be incorporated, and if this is achieved within one's teaching and in curriculum development, then children who may have weaknesses in some aspects of language or other processing (such as dyslexic children) will benefit. This essentially turns the concept of deficits on its head, and as Gardner points out, every child has the potential for effective learning but their learning preferences and strengths need to be accessed. The eight intelligences can be summarized as follows:

♦ *verbal/linguistic* – involves language-processing
♦ *logical/mathematical ability* – associated with scientific and deductive reasoning

Dyslexia

♦ *visual/spatial* – deals with visual stimuli and visual planning
♦ *bodily/kinesthetic* – involves the ability to express emotions and ideas in action (such as drama and dancing)
♦ *musical/rhythmic* – the ability to recognize rhythmic and tonal patterns
♦ *interpersonal* – involves social skills and working in groups
♦ *intrapersonal* – involves metacognitive-type activities and reflection
♦ *naturalist* – relates to one's appreciation of the natural world around us, the ability to enjoy nature and to classify (for example) different species of flora, and how we incorporate and react emotionally to natural environmental factors such as flowers, plants and animals.

Each of these intelligences can be incorporated into teaching and learning and into curriculum development. It is important therefore that the skills and preferences of, for example, children with dyslexia are utilized within a multiple intelligences curriculum. Lazear (1999) has made considerable effort to highlight the potential of multiple intelligences within daily classroom activities. For example:

♦ *verbal linguistic* – creative writing, poetry and storytelling
♦ *logical/mathematical* – logic and pattern games, problem-solving
♦ *visual/spatial* – guided imagery, drawing and design
♦ *bodily/kinesthetic* – drama, role-play and sports
♦ *musical/rhythmic* – classroom activities relating to tonal patterns, music performance
♦ *intrapersonal* – thinking strategies, metacognition and independent projects
♦ *naturalist* – fieldwork projects on conservation, evolution and the observation of nature.

Multiple intelligences as a guide to classroom practice can be very helpful in ensuring that the curriculum and the learning and teaching provide the opportunity for the child to display and extend his or her natural abilities in many areas. Historically, there has been considerable preoccupation with the verbal/linguistic aspects of intelligence, and this has resulted in a curriculum and examination system that appears to give a preferential status to these areas. This can be disadvantageous to children with dyslexia. It is interesting to note the comment by Pringle-Morgan made as long ago as 1896 (Pringle-Morgan 1896) that there is a group of otherwise intelligent people who have difficulty in expressing their understanding of a situation in writing, and if this group were provided with the opportunity to present their knowledge in some other form (such as orally) they would score considerably higher in examinations. Over 100 years later this message is beginning to get through, but there have been many casualties along the road, and children with dyslexia can account for some of these.

> It is important that people with dyslexia are able to demonstrate their skills in some way. They should not be restricted by the examination system.

Study Skills

Study skills should be considered when developing a programme for dyslexic children. There is evidence that dyslexic children require help in this area principally due to their organizational and memory difficulties. A well-constructed study skills programme is essential and can do much to enhance concept development, metacognitive awareness, transfer of learning and success in the classroom.

Programmes will vary according to the age and stage of the learner. A study skills programme for primary children, for instance, would be different from one to help students cope with examinations at secondary level. Well-developed study skills habits at the primary stage can provide a sound foundation for tackling new material in secondary school and help equip the student for examinations. Some of the principal factors in a study skills programme include:

♦ organization of information
♦ sequencing of events, arranging text into logical sequence
♦ the use of context – memory strategies, using familiar items, thinking about the purpose of learning
♦ the development of schemata: this provides a framework for learning and suggests that the meaning and the understanding of the material to be learnt is important
♦ the development of self-confidence and motivation – learners will be more successful if they have intrinsic motivation. There is also a great deal of evidence to suggest that self-confidence is one of the most important determinants in successful learning.

Organization

Children with dyslexia require help with organization. A structure should therefore be developed to help encourage this. This involves not just

Dyslexia

physical organization, but also how they organize their thinking, learning and retention.

Children may need help with the organization of responses (output), and this can in turn help to organize learning through comprehension (input). The teacher can develop a framework to help develop this type of organization. For example, when discussing a book that has recently been read, a possible framework will include the following questions:

♦ What was the title?
♦ Who were the main characters?
♦ Can you describe the main characters?
♦ What did the main characters try to do?
♦ Who were the other characters in the story?
♦ What was the story about?
♦ What was the main part of the story?
♦ How did the story end?

In this way a structure is provided for the learner to retell the story. Moreover, the learner will be organizing the information into a number of components, such as 'characters', 'story' and 'conclusion'. This will not only make it easier for the learner to retell the story orally, but will help to give him or her an organizational framework that will facilitate the retention of detail. The learner will also be using a strategy that can be used in other contexts. This will help with the new learning and the retention of new material.

> Children with dyslexia will need a structure and a framework to guide their responses to a task.

Sequencing

Dyslexic children may have some difficulty in retelling a story or giving information orally in the correct sequence. It is important that sequencing of information should be encouraged, and exercises that help to facilitate this skill should be developed. For example, in the retelling of a story, children should be provided with a framework that can take account of the sequence of events. Such a framework could include:

♦ How did the story start?
♦ What happened after that?
♦ What was the main part?
♦ How did it end?

Various exercises, such as the use of games, can be developed to help facilitate sequencing skills.

The use of context

Contextual aspects are also important elements in acquiring study skills. Context can be used to help the learner in both the sequencing and organization of materials, as well as providing an aid to comprehension.

Context can be in the form of syntactic and semantic context. In study skills, semantic context can be particularly valuable as a learning and memory aid. If the learner is using or relying on semantic context, this provides some indication that the material is being read and learnt with some understanding. The context can therefore help to:

♦ retain information and aid recall
♦ enhance comprehension
♦ transfer learning to other situations.

The development of schemata

The development of schemata helps the learner organize and categorize information. It also ensures the utilization of background knowledge. This can aid comprehension and recall.

When children read a story or a passage, they need to relate this to their existing framework of knowledge – i.e. to their own schema. So when coming across new knowledge, learners try to fit it into their existing framework of knowledge based on previous learning, which is the schema they possess for that topic or piece of information. It is important for the teacher to find out how developed a child's schema is on a particular topic, before providing more and new information. This helps the teacher to ensure that the child develops appropriate understanding of the new information. Thus, some key points about the passage could help the reader understand the information more readily and provide a framework into which the reader can slot ideas and meaning from the passage. A schema can help the learner:

♦ attend to the incoming information
♦ provide a scaffolding for memory
♦ make inferences from the passage which also aid comprehension and recall
♦ utilize his or her previous knowledge.

There are a number of strategies that can help in the development of schemata. An example of this can be seen in an examination of a framework for a story. In such a framework two principal aspects can be discerned: the *structure* of the story and the details related to the components of the structure.

The *structure* of a story can be seen in the following components:

♦ background
♦ context
♦ characters
♦ beginning
♦ main part
♦ events
♦ conclusion.

The *details* relating to these components can be recalled by asking appropriate questions. Taking the background as an example, one can see how appropriate questioning can help the learner build up a schema to facilitate understanding of the rest of the story:

♦ What was the weather like?
♦ Where did the story take place?
♦ Can you describe the scene?
♦ What were the main colours?

Background knowledge is an important aid to comprehension, although it is postulated that background knowledge in itself is insufficient to facilitate new learning; it must be skilfully interwoven with the new material being learnt. It is important that the learner is able to use the new information in different and unfamiliar situations. Hence, the connections between the reader's background knowledge and the new information must be highlighted in order for the learner to incorporate the new knowledge in a meaningful manner.

The ideas contained in a text therefore must be linked in some way to the reader's background knowledge, and the ideas need to be presented in a coherent and sequential manner. Such coherence and sequencing of ideas at the learning stage not only allows the material to be retained and recalled, but also facilitates effective comprehension. Being aware of the learner's prior knowledge of a lesson is therefore of fundamental importance. Before the learner embarks on new material, prior knowledge can be linked with the new ideas, in order to pave the way for effective study techniques and for strategies to enhance comprehension and recall (Reid and Green 2007).

Self-confidence and motivation

One of the most important ingredients in any intervention programme for children with dyslexia is self-esteem: without a positive self-concept, children with dyslexia will soon opt out of learning. It is important therefore that all teaching should be directed at enhancing self-esteem. There are several ways of achieving this.

There are some programmes that have been specifically developed to boost self-esteem, and others that can indirectly boost self-esteem through the students' achievements. Of the first type, some of the best-known are the circle time programmes (Mosley 1996). There have been many variations on these programmes but essentially they involve a degree of positive feedback, and place a high focus on the individual person. They also promote group work, peer support and conflict resolution (Lannen 1990). These can be particularly suitable for children with dyslexia because they are whole-class activities, and so while they can be beneficial in boosting the self-esteem of children with dyslexia, they have the added benefit that the dyslexic child is not being given different activities.

Self-esteem can also be boosted through achievements in literacy or any other area of the curriculum. Some of the programmes based on behavioural principles with targets and goals to achieve can be extremely useful in this respect. One such programme is Phonic Codecracker (Russell 1992). This programme provides opportunities for students to monitor their own learning and their progress. Indeed, they may get some tangible reward (such as a certificate) for completing a particular objective. It is important that children with dyslexia can see that they are making some progress – however small that progress may seem. A programme operating in this manner is usually developed through a step-by-step approach, and is based on mastery learning. One of the benefits of this for children with dyslexia is that it can also promote over-learning and therefore help to achieve automaticity. It is important for children with dyslexia to attain a degree of automaticity because there is a tendency to forget, for example, spelling rules if these are not used. Automaticity can be achieved by using these rules, or indeed any skill, in different learning contexts. So, for example, if a new word is being learnt it should be introduced into different subject areas and in different ways. Using the new word in this way will help with automaticity as well as in the development of comprehension skills. Programmes based on mastery principles or behavioural objectives can therefore help to achieve this as they can quite readily be adapted to develop automaticity.

Programmes that boost self-esteem have a beneficial effect on confidence and motivation. Such programmes enable the student to succeed. This is important, as the learner needs to have some initial success when beginning a new topic. Success builds on success, and early and significant success is an important factor when new material is being learnt.

These programmes also encourage independent thinking, independent decision-making and help students come to conclusions without too much direction from the teacher. These abilities can also develop confidence in a learner, and help to motivate the learner to tackle new material.

Some of the above study skills can be achieved through the use of thinking skills programmes, such as the CORT programme devised by Edward De Bono (De Bono 1986). These do not only help to enhance thinking skills, but also encourage students to use these skills by helping them to structure their own studying. This can aid the development of appropriate study habits and maximize retention and transfer of information.

Transfer of Knowledge and Skills

A key aspect of effective study skills training is the transfer of skills to other curriculum areas. A number of studies support the view that, in order to achieve this, attention must be given to the context in which learning takes place. Study skills should be integrated into day-to-day teaching in a meaningful way, and not as a separate curriculum area.

Visual skills

Children and adults with dyslexia may have orientation problems, which may be evident in directional confusion. This aspect, even though it may not directly affect every aspect of the curriculum, can lead to a loss of confidence that may permeate work in other areas. To what extent can the teacher help to promote and enhance visual and orientation skills in children with specific difficulties?

According to the principles of skill transfer, it is important that such enhancement takes place within the curriculum and is contextualized within a meaningful task.

Games or specific exercises in mapping and orientation can help to build up confidence in the learner, but there is some uncertainty as to whether such exercises, in isolation, would have a significant skill enhancement effect, and so it is important to use directional and visual cues as much as possible within the context of the curriculum. It may be advantageous to develop specific exercises from materials the learner is using.

Lazear (1999) suggests that visual/spatial skills can be developed through multiple intelligence training that is integrated into everyday classwork. This can be done through exercises involving active imagination; creating patterns with colour pencils and paper; forming mental images and describing these; developing graphic representations; and using perceptual puzzles in games involving spotting similarities and differences.

Lazear (1999) suggests that our education system, which has an emphasis on reasoning, can diminish the importance of imagination. Often the imagination is very fertile in young children but that quality can be lost in the shift to the importance of logic and reason as they progress through school. Lazear emphasizes the importance of awakening the visual/spatial intelligence and suggests that this can be developed in everyone. This is particularly important for children and adults with dyslexia, as they can have significant abilities in the visual area (West 1997) and need to have the opportunity to develop this strength.

Memory skills

Children with dyslexia may have difficulty remembering, retaining and recalling information. This may be due to working memory and short-term memory problems, or naming difficulty, particularly at speed (i.e. difficulty in recalling the name or description of something without cues). It is important therefore to encourage the use of strategies that may facilitate remembering and recall. Such strategies can include repetition and over-learning, the use of mnemonics and Mind Mapping©.

Repetition and over-learning

Short-term memory difficulties can be overcome by repetition and rehearsal of materials. This form of over-learning can be achieved in a variety of ways, and not necessarily through conventional, and often tedious, rote learning.

In order to maximize the effect of repetition of learning, it is important that a multisensory mode of learning is utilized. Repetition of the material to be learnt can be accomplished through oral, visual, auditory and kinesthetic modes. The learner should be able to see, hear, say and touch the materials to be learnt. This reinforces the input stimuli and helps to consolidate the information for use, meaning and transfer to other areas. There are implications here for multi-mode teaching, including the use of movement, perhaps drama, to enhance the kinesthetic mode of learning.

Mnemonics

Mnemonics can be auditory, visual or both. Auditory mnemonics may take the form of rhyming or alliteration, while visual mnemonics can be used by relating the material to be remembered to a familiar scene, such as the classroom.

Mind Mapping©

Mind Mapping© was developed by Buzan to help children and adults develop their learning skills and utilize their abilities to the greatest extent possible. The procedure is now widely used and can extend one's memory capacity and develop lateral thinking (Buzan 1993). It can be a simple or a sophisticated strategy, depending on how it is developed and used by the individual. It is used to help the learner remember a considerable amount of information and encourages students to think of, and develop, the main ideas of a passage or material to be learned.

Essentially, mind maps are *individual* learning tools, and someone else's mind map may not be meaningful to you. It is important, therefore, that children create their own, in order to help both with understanding of key concepts and with the retention and recall of associated facts.

Mind Mapping© can help children not only to remember information, but also to organize that information, and this exercise in itself can aid understanding. Elaborate versions of mind maps can be constructed using pictorial images, symbols and different colours.

Starting to mind map
It is best to start a mind map with something very familiar, such as events that have been recently experienced or a film the student has recently seen.

Example: My weekend
1. Brainstorm all the things you did at the weekend.
2. Place them under categories, such as: family, friends, school, recreation, other things.
3. Make a central image in the middle of the page. This could be a drawing representing the phrase 'my weekend' or a drawing of you.
4. Place all the categories around the image.
5. Extend each of the categories into sub-categories – so, for example, for friends you may have sub-categories, such as: activities with friends, where they took place, conversations.

6. Each of these sub-categories can then be sub-divided into other headings, so 'activities with friends' can be divided into sport, cinema, etc. and for cinema the specific film could be another sub-heading.
7. Finally, once all the information has been put down into a mind map, additional images can be made to represent the words. These need not be works of art, but whatever makes sense to you.

The idea is that the mind map helps the student remember the information and organize it for easier recall. It is also good practice in lateral thinking as it helps the student make connections and extend thinking.

> Metacognitive strategies and study skills are important for children with dyslexia. It is therefore essential that the development of these skills in children with dyslexia is given a high priority in the curriculum.

In this chapter we have considered effective learning approaches for students with dyslexia. Effective learning approaches should all incorporate the following:

♦ communication skills
♦ organization and planning skills
♦ sequencing skills
♦ using context
♦ recognizing the need to develop schema and language concepts
♦ developing confidence, motivation and self-esteem
♦ ensuring the transfer of skills to other areas of the curriculum
♦ developing memory strategies
♦ encouraging learner independence
♦ acknowledging the individuality of the student.

9

Dyslexia in the Secondary School: Making Inclusion Effective

There are many features about secondary schools that can provide a number of challenges for students with dyslexia. The size and range of subjects offered can pose immediate problems for the young person with dyslexia. Additionally, support may not be available in the same way as it was in primary school and very quickly the young person with dyslexia has to become accustomed to a range of different teaching styles. These all require a period of adjustment and yet transition arrangements from primary to secondary school are not always given a high priority.

Some areas of concern for the student with dyslexia include the following:

♦ variety of subjects on offer
♦ availability of learning support and pastoral care
♦ the timetable – how it operates and the break times
♦ orientation – finding their way around the school and finding their friends who may be in different classes
♦ homework – particularly the amount of homework and ensuring it is copied down correctly
♦ who to ask for help if the teacher is not available
♦ additional learning strategies required, particularly memory strategies
♦ planning a balance between homework and other extracurricular activities
♦ remembering items needed for different subjects and school trips.

It is important that advice is available on these aspects and that they are considered when planning induction programmes for new students.

School Support

Many schools are now setting up transition arrangements to help new students at secondary school. These arrangements are very helpful for students with dyslexia. According to Hunter (2009) many schools have programmes where all new students come to the secondary school for a visit late in the summer term and this serves as the first stage in the orientation process. As this can be both exciting and overwhelming, additional meetings are often planned and these can be helpful for students with dyslexia as they can often involve subject teachers and the learning support staff.

Provision and Practice

The gradual acceptance of responsibility on the part of the student is one of the key issues in secondary or high school education. It is important to ensure that students with dyslexia are supported throughout this process and that all members of staff are fully aware of the needs – educationally, socially and emotionally – of young people with dyslexia and are fully involved in this process.

School management has a key role to play and they need to ensure that the following are considered:

♦ The ethos of the school is supportive. The philosophy of the school together with attitudes and actions must be known to all staff, including part-time support and other staff.
♦ All staff should be encouraged to acknowledge that with effective differentiation the curriculum can be accessed by dyslexic students.
♦ All teaching staff need to be supported in order to utilize some of the suggestions made in previous chapters in relation to planning, presentation and the development of materials.
♦ Parents need to be considered. Parents are a very rich support of information and support and it is important that collaboration between home and school is ongoing.

It is important to provide a supportive environment to encourage the young person to assume responsibility for their own learning. This means that they should become less dependent on learning support staff but this can only become a reality if they have the learning skills needed for coping with the range and the quantity of work in secondary schools.

Setting up pastoral care systems and a supportive school ethos is necessary but these can only be effective if there is a simultaneous emphasis on developing independent learning skills. For that reason, modules and units on effective learning are highly beneficial in secondary school and particularly so for students with dyslexia. Examples of this are shown in Chapters 8 and 10 and examples of making learning more accessible for different subjects are highlighted throughout this chapter.

Accessing Subject Content

If the subject materials and teaching plans are developed and implemented in a manner that is compatible with the dyslexic child's abilities, the student should be able to perform on the same terms as his or her peers. Although most of the subject content is determined by examination considerations and prescribed curricula, much can still be done to identify the potential areas of the curriculum that may present difficulties for dyslexic students.

There is therefore no reason why the content of all subjects cannot be developed in a dyslexia-friendly manner. It can be argued that the principles for making information dyslexia-friendly are the same for every subject – that is, forward planning, together with an awareness of dyslexia. This also implies an awareness of differentiation, learning styles and dyslexia-friendly assessment procedures.

The Northern Ireland report called the 'Education of Children and Young People with Specific Learning Difficulties' – the report of the task group on dyslexia (2002), see also Republic of Ireland task force report (2001) – recommended that all teachers and support staff have a good general understanding of the nature of dyslexia and of the difficulties that a dyslexic child may have when coping in the school environment. It is important that recommendations which promote a clear understanding of the nature of those difficulties are put into practice.

Norwich, in an international study comparing teachers perceptions of learning difficulties in the US, UK and the Netherlands, found that 'changed attitudes to SEN/disability' was one of the issue categories that were high among the three countries. The implication of this is that the changed attitudes would promote a normalization of SEN and disabilities such as dyslexia so that teachers adapted and accommodated to them in the classroom as a matter of routine. This would make it more possible to plan and to anticipate the types of challenges that children with dyslexia will likely experience in secondary schools. A good example of this is the series of guides produced by Thomson (2006) in conjunction with Dyslexia Scotland. These guides for all teachers in secondary schools outline, in plain straightforward language, what they need to do to support students with dyslexia.

The emphasis is on what learners with dyslexia *can do* rather than what they 'can't do'. The difficulties experienced by learners with dyslexia are seen as 'barriers to learning' with much attention given to supporting learners overcome these barriers. This places the responsibility firmly on the professionals working in schools. These guides reiterate the view that dealing with dyslexia is a whole-school responsibility and it is important that all teachers are aware of this and the potential impact of dyslexia on the student. Only then will they be able to anticipate the challenges of dyslexia and put adequate accommodations in place.

> The difficulties experienced by students with dyslexia can be antici-pated. Forward planning therefore is necessary to prevent these difficulties becoming obstacles.

Thomson (2006) argues that it is important to consider the underpinning skills necessary to help students understand and access the materials in different subject areas of the curriculum. She suggests that these underpinning skills include:

♦ *Communication skills* – reading, writing, listening, talking and study skills
♦ *Memory skills* – short-term (working) memory, sequencing; shape/symbol/directional confusion; accessing alphabetical rules; reversals of letters and numbers; time and positional difficulties
♦ *Coordination and organization* – handwriting, team games, use of tools and equipment.

She also argues that it is a relatively simple process to initiate adjust-ments to ensure that dyslexic students can access print more easily. For example, in order to minimize visual difficulties, she suggests:

♦ enlarging print or changing font and line spacing
♦ providing text on coloured paper
♦ allowing the use of coloured overlays or reading rulers
♦ providing audio versions of longer texts
♦ scanning shorter text into a computer to take advantage of text-speech software
♦ seating pupil out of direct sunlight and away from fluorescent lighting.

These accommodations are well within the reach of all teachers.
    Similarly in the case of reading for information, which students with dyslexia can find tiresome and offputting, she suggests:

- highlighting key words/information in text
- using a variety of teaching styles
- providing opportunities for discussion of topics
- using video or audio recordings to support/illustrate text content
- numbering lines and paragraphs and providing specific references of location of information
- ensuring that all text materials are clear and legible
- arranging access to a scanner and computer with text-to-speech software
- providing electronic dictionaries and other electronic equipment and software that can help to access text.

Again it is quite feasible for all teachers to take these guidelines into account when planning lessons and the subject curriculum.

Another good example of adopting a whole-school approach to promote curriculum access and teacher awareness is provided by Fife Education Authority in Scotland (2005) in their document 'Specific Learning Differences: Guidance for Teachers and Parents'. In this document the authors emphasize the need for considering a variety of learning and teaching approaches for all students with dyslexia.

Some examples of this approach include:

- thinking skills and discussion using content-free materials that involve minimal reading
- memory and study skills training to help make learning and studying effective
- mind mapping© – utilizing the visual skills of students with dyslexia
- the use of symbols around the school – to help with orientation and finding classes
- the use of appropriate ict hardware and software
- using a reader, scribe or dictaphone
- using multimedia
- working within pairs/groups
- redesigning the classroom layout to allocate areas requiring more room, calm or discussion
- having a whole-school uniformity – in terms of symbols, signs and layout – as this can minimize confusion.

The Fife guidelines emphasize that class teachers should collaborate with the senior management team and the learning support teacher to build in approaches and resources to meet the learning needs of students with dyslexia. They also emphasize that a mutual trust and respect should be for the goal between all those involved in the education and social wellbeing of students with dyslexia.

Principles of Good Practice

Some of the key principles mentioned in this document provide a good blueprint for practice elsewhere. Some of these include:

♦ close parental and pupil involvement
♦ regular planning and review systems
♦ alternative assessment arrangements
♦ enhanced training for all teachers
♦ good linkage and collaboration between class teachers and support staff.

These points emphasize the fact that supporting students with dyslexia is a whole-school responsibility and resources need to be provided to make that a reality.

Some examples of how this can be done in each of the secondary subjects are shown below.

English

In English it is important to use a range of sources. For example, in regard to literature, it is often best to begin with a discussion so that the overall story and plot can be understood before any reading begins. This fits in with the learning style of many dyslexic children – that is, holistic as opposed to analytical processing. This means that the child would need to understand the ideas and the background to the novel before reading it, which also helps to build concepts and a schema (schema essentially refers to the student's own understanding of a situation or an event). It is important therefore that the child with dyslexia has an appropriate schema before commencing to read. Having a schema or framework will help the reader use context and understanding to read difficult words and understand the novel without actually reading every word.

There are many aspects relating to English that can be challenging for students with dyslexia – expressive writing, spelling and grammar, as well as reading accuracy and fluency. It is important to acknowledge the different types of reading activities and the different strategies that can be used for each. Reading for examination questions and reading instructions requires a detailed and accurate form of reading. For the child with dyslexia this will mean that additional time is necessary, and the child can produce a checklist to ensure that he or she has understood the instructions. Such a list can include: What is actually being said/asked? What is required of me? How will I know if I am right? In other words, the teacher is encouraging the child to think about the implications of the instructions and to consider the information gleaned in different ways. By doing this it should become apparent to the student if the question has been misread.

Similarly, in reading for facts the reader can make a checklist of different types of information under different headings. It may also be helpful if the teacher actually provides the headings for the student. The child with dyslexia needs to practise scanning and reading to obtain a general overview or impression of the text. One way to help the child practise scanning is to give him or her a passage to read but not sufficient time to read it. This means the child will be forced to read only the key words.

These factors emphasize the importance of forward planning and breaking challenging areas down into smaller components so that the teacher can identify which of these presents the most challenge, and then work through the range of strategies that can be used for these areas. Some of the strategies include those that can be used for good teaching in general – teaching in a multisensory manner, helping to boost the student's memory through the use of mnemonics, personal spelling notebooks, the use of ICT to help with reading, and the use of the internet to investigate topics, for example. It can sometimes be useful if the child with dyslexia can work in groups, as he or she can share skills with others in the group: the reading part can be done by someone else in the group while the dyslexic child can deal with some of the other aspects of the task.

Reciprocal reading

Reciprocal reading is another way of doing this. It encourages students to check their own understanding and bring active meaning to the text. The teacher goes first, modelling the read-aloud and think-aloud process. It is best to present small units at a time. If a pre-reading discussion is necessary this can be done first.

The procedure is to *read* aloud – the student follows along – then *summarize* what you have read. Teachers can point out important details and paraphrase in a way that helps the student understand the main ideas. This step ensures the student understands what was just read.

Clarify anything confusing or complicated, such as: unfamiliar vocabulary, new or difficult concepts, losing track of the story or meaning. Some strategies that may restore meaning are: re-reading, looking up words in the dictionary/thesaurus or discussing phrases that may be unfamiliar, confusing or difficult to understand.

Ask any *questions* you might have about the text. This stage could lead to additional questions and result in a dialogue by offering possible solutions or providing relevant information.

Make a *prediction* about what will happen next. This stage will provoke imagination and can also provide an opportunity to critically assess the author's intent. This also provides a purpose for continuing to read. Further reading will confirm or reject predictions.

Now the student repeats the same process.

Eventually the student will learn to go through this process without the support of the teacher. This technique takes a lot of modelling and practicing but it can help the student see print in a different and more thought-provoking and meaningful way.

Inferential questioning
Inferential questioning can be a good exercise for students with dyslexia as often this type of questioning can enrich the piece of text and is often overlooked by students with dyslexia as they are too firmly focused on accuracy.

Inferential questioning includes questions such as: What do you think will happen next? Why do you think he said/did what he did? What kind of person was he? Why did that happen?

This will help students develop insights into the text and provide a deeper sense of understanding. To develop inferential thinking, students with dyslexia should be encouraged to:

♦ think aloud and articulate their thoughts as they read or are read to
♦ ask and answer questions that show how they have monitored their own comprehension.

There are a number of strategies that can be used to help students practise using inferences, such as choosing an article and writing down sentences that are either facts from the story or inferences. If the sentences are facts, they can mark them in one colour and if inferences use a different colour.

Another strategy involves choosing a short movie clip and discussing with the student what could be inferred from the clip, e.g. facial expressions, voice tone and the sequence of events.

Creative writing
Many students with dyslexia have difficulty getting started with a piece of writing. This difficulty can be overcome by using prompts as well as providing structure words that can help to inspire, expand and develop storylines.

A prompt can be a key word, a storyline or an event that can inspire a story. Prompts may get the story started but students will need guidance to sustain the story. Prompts can be a title, the first sentence in a story or a description of an event that the writer has to put into context and expand on. Some prompts can include the following:

♦ close your eyes and describe an object in the room
♦ find an old picture from a book or an art gallery and write about the people in it and the type of life you think they experienced
♦ select four words randomly from the dictionary and see if you can use these words in a story.
♦ choose a poem that you like and take one of the lines from the poem as the opener to your story.
♦ write about a weird day at school
♦ write what you would do with three wishes
♦ write about your first toy – or at least the one you can remember most vividly
♦ begin the story with the phrase 'I wish someone would have told me'.

Geography

Geography is a subject that many dyslexic children find accessible. It has the potential to be highly visual and the subject content relates to the study of people and activities in the community and the world around us. In other words, it is a subject that has direct relevance to living in today's world. This means that information in geography can be accessed in a variety of ways – through field trips, visually, or through visits, interviews and observation, quite apart from reading materials.

Additionally, the geography curriculum lays emphasis on the enquiry approach in developing geographical knowledge and understanding, through knowledge of environments throughout the world, an understanding of maps, and using a range of investigative and problem-solving skills. These activities can take place both inside and outside the classroom.

In geography, as in many of the other subject areas, alternatives to the written answer can be used to a great extent. Students with dyslexia usually have skills in the visual/kinesthetic areas as opposed to the auditory area. This means that they will learn more effectively by active learning through projects, field trips and interviews. They may also work well in groups.

It is important to ensure that students with dyslexia can present their work in a variety of ways using multi-media, including tapes, videos and ICT.

Geography is underpinned by understanding, and this is why active participatory learning is essential for dyslexic learners. It is crucial that the skills and abilities of dyslexic students in the areas of visual processing and understanding are not restricted because of lack of access to print materials.

History

History is a subject that can be stimulating and engaging for the dyslexic student. It essentially demands investigation and skills in problem-solving, but too often the actual demands placed on the student relate to memory demands and the learning of massive amount of facts. This of course need not be the case, and it is necessary to consider ways in which the student might acquire the necessary information without resorting to rote memorization.

Dargie (2001) suggests that discussion is the key to this. Talking about an issue, he suggests, can help students rehearse the separate components of a topic and develop an argument that they can then use in written work.

Contributing to a discussion exercise or a group presentation can have positive consequences for the dyslexic learner's self-esteem. Working in groups can also provide the child with practice at experimenting and becoming more familiar with his or her own learning style. It is important, according to Dargie, that students with dyslexia gain experience in the range of specific skills needed for history, such as the ability to question, infer, deduce, propose, estimate, guess, judge and think.

Learning to talk about history can provide a launch pad for reading and writing about history. Similarly, paired homework, with an emphasis upon pupils having to check that their partner can readily explain topic vocabulary, can also provide the confidence to write.

It is important to plan and anticipate the type of difficulties the student with dyslexia may experience in history. One example of this can be listening skills. These can be enhanced by providing dyslexic children with topic content in audio cassette form for individual use in Walkman-type players. According to Dargie (2001), it is also important that history departments plan a reading strategy that seeks to create more self-aware readers, who understand the purpose of their reading and appreciate how and why the text in front of them is shaped in the way that it is. An effective reading strategy in history might include features (taken from Dargie 2001) such as:

♦ Consistent teacher pre-checking of text material and calculation of reading age to ensure students encounter historical text in a planned, progressive way.
♦ A focus upon concept vocabulary and upon discursive connectives that develop historical argument.

Dyslexia

- The selective use of word-processing functions, such as emboldening and/or increasing point size, to highlight the way historical text works.
- The planned reading of material as homework to increase pupil familiarity with the demands of the text by using scissors and highlighter pens to analyze how different kinds of historical text are constructed.
- Highlighting photocopied text to given criteria, for example in search of key phrases.
- Persistent teacher questioning in order to check comprehension. This is particularly important when working with dyslexic readers who may only have partially automatized the decoding of print, and who may not yet be self-generating questions as they read.
- Teacher awareness of the different preferred reading styles of pupils, and of the interactive nature of effective reading.
- Teacher awareness of the difficulties posed by 'weasel words' in history, such as: class, state, party and church, which have an abstract historical usage in addition to their more familiar concrete meaning.
- Teacher alertness to the difficulties posed by subject-specific conventions such as 'c.' for circa, 'IV' for fourth, 'C.' for century, etc.
- Teacher awareness of the need to structure the teacher's own text to meet the needs of different learners, e.g. by avoiding long, multi-clausal sentences, avoiding overuse of passive-voice constructions, planning ways of explaining unfamiliar vocabulary and ideas (e.g. word boxes and marginal scaffolding), keeping text concrete where appropriate rather than abstract, minimizing the use of metaphorical language, being alert to the range of tenses used in history to describe actions in the past.

Examinations can cause considerable anxiety for students with dyslexia, and this can be dealt with by the department through recognition of the type of exam anxiety and perhaps by providing specific study skills aimed at examination revision and by ensuring that the student revises effectively and uses the available time efficiently. It is often the case that children with dyslexia spend a considerable length of time revising but often to no avail – it is important then that the effort made by the student is rewarded. Guidance and support in study and study techniques is therefore as crucial as the student's knowledge and understanding of the actual content of the subject.

Physics

Physics is a subject that can present some difficulties to dyslexic students, but it is also one in which they can do well because it may involve less reading and a high degree of scientific understanding. Holmes (2001) suggests a top-down approach, providing a whole-school awareness of dyslexia and allowing teachers to reflect on the implications of providing for dyslexic students in their own subject.

Other factors that Holmes considers include building a bank of support materials that can become a whole-school resource and recognizing the implications of secondary difficulties that can affect a student's performance in a particular subject – for example, the relationship between mathematics and physics can mean that the student's difficulties in physics are a consequence of mathematics difficulties. This emphasizes the need for a whole-school approach in dealing with dyslexia.

Drama

Drama is a subject that should be enjoyable and accessible to students with dyslexia. However, this is often not the case. There is much more to drama than reading plays and it is important that the dyslexic person becomes actively involved in all aspects of drama. This can include planning the sets and designing costumes. Eadon (2005) suggests that many ideas can come from students themselves, and it is important to allow students to take some initiative, especially since children with dyslexia can have innovative ideas. This of course can also help to boost self-esteem.

It can be very useful to present scripts in a larger-than-normal font size. It is also helpful to use a dyslexia-friendly typeface, such as Comic Sans, Times New Roman or Sassoon. The script should also be spaced out to improve readability – in fact, each sentence can be on a new line.

One of the important aspects about drama is that it has cross-curricular implications. Drama can have a positive spin-off effect in English, art and other subjects, since it has the potential to boost a student's self-concept, and this will have a transferable effect to other subject areas.

Most of the content in all subjects can be made dyslexia-friendly. Often these approaches will benefit all students, and not only those who are dyslexic.

Differentiation

Differentiation can be described as the action necessary to respond to the individual's specific requirements for curriculum access. Essentially, therefore, the differentiation required for dyslexic students should be seen not as a 'special case', but as an essential component of preparation that should be carried out for all pupils. Williams and Lewis (2001), in relation to geography, recognize that differentiation can take place

♦ by task, i.e. providing the student with a range of tasks from which to select
♦ by outcome, which means using a range of assessment strategies so that the dyslexic student can demonstrate his or her knowledge and understanding of the subject
♦ by support – this can include support staff but also parents, school management and collaboration.

It is suggested that differentiation does not mean writing worksheets with reduced content. The following factors can be useful:

♦ knowledge of the 'readability' levels of text and sources of information
♦ paying attention to the design of resources, including the layout and the use of (clearly-labelled) diagrams
♦ provision of printed materials, such as notes and maps, to prevent tracing and arduous note-taking
♦ provision of key words – this can help provide the student with a framework and prevent any difficulties with word recollection
♦ specialized vocabulary spelling lists – important for any subjects that utilize technical terms
♦ tape recordings of key passages – these can obviously be replayed by the student.

Revision

Revision can be taxing on students' memory, particularly students with dyslexia. However, memory problems can be overcome by systematic, planned revision. The object of revision is not to memorize the complete course but rather to enhance understanding of the issues and to be able to develop important points in written work. The key to success for the person with dyslexia is organization. A study plan should be made in detail.

For each topic a programme of multisensory revision should be undertaken. It is possible to identify a number of helpful steps:

- Step 1: Compile notes for the topic. Check that class notes are complete. Are comments on prescribed reading included?
- Step 2: Dictate key points and issues, using a voice-activated tape-recorder.
- Step 3: Listen to information gathered on the tape.
- Step 4: Listen a second time but on this occasion enter the information on a prepared mind map or diagram.
- Step 5: Write linear notes from the diagram.
- Step 6: Put key words for each section on index cards.
- Step 7: Place titles of topic and three or four headings on a postcard.

> Revision, it must be remembered, is an active process, not simply a reading exercise.

Key Issues

Some of the key issues relating to supporting students with dyslexia at secondary school include:

- subject content – ensure it is accessible for all students with dyslexia
- subject delivery – ensure presentation of curriculum acknowledges the learning style and strengths of students with dyslexia, and that the planning takes into account the potential difficulties they may experience with the subject area
- assessment – use a wide range of assessment strategies including oral assessment, or poetry and drama, using all the modalities
- cross-curricular aspects – provide opportunities for collaboration with other subject teachers as this can promote cross-curricular knowledge and concept sharing
- learning styles – acknowledge that *new* learning is presented in a manner that suits the student's learning style
- training – all staff should have at least an awareness of dyslexia
- awareness – the recognition that dealing with dyslexia is a whole-school responsibility.

It is important that these issues are fully addressed so that the student with dyslexic difficulties can achieve some success in different subject areas.

Teaching and learning should be planned together. This implies that knowledge of teaching strategies and of the learner's individual strengths, difficulties and learning style are all necessary in order for planning and presentation of learning to be effective.

Hunter (2001), in referring to the layout of the science classroom, highlights potential pitfalls, particularly relating to organization of group work, that can result in the dyslexic student missing vital information if, for example, the student is seated out of view of demonstrations or even the board. There are organizational implications here, particularly if there are booklets and materials to refer to, which need to be readily accessible and identifiable. The laboratory setting can, however, be very compatible with the learning style of a dyslexic student as it provides scope and space for group work, and flexibility in approaches to learning.

Other subjects, such as modern foreign languages, English, art and drama, which can prove challenging in terms of the amount of reading required, can lend themselves quite easily to kinesthetic approaches by focusing on experiential learning activities. For example, in modern languages – often seen to be a source of considerable difficulty for the dyslexic student and consequently of frustration for the teacher – Crombie and McColl (2001) show how by use of appropriate strategies and consideration of the mode of presentation, dyslexic students can achieve success. They suggest the following:

♦ the use of charts and diagrams to highlight the bigger picture
♦ adding mime and gesture to words
♦ adding pictures to text
♦ using colour to highlight gender or accents
♦ labelling diagrams and charts
♦ using games to consolidate vocabulary
♦ making packs of pocket-size cards
♦ using different colours for different purposes
♦ combining listening and reading by providing text and tape
♦ using mind maps or spidergrams
♦ allowing students to produce their own tapes
♦ presenting information in small amounts, using a variety of means, with frequent opportunities for revision
♦ providing an interest in the country, through showing films, and highlighting literature and culture.

It is important in most subjects for instructions to be short and clear, preferably using bullet points. Also consider the use of labels and key terms to highlight various points. The dyslexic student often has word-finding issues and may need some of the terms used in some subject areas to be reinforced.

Other Considerations

Thinking skills

It is important to consider the development of higher-order thinking skills when teaching children with dyslexia. There may be a tendency to overlook these types of programmes in preference for a more direct decoding/literacy acquisition type of intervention. Some forms of assessment, such as dynamic assessment, which involves providing the learner with assistance during the assessment process, offer an opportunity to utilize thinking skills. This form of assessment encourages the learner to articulate the thinking process, for example, why he or she thinks a certain response is correct. This approach essentially links assessment and teaching, and highlights the child's learning process.

Multilingualism

Usmani (1999) suggests the bilingual, bicultural child may have a broad range of thinking skills that may go undetected if the professional is unaware of the cultural values, or fails to understand them in relation to the assessment and teaching programme.

Bilingualism, or multilingualism, is an area that can present a challenge to those involved in assessment and teaching of learners with dyslexia. Although considerable progress has been made in the development of teacher-friendly assessment and teaching materials for dyslexia, it has been assumed that these materials would be suitable for all children with dyslexic difficulties, irrespective of their cultural and social background. This may not be the case.

The British Psychological Working Party Report (BPS 1999) emphasizes the importance of culturally relevant materials for children with dyslexia, and particularly of culture-fair assessment. Dyslexia, the report suggests, may be 'masked by limited mastery of the language of tuition' (p. 60). It is acknowledged in the report that dyslexia can occur across languages, cultures, socio-economic statuses, races and genders. Yet the report notes that the tools needed to uncover the masking of dyslexic difficulties are not readily available. Furthermore, the message that this gives to teachers is that the key reason why a child is not acquiring literacy skills in the language being taught relates to the bilingual dimension, and not due to any other factor – such as dyslexia.

Many of the teaching approaches suggested for bilingual children are essentially an adaptation of those suggested in Chapter 3, which are aimed mainly at monolingual dyslexic learners. It is important that this adaptation occurs following consultation with school staff, support staff and specialist teachers, and is contextualized for the bilingual child. However, as Deponio, Landon and Reid (2000) indicate, care should be taken to note that some bilingual learners may have difficulty articulating some sounds, especially English vowels and final consonantal morphemes, and speakers of syllable-timed languages such as Cantonese may have difficulty in hearing unstressed syllables in stress-timed English utterances. Previous experience of reading logographic, as opposed to alphabetic, script may also cause difficulties with analogical reading for a literate Chinese pupil. Therefore, more practice in recognizing rhyme and syllable may be necessary for learners from certain language backgrounds.

Berryman and Wearmouth (2009) report on a study conducted in New Zealand. This literacy project aimed to raise the reading achievement of Māori students in two New Zealand bilingual schools and was conducted using a tape-assisted reading resource for students learning to read in the Māori language (Berryman and Woller 2007). In School One, students were encouraged to use the resources with family members for two terms in their homes; while in School Two, the programme was maintained in the school for two terms. Both schools managed to complete two terms of approximately ten weeks in each programme. In each school, the same researcher was able to conduct assessments prior to the intervention and afterwards.

After two consecutive terms of being in the programme, the results indicated that, for students reading at the lowest levels in both schools, improvements were of statistical significance and that they were also much greater than typical. The results indicate the worth of oral language tasks, in collaboration with competent speakers of Māori.

This is a good example of a classroom-focused research project that takes into account the significance of culture for students who find accessing print challenging.

Berryman and Wearmouth (2009) argue that the way in which schools respond to family culture and background and the kind of teacher–student and home–school relationships that exist can serve to either include or alienate students, parents, families and communities. It is important, they argue, for schools to recognize any preconceptions and assumptions in order to negotiate more effective home-school literacy initiatives.

They suggest that research shows the benefits to literacy learning that accrue when schools work to address issues of cultural understandings between themselves and their home communities.

Guise (2010) found in her research in a Higher Education Institution that a more open and explicit process of communication needs to be encouraged. Her research supported the view that students often feel unable to challenge lecturers. This is an area that needs to developed in relation to general critical thinking which should take place in secondary schools.

Awareness-raising

The key to successful planning and presentation of the curriculum and differentiation for dyslexic children is for all staff to have an understanding of the characteristics of dyslexia and the processing style of the individual dyslexic children in their class. This can be done through awareness-raising staff training that can be directed to all staff, and not just to a few specialists (as has been the case in many schools). This is a list of the potential topics that can be included in awareness-raising staff development:

♦ what is dyslexia?
♦ identification and assessment of dyslexia in the classroom
♦ teaching programmes
♦ teaching strategies
♦ learning skills and learning styles
♦ differentiation
♦ using a reading scheme effectively with dyslexic children
♦ planning and presenting curricular materials
♦ thinking skills and the implications of these for dyslexic children
♦ multilingualism and cultural influences
♦ role of parents
♦ whole-school programmes
♦ study skills
♦ role of computers.

Awareness-raising training should be more than a one-off snapshot. Rather, it should be a carefully constructed and contextualized course over a period of time. This can pay dividends as it is very likely that every teacher will have at least one child with dyslexia in his or her class.

This chapter has addressed the following:

♦ There is no 'off-the-shelf' answer to dealing with dyslexia. Ideally a curriculum perspective should be adopted, placing the onus on the teacher to ensure that the curriculum and the tasks are suitably planned, presented and differentiated for children with dyslexia.

♦ For the teacher, working with a child with dyslexia involves knowledge of the child and his or her individual learning and processing style. A comprehensive and curriculum-contextualized assessment is necessary before planning commences.

♦ Contextualized assessment can be conducted by the class teacher, with support from specialists, if available. The class teacher will acquire knowledge of the child in the normal course of teaching the class, and this knowledge is essential to the planning and presentation of the curriculum for children with dyslexia.

♦ Most classroom and teaching adaptations can be put in place quite readily and with minimal resource outlay.

♦ Perhaps the most crucial aspect to consider is the awareness of teachers and management. It is important that all appreciate that students with dyslexia *can* be supported within a whole-school inclusive context. This of course rests on the availability of appropriate training and a commitment from management and governments to provide the resources for this.

10

Specific Learning Difficulties: Overlap, Continuum and Intervention

One frequently asked question is, what distinguishes dyslexia from other specific learning difficulties? Further, what do we mean by 'specific learning difficulties'? Specific learning difficulties are particular processing functions that are significantly discrepant in relation to an individual's other processing abilities. Some of these discrepancies have a profile with a label, such as: 'dyspraxia', 'dysgraphia' and 'dyscalculia'.

Weedon and Reid (2002, 9) identified 15 specific learning difficulties during the development work for a screening procedure for specific learning difficulties called SNAP (Special Needs Assessment Profile V3). It was indicated during the piloting of the instrument that at least seven of these had strong cross-correlations with each other (Weedon and Reid 2003, 2005).

The specific learning difficulties identified in SNAP (Weedon and Reid 2003, 2005, 9) included the following:

♦ coordination difficulties
♦ hyperlexia (low comprehension but good decoding skills)
♦ language and communication difficulties
♦ dyslexia
♦ auditory processing difficulties
♦ hyperactivity
♦ attention difficulties
♦ dyscalculia
♦ working-memory difficulties
♦ information-processing difficulties
♦ non-verbal difficulties
♦ literacy difficulties
♦ phonological processing difficulties
♦ visual difficulties
♦ social awareness difficulties.

Dyslexia

Generally, however, the broad range of specific learning difficulties can be grouped into:

♦ language-related difficulties
♦ attention difficulties
♦ motor difficulties
♦ social difficulties.

Like dyslexia, many of the other specific learning difficulties can be seen within a continuum. The term 'co-morbidity' is now used to describe the overlap between the different specific learning difficulties. It is not unusual, for example, for dyslexia, dyspraxia and, to a certain extent, attention deficit hyperactivity disorder (ADHD) to share some common factors.

Perhaps the syndrome which has attracted the most interest in terms of co-morbidity is ADHD, yet this syndrome itself is subject to controversy and debate about whether it has a distinct aetiology. Some of the specific learning difficulties that can overlap with dyslexia are described as follows.

Dyspraxia, or Developmental Coordination Disorder

Dyspraxia and Development Coordination Disorder (DCD) affect motor/coordination functions. DCD can range from mild to severe and can affect fine motor activities, such as pencil grip and scissors control, and gross motor activities, such as movement and balance. According to the classification in DSM-IV (American Psychiatric Association 2000), DCD is recognized by a marked impairment in the development of motor coordination, particularly if this impairment significantly interferes with academic achievement or activities of daily life.

Children with DCD may, however, have a range of other difficulties that can be associated with other types of specific learning difficulties. It may, therefore, be more useful for the teacher to be aware of the specific characteristics of an individual child's profile, rather than labelling them. This also highlights the view that children can have different profiles for the same difficulty. For example, some children with characteristics of DCD may also have significant difficulties in working memory, while other children may not.

Characteristics for a number of specific learning difficulties can include, to a greater or lesser extent, aspects relating to:

♦ working memory
♦ auditory processing
♦ fine motor skills

154

♦ phonological skills
♦ non-verbal skills
♦ literacy skills.

These processing difficulties relate to skills that are necessary for a range of learning tasks and that affect attention, memory and reading. It is not surprising, therefore, that some overlap exists between them. One common element shared by all the special learning difficulties is the resulting low level of self-esteem often experienced by children. This can be addressed without recourse to a label, as a self-esteem programme can have a beneficial effect on all children. Jones (2005) suggests that even low-level intervention significantly increases self-esteem and has the secondary effect of improving classroom performance. This point is reinforced by Kirby (2003), particularly in relation to adolescents. Kirby suggests that adolescence is a difficult period for most children, but for an individual with DCD it can be twice as hard. Amanda Kirby, the Medical Director of the Dyscovery Centre in the UK and the mother of a DCD child herself, suggests it is important that the child with DCD obtains support and practice in building relationships and coping with secondary or high school.

Dyspraxia

The term dyspraxia is more popular than DCD although the terms can be used interchangeably. According to Macintyre (2009), dyspraxia is primarily a difficulty in achieving motor milestones at the correct times – meaning, therefore, that carrying out many of the activities fundamental to living and learning will be delayed and difficult.

In the table below, 'movement skills' lists everyday activities and 'planning skills' lists the control the student needs over each activity. People with dyspraxia often do not have this control.

Movement skills	Planning skills
Balancing: being able to sustain an upright posture and recover poise.	Knowing what to do and where to go, i.e. using environmental cues.
Coordinating different body parts to effect balance. Knowing where these parts are in relation to one another. Appreciating body boundary, i.e. where the body ends and the outside world begins.	Remembering, reflecting and building on previous similar experiences in the memory to inform the new experience. This is called habituation.

(continued)

155

Dyslexia

(*continued from previous page*)

Movement skills	Planning skills
Controlling the pace and timing of movement so that a rhythm emerges.	Sequencing the order of actions, i.e. knowing what comes first and what follows.
Using the correct amount of strength, speed and space to organize an efficient movement pattern.	Using immediate feedback from one attempt to improve the next.

Macintyre (2009) provides a number of pointers for identifying dyspraxia:

Body boundary

Some dyspraxic children have difficulty differentiating where they end and where the environment begins. These children usually bump and barge – not because they are uncaring of others, but because they don't naturally recognize where their bodies finish. Their body and spatial awareness is poorly developed.

Use of feedback

This refers to activities such as running to jump over a puddle. Usually, when they first undertake this type of activity, children will save that movement in their memory store and the next time they try they will build on that experience to amend their first try. This ensures that they make progress. So, if on their first attempt they landed in the puddle, they would run faster and use the increased momentum to jump higher so they would be more successful in clearing the obstacle. Children with dyspraxia don't seem to be able to do this. They repeat the same movement errors again and again. They do not use self-feedback. This means that each repeated action is like a first-time try. Mistakes are repeated again and again.

Transfer of learning

Linked to use of feedback is the ability to understand (intuitively) that acquired skills can be used in more than one situation/environment. So, in non-dyspraxic children, climbing one set of stairs eases coping with another even when the riser and tread are different. They transfer the balance and coordination from one setting to the next. For them, learning to draw a large circle embeds the shape in their memories so that writing cursive letters is eased. But many children with dyspraxia do not have the ability to appreciate that transferring skill from one environment to another is possible. Macintyre reports on how a teacher, eventually having taught a child with dyspraxia to swim in the school pool was amazed to be asked, 'Now can you come and teach me to swim in the pool at home?' The child had no notion that the skill could be used again in another venue with no further instruction.

Dyspraxia as a difference

The Dyspraxia Foundation describes dyspraxia as a specific learning difficulty or learning difference that relates to an impairment or immaturity in the organization of movement. This leads to associated problems with language, perception and thought.

Dyspraxia is considered to be a specific learning difficulty because dyspraxic children's performance score on motor tasks is lower, often significantly lower, than other aspects of their development. Children and adults with dyspraxia do not necessarily have a pervasive developmental disorder, i.e. an all-over low level of attainment, but they can be surprisingly low on one aspect. Recognizing this, the Irish Support for Learning Association (2007) suggests that dyspraxia means that some children, despite adequate teaching, a stimulating environment and a normal intellect, have constant difficulty in moving well. They recognize that children with dyspraxia are intelligent, but that movement difficulties prevent them fulfilling their potential. This means that a diagnosis of dyspraxia is best carried out as early as possible.

Critical periods

There are critical learning times when movement patterns are more easily acquired. Generally, this is in the first four to seven years of a child's life, when the brain is using more glucose than at any other time in its life.

The vital importance of early years' education has long been highlighted – when all the building blocks are put in place and children begin to develop a sense of self. In these early years, however, children tend to be egocentric. This means they are less likely to compare their motor skills to those of others. The aim of intervention is to reduce the children's difficulties before they impact on their confidence and self-esteem.

Children with dyspraxia can look just the same as their peers. Kirby (2006) explains that dyspraxia is a hidden handicap and this means that often the difficulty may not be noted by others. While there are some advantages to this it is usually disadvantageous. Children with dyspraxia may have low self-esteem because they feel different from their peer group. They may not be good at sport and this can isolate them from their peer group and, for example, they may be the last to be chosen for team games.

As indicated previously dyspraxia can be referred to as Developmental Coordination Disorder (DCD). The term DCD appears in the American Psychiatric Association's (APA) Manual for Mental Disorders (1994).

The essential feature of Developmental Coordination Disorder is described as 'a marked' impairment in the development of motor coordination (criterion A). The diagnosis is made only if this impairment significantly interferes with academic achievement or activities of daily living (criterion B). The prevalence of DCD has been estimated as high as 6 per cent for children in the age range of 5–11 years (American Psychiatric Association 1994). The problem affects more boys than girls in a ratio of 3–4: 1 (Sugden 2008).

Keeping positive – the issue of labelling

Although dyspraxia brings a number of problems and many frustrations, if parents and teachers focus on things the children can do, this prevents children building negative self-evaluations and coming to believe that they are no use at all. This raises the important question as to whether young children should be given a label and, if so, what label?

There are no blood tests that show whether a child has dyspraxia and there are no clear cut-off points within tests that indicate that one child has the condition while another does not. No two children will be the same. There is not one 'typical' dyspraxic child. This causes confusion in making a diagnosis and giving accurate labels. Sometimes bewildered parents will wonder why their child has been told he has dyspraxia while his friend 'who is just the same' is told he has dyslexia. Perhaps this is why some education authorities insist on psychologists being involved.

Sometimes this confusion and a reluctance to give a label, delays early intervention as some parents and teachers decide to wait and see if maturation will reduce the difficulties. Interestingly, some children can pass a test when they concentrate on one thing at testing time, but when simultaneous movement demands are made in everyday coping skills or in changing environments, their true skills, or lack of them, are revealed. This is why those in daily contact with the child are often best placed to make assessments. They can build a profile of the children's coping skills as they occur naturally in the day and they can focus on the things the children do well in a reassuring environment.

They can help keep their difficulties in proportion. The difficulty with not giving a label is that children may self-blame. At the same time, if they are given another label, e.g. being stupid or lazy, that will be very hurtful and of course untrue.

Observing the signs of dyspraxia – screening and assessment

The variation in level and kind of difficulties means that there is not one typical child with dyspraxia. Observing the children over a variety of activities at different times of the day, with different people around and if possible in different environments, is essential. If video clips can be dated, then a movement record showing progress or recession is possible. This type of record can provide an accurate profile of the children's difficulties. Seeing movement is much easier than hearing someone describe it.

Testing

The Movement ABC Test Battery (Henderson and Sugden 1992, Sugden 2008) is one of the most well-known standardized tests used by a range of professionals including advisory teachers and specialist PE teachers. The ABC movement may be administered by professionals with a wide range of expertise and experience. From the education professions, psychologists, physical education teachers, teachers in special education and classroom teachers may find it helpful; and from the health professions, pediatricians, and physical, occupational and speech therapists may find it provides them with useful information.

To use the Test and Checklist in their standard format, no special training is required. Examiners require familiarity with the general procedures of standardized testing and some experience of working with children, especially preschoolers and children with special educational needs. Using the Movement ABC Test with the qualitative observations is more difficult and requires skill and experience in observing children. For some professionals, these skills will have been developed during their specialist training; for others, additional training may have to be sought.

The Battery has the following features:

♦ It is concerned with the identification and description of impairments of motor function in children.
♦ The Test provides objective quantitative data on performance. Its score indicates the extent to which a child falls below the level of

159

his or her age peers. No attempt is made to differentiate between children who perform above this level. Age norms are provided for children aged 4–12, based upon a representative sample of over 1200 children.

♦ Administration of the basic form of the test takes 20–40 minutes depending on the age and degree of difficulty experienced by the child.

♦ The formal assessment is paralleled by an observational approach designed to help the examiner observe how the child performs each task in the test, and to pinpoint emotional and motivational difficulties the child may have in relation to motor tasks.

♦ It provides a structured framework within which to identify a child's strengths and weaknesses and to indicate directions for further assessment or remediation.

♦ The Manual includes a complete section designed to support the management and remediation of movement difficulties.

♦ It may be used by professionals with a variety of backgrounds and training from both the educational and medical fields.

How soon can one tell if dyspraxia is present?

This varies according to the severity of the condition and the awareness of the parents and pediatricians the baby meets. One of the earliest signs is that the baby is hypotonic, i.e. showing poor muscle tone. This lack of strength becomes even more evident when the baby is late in achieving his/her motor milestones. If the muscles lack tone, they do not hold the joints firm and so movement is delayed or distorted. Some education authorities, however, will not provide labels before children are six years old. This is because it provides an opportunity for maturation of the nervous system, which can reduce the difficulties. It is perhaps preferable to acknowledge a difficulty early so that support can begin at the critically important time.

Some characteristics of dyspraxia

Children with dyspraxia may:

♦ move in an ungainly, uncoordinated way
♦ appear reluctant to try new movement activities
♦ bump into things because they have misjudged the space between them
♦ get tired and irritable easily
♦ ignore instructions
♦ begin a task then forget what comes next

♦ make the same mistakes over and over again
♦ have difficulty articulating clearly
♦ find it impossible to manage fiddly jobs such as doing up zips and buttons
♦ make two hands work together at the midline of the body
♦ stand or sit still and wait for a turn.

Checklist for motor development

The child may:

♦ appear uncoordinated
♦ have difficulty naming and locating body parts
♦ have trouble judging the force needed to throw balls
♦ demonstrate a lack of control and direction when throwing a ball
♦ have poor balance, both static and dynamic
♦ have poor posture and muscle tone
♦ use either foot to kick
♦ have problems with running and jumping
♦ experience difficulty with handwriting and scissor skills
♦ not be able to sit appropriately on a chair
♦ possess low self-esteem.

Motor organization

The child may have difficulty with:

♦ the order of garments when dressing
♦ organizing work, often losing and dropping things
♦ remembering the right school books, often leaving homework at home, difficulty managing time
♦ telling directions, getting lost easily – may have difficulty finding way around the school.

Visual perception

The child may have difficulty with:

♦ planning; and layout of work may be poor
♦ consistently spacing words and sizing letters. This may vary from day to day
♦ remembering an image when it is removed, for example: copying from the board
♦ remembering a series of visual images in order.

Auditory perception

The child may have difficulty with:

- distinguishing appropriate sounds in the classroom, e.g. teacher's/children's voices
- discriminating and focusing on appropriate sounds and ignoring background noise
- recalling sounds in order, including following directions.

The Role of Fatty Acid

Portwood's (2006) research into the effects of fatty acid supplementation found that 60 per cent of children with movement difficulties were helped by a nutritional supplement that can be bought over the counter at chemists. This was not a medication so there are no unknown long-term effects to worry parents. After six months, children taking the supplement were calmer and more controlled in carrying out their movement patterns.

Comment

Irrespective of the approach adopted and the conceptual understanding and the intervention advocated for DCD (and the other specific learning difficulties), it is important to see the bigger picture. This means viewing the child in relation to the learning environment in a holistic and global manner. Importantly, it is crucial to identify the high-risk factors as early as possible and this can put some responsibility on the class teacher but at the same time the identification and intervention for DCD and dyspraxia should be seen as a whole-school responsibility (Portwood 2000, 2001).

Dysgraphia

You will have noted above that dyspraxia can include children with fine motor difficulties as well as difficulties in movement and coordination. Those children who also have fine motor difficulties will find writing and sometimes keyboard skills challenging. This means that some children with dyspraxia will also have dysgraphia. At the same time some children may only have dysgraphia and be well coordinated in other areas of movement and may even play sport and other physical activities well.

The Importance of Handwriting

Handwriting is an important element of communication. Even though computers can now replace handwriting for many of the main communication functions, handwriting is still required for many day-to-day purposes. Children who have severe difficulties in this area are therefore at a considerable disadvantage in the school system and in their lives outside the school. Learning to spell is aided by the motor patterns of letters becoming reinforced as the child learns to write them. Writing is a social skill in most cultures so it is important that any children who have difficulties in this area have these difficulties investigated and plans made to bring their handwriting to an acceptable level of legibility. These plans should be included in the Individual Education Plan if the child is dysgraphic.

Writing difficulties are the most regularly reported problems in children who have Developmental Coordination Disorder (DCD). According to Smits-Engelsman and Van Galen (1997), 'the common feature of dysgraphic children is that even with the proper amount of instruction and practice, they fail to make sufficient progress in the acquisition of the fine motor task of handwriting' (p. 165). Dysgraphia is characterized by illegible handwriting with letters wrongly sized or spaced incorrectly. Words are frequently misspelled even though the child may be able to read the word correctly. First signs of dysgraphia are generally there when the child first starts to write their name at nursery stage. Often there is overlap with other syndromes such as dyslexia, DCD and ADHD. This is only to be expected as dysgraphic difficulties relate to motor skills as well as to processing skills. Children need to learn both the thinking skills to enable them to communicate on paper and the motor skills and spatial skills to enable them to set out their work in a legible form.

Checklist

Signs of dysgraphia include:

♦ poor pencil grip
♦ too much/little pressure on pencil
♦ poor letter formation and spacing between words (despite practice)
♦ inconsistencies in style (mix of cursive and print in the same word with a mix of upper- and lower-case lettering)
♦ unfinished words or letters, words omitted
♦ awkward seating position when writing
♦ difficulty writing numbers and copying geometric shapes

Dyslexia

♦ difficulty with practical tasks like using scissors
♦ content out of character with the appearance of the work.

Motor organization

Children with dysgraphia often:

♦ have difficulty with the order of garments when dressing
♦ have difficulty organizing work, losing and dropping things
♦ get mixed up about the right books to take to school
♦ have difficulty organizing time schedules and understanding the passage of time – e.g. don't realize that having work ready for Wednesday means that it will need to be done by Tuesday
♦ get lost easily – may have difficulty finding way around school
♦ difficulty understanding and/or giving directions.

Visual perception

Children with dysgraphia often have:

♦ poor planning and layout of work
♦ variable presentation regarding the size and shape of the letters – difficulties may seem to differ from day to day
♦ difficulty remembering an image when it is removed, for example: copying when the image is not immediately in front of them
♦ poor visual sequential memory – remembering a series of visual images in order.

Auditory perception

Children with dysgraphia often have:

♦ difficulty discriminating appropriate sounds in the classroom, e.g. teacher's/children's voices
♦ difficulty discriminating and focusing on appropriate sounds and ignoring background noise
♦ difficulty recalling sounds in order, including following directions.

Approaches and strategies for dysgraphia

Strategies aimed at tackling the difficulties associated with dysgraphia can be dealt with under three main headings:

Direct teaching
Providing focused instruction designed to tackle the difficulties encountered. (Precise assessment of the actual difficulties is required to ensure the teaching is of the right nature – for example, look at specific letter formation and identify the letters that are incorrectly formed, then teach the letter shapes in a multisensory way.)

Accommodations
Putting steps in place to avoid the most difficult tasks and to enable the children to show what they can do when the writing task is avoided.

Modifications
Changing the medium used for communication – handwriting to typing or speech input on a computer.

As a first stage in tackling the difficulties associated with dysgraphia (as for the other syndromes), it is best to ensure that eyesight is all right and that there are no other problems with the eyes. This check should include a test from an orthoptic specialist to ensure that the eyes are well coordinated as this could in itself be causing difficulty. Any difficulties with binocular vision or eye movements may be able to be treated and advice from a specialist should be followed and used to inform the teaching.

Direct teaching approaches

Teaching approaches for dealing with dysgraphia will depend on the exact profile of difficulties exhibited, but if the child has significant motor difficulties overall then it is likely that help from an occupational therapist should be sought. The therapist can advise on the best course of action that should be linked to the teaching programme. This is likely to include physical exercises aimed at developing fine motor skills and from there an improvement in handwriting could be expected. The programme may then require a re-teaching of letter shape patterns as the child may have got into bad habits from seeing unrewarding images each time he/she writes. It is usually best to teach the letter shape patterns by starting big (writing in the air) and then working down to smaller (writing on the board), and then on to paper.

Difficulty in understanding spatial relationships (sometimes called spatial dysgraphia) may benefit from physical exercises designed to help the child to orientate him/herself in space. Further strategies for direct teaching are shown below.

Dyslexia

Cursive writing
The writing will start to flow more easily if the child doesn't have to think where to begin and end the letters. Ensure each letter begins on the line. The child will need to be taught how joins are made and the correct letter formation patterns.

Pencil grip
Depending on the age and stage of the child, encourage the correct pencil grip. There are many grips and specially shaped pencils and pens on the market. Allow the child to try these out. For older children, sometimes a triangular pencil is easier to hold correctly and other children are not so aware of the difference.

Sitting position
Teach the child how to sit in an appropriate position, holding the writing paper or jotter in place with one hand and using the other for writing. The positioning will depend on whether the child is right- or left-handed. If the child's difficulties are severe, a sloping board for handwriting might help. Insist on legibility over speed.

Multisensory approach
Always encourage a multisensory approach, getting the child to: see what they are writing (a letter or word); say what they are writing (at first to establish letter shape – for example, saying, 'up, down and round', then the letter sound or name and later spelling out the word); hear the sound of their own voice saying it; writing it (air writing, tracing in sand or any other medium that feels good to the child). Young children can pretend to be planes in the gym, and fly the shape saying out the pattern as they do.

Some types of dysgraphia do not seem to readily respond to direct-teaching programmes and, if this is the case, then you will certainly want to ensure that you take account of the different types of strategies mentioned above. Even if you do see an improvement in handwriting, you will still probably wish to consider the other approaches as the child will tire easily from the effort required to produce acceptable written work.

Accommodation approaches
There will probably come a point in the teaching when you feel it is appropriate to put in support that will ensure that the child or young person is able to show what they can do without always having to rely on handwriting. Appropriate accommodations will of course vary according to the age and stage of the children. The following bullet points will give you some ideas of the accommodations that can be made to take account of a child's needs.

Scribe
Organize a scribe to do the writing for the dysgraphic child. In this case the child will use their own idea(s), and the other person will do the writing. Care has to be taken to ensure that this does not affect self-esteem, so any partner or peer supporter has to be chosen with care.

Headstart
Allowing the student to begin their work ahead of the rest of the class may provide them with the incentive they need as they know there will be time to get through the tasks of writing without undue pressure. Sometimes it may also be desirable to allow the student to start preparing a piece of work at home, and then allow them to finish it off in class. Expecting slightly less work from the student with dysgraphia too will help ease the pressure and allow more time to concentrate on the writing skills and presentation. You might also be able to allow the student to use abbreviations for some longer words to minimize the amount of writing required.

Special paper and templates
Allow students to use paper with raised lines to help keep writing on the line. Allow students to use graph paper or boxes for number work. Provide templates where possible so the child does not have to spend time planning out work. This is particularly important for any student with spatial dysgraphia.

Mind maps
Encourage the use of mind maps as tools for planning. Students can brainstorm their ideas, and then sort them by numbering into a logical sequence.

Divide tasks into steps
Break down the tasks of writing into a series of manageable stages. This can involve drawing the mind map, drafting, editing and proofreading. If a longer piece of work, this should be done on the computer to make the task easier.

Provide notes
Provide the student with a set of notes to avoid them needing to take notes while they are listening. Automaticity as we have seen in the other parts of this course is something that students with special learning difficulties find very difficult. Alternatively, allow the young person to record your voice while you are speaking so that separate notes are not required.

Dyslexia

Mark for content only

Mark for content and not presentation or spelling. Ensure that you praise the child for good attempts. Have an understanding peer help with spelling and/or allow the use of a speaking spellchecker. Headphones will be needed for use in class.

Modification approaches

Possible modifications for children with dysgraphia would be to accept the young person's work in a different medium.

Digital voice recorders

Digital voice recorders are useful for all children and it need not only be the dysgraphic child who presents their work in another medium. Be prepared to accept children's work in a form that suits them. This may initially seem like hard work for the teacher, but with some help and support the children can generally learn to present their work without the need for a lot of help. Digital recording software can be organized and downloaded, or else children may type directly on to the computer. Keyboard skills will be required, but if the child's difficulties are such that coordination is very poor on the keyboard as well as in handwriting, it may be best to opt for a word processor that will accept voice input. Examples of this type of software are given in Chapter 8, but some are also included at the end of this chapter.

Accept one-word answers

Be prepared to accept one-word answers instead of a whole sentence, or to insist on the first answer being a sentence and thereafter one-word answers. Adjust the demands depending on the specific needs of the child or young person.

Group/pair work

Encourage paired or group work where cooperative writing is positively encouraged.

Modify the length and style of assignments

Why does everyone need to write 1,000 words? Could you accept the assignment in note form? The student may need to understand that this may not be acceptable to every teacher. Set out a format that will be acceptable depending on the topic and/or genre. Introduce five rules:

1. It must contain two ideas.
2. It must mention four people.
3. It must say where, when, why and how.

4. It must say what happened.
5. It must say how it ended.

Introduce the motto: 'Quality not Quantity' and apply it to content, rather than handwriting.

Handwriting checklist

Note the observations made by Jones (2005) regarding how to observe handwriting in the classroom. Make an attempt to apply this checklist in your place of work. Reflect on how easy or difficult you found it. What might you add to this to get the information you need to develop an IEP for a child with dysgraphia?

Observations	Yes/No	Consider
Does the child seem unsure which hand to hold the pencil in?		Hand dominance
Is the pencil held in an abnormal grip?		Grip
Does the child sit appropriately on a chair when writing?		Posture
Does the child slump forward onto the table when writing?		Posture
Does the child position the paper awkwardly when writing?		Paper position
Does the child lift their wrist off the paper when writing?		Grip
Is too much pressure applied through the pencil?		Grip
Is too little pressure applied through the pencil?		Grip
Are letters formed appropriately?		Letter formation
Are reversed or inverted letters evident?		Letter formation

(continued)

Dyslexia

(continued from previous page)

Does the child commence writing at the left side of the page?		Left to right
Does the writing slope downwards across a page rather than follow a horizontal direction?		Letter formation
Are inadequate spaces left between words?		Spacing
Are the sizes of letters erratic?		Size of letters
Are letters incompletely formed, i.e. the cross bar is missing from the 't'?		Letter formation
Does the child's writing contain an erratic mixture of upper- and lower-case lettering?		Letter formation
Do you struggle to identify distinct ascenders and descenders in the child's writing?		Size of letters
Does the child struggle to join letters appropriately?		Joins
Does writing appear slow and laboured?		Speed
Is the speed of writing slow?		Speed

Handwriting Speed and Legibility Test (from Jones 2005)

In order to collect the information listed on the handwriting checklist the following legibility and speed test could be administered. You will need the following equipment:

◆ legibility and speed sheets
◆ pen/pencil
◆ stopwatch.

When testing an individual the activity should be timed. The duration of the test is 3 minutes. The pupil from the junior sector is asked to copy the sentence: 'The quick brown jumps over the lazy dog.' Pupils from the infants sector copy the words 'cats and dogs'. This should be done:

♦ as quickly as possible
♦ without correcting
♦ as neatly as possible.

Norms for handwriting speed suggest that:
   A child of 7 years writes 28 letters a minute
 8 36
 9 45
10 52
11 60
12 67
13 75 letters or 13–15 words

Resources

Computer software

♦ *Iansyst* have a selection of suitable software including *Dragon* and *MacSpeech Dictate* (speech recognition software for PC and Mac).
♦ *Audio Notetaker* will enable notes to be made through audio recording. The program will help annotation and organization of notes and audio files. Recordings of notes can be edited and exported to Mac.

Stationery

Jones (2005) provides the following list of potential resources to help students with dysgraphia:

♦ Handhugger pens/pencils
♦ Chunky crayons/coloured pencils
♦ Ultra-pencil grips
♦ Ridged comfort grips
♦ Ridged ruler
♦ Selection raised line paper
♦ Plastic lower-case letters
♦ Left-handed ruler
♦ Angle board
♦ Plastic lower-case letters
♦ Selection of pencil grips (tri-glo grip, comfort grip, stubbi grip, triangular grip)
♦ Handwriting whiteboard
♦ Handwriting demonstration sheet

Dyslexia

♦ Copycat handwriting practice sheets
♦ Eye-hand integrated cards
♦ Tracing/colouring/maze books
♦ Berol Handhugger pens

Exam success

Allcock (2001) studied over 2,000 students aged 11–16 years and found that exam success depended on:

♦ Thorough subject knowledge and understanding.
♦ This depends on the tuition and revision methods and revolves around study skills.
♦ The ability to read and interpret questions correctly in a limited time-frame. This is the complex skill of reading and includes accuracy, comprehension and rate.
♦ The composition and execution of the writing, which proves that the candidate has subject knowledge and understanding.

Slow handwriting

Slow handwriting speed is a major factor, which prevents many students achieving the success they deserve. Slow handwriting may be due to:

♦ delays in information processing
♦ problems with spelling
♦ motor coordination difficulties
♦ labour-intensive style, which results from lack of tuition in handwriting skills.

She suggests that students must first be identified, efforts made to improve their speed, raise their self-esteem and provide equal opportunity for achieving success. Ideally all students should be tested annually and this would provide evidence to support special arrangements in all written exams. It would also bring them to the attention of staff in schools.

Allcock (2001) suggests that the average for Year 11 is 16.9 wpm. The ART (Adult Reading Test), which uses a 2-minute writing task, gives 22–23 wpm as the average for adults. The main difficulty with using a 2-minute test is that it bears little resemblance to answering an examination question and the speed over 20 minutes would be appreciably slower. No data has been collected, in a sample representative of the entire population for a 20-minute writing task, covering the older age range. Without hard data we can only fall back on the predicted increase in speed from Y11 as shown in the projection based on data collected by Allcock (2001).

On projected scores the average for Year 12 is 17.8 wpm and for year 13 it is 18.6 wpm. It should be noted that handwriting speed will only improve with continuing practice as with any other skill.

Dyscalculia

There is a growing acceptance within the research world that there are some students who present with dyslexic characteristics, dyscalculic characteristics or aspects of both conditions. The guidance to support pupils with dyslexia and dyscalculia (DfES 2001) suggests that purely dyscalculic learners who have difficulties only with numbers will have cognitive and language abilities in the normal range, and may excel in non-mathematical subjects. It is more likely that difficulties with numeracy accompany the language difficulties of dyslexia.

Literacy is also involved in maths and this can also have an impact on the student with dyscalculia who may also have some literacy difficulties.

Chinn (2009) suggests that mathematics makes considerable demands on learners. These include mathematical memory, working memory and the ability to generalize and see patterns and links. Additionally, he argues that emotions can compound the problems created by these cognitive skills. Lack of confidence as is the case with children with dyslexia can also have an impact on dyscalculia. Henderson, Came and Brough (2003) suggest that weak understanding of mathematical concepts in addition to an uncertainty about procedures and methods in maths can result in a lack of confidence in applying their skills to maths problems.

In relation to diagnosis and acceptance of the condition of dyscalculia, Chinn (2009) argues that the publication of Brian Butterworth's Screening Test for Dyscalculia (2003) and the inclusion of dyscalculia as a specific learning difficulty on the UK government website have helped to highlight dyscalculia as a discrete condition.

Chinn (2009) suggests that some of the characteristics of learners with dyscalculia include:

♦ Difficulty remembering basic addition facts.
♦ Finding it much harder to count backwards instead of forwards.
♦ Inability to fluently count less familiar sequences, such as: 1, 3, 5, 7, 9, 11; or 14, 24, 34, 44, 54, 64.
♦ Can only recall the 2, 5 and 10 multiplication tables. May be able to learn the other multiplication tables, but will forget them overnight.

Dyslexia

♦ Inability to estimate.
♦ Weak at mental arithmetic.
♦ Forgets the question asked in mental arithmetic.
♦ Finds it difficult to progress from the materials (counters, blocks) to symbols.
♦ Poorly organized written work, for example: columns of numbers are not lined up.
♦ Anxious about doing any mathematics.
♦ Does not recognize patterns or generalizations.
♦ Impulsive when doing maths, rather than analytical, starting at the first information rather than over-viewing all the information.

The organization and presentation of work can also be an issue for students with dyscalculia as they often have difficulty being in the right place at the right time with all the things that they might need. They may have untidy writing and find the neat presentation of work and organizing their files challenging. This can lead to confusion for both student and teacher.

Some of the difficulties experienced by students include: difficulty linking mathematical words to numerals; difficulty transferring from the concrete to abstract thinking; difficulty understanding mathematical concepts; difficulty copying numbers correctly; difficulty with place value; difficulty remembering maths rules and formulae; difficulty sequencing the order and the value of numbers; and they may be inconsistent from day-to-day in their performances.

The issue of co-morbidity also needs to be considered when identifying dyscalculia. There is clear evidence from both research and practice that some of the characteristics of dyslexia can have an impact on mathematics. It may therefore be useful to identify the presenting characteristics in relation to maths and to adopt a type-of-problem-to-solution approach by identifying the barriers experienced by the student and looking at specific ways of dealing with these. A useful general web link is www.dyscalculia.org.uk. Details of the dyscalculia screener can be found at www.gl-assessment.co.uk. Further information can also be located on the UK government website www.standards.dfes.gov.uk/numeracy/about.

Attention Deficit and Hyperactivity Disorder (ADHD)

There has been considerable debate regarding the concept of attention disorders, covering the medical, educational and social perspectives. It is, however, interesting to note that in the American Psychiatric Association's *Diagnostic and Statistical Manual of Mental Disorders* (2000), ADHD is noted as the most prevalent neuro-developmental disorder of childhood. The manual provides criteria for diagnosis, which includes factors relating to inattentiveness, hyperactivity and impulsivity, such as: 'often has difficulty in sustaining attention in tasks or play activities', 'often runs about or climbs excessively' and 'often interrupts or intrudes on others'. These factors need to have persisted for at least six months, and to a degree that is maladaptive and inconsistent with developmental level.

Although there has been a considerable amount of literature on ADHD, there is still controversy regarding its unitary model as a discrete syndrome. There is also some debate on the nature of the syndrome, and particularly on its primary causes and the intervention needed (Reid 2006). For example, Barkley (1997) suggests that it is a unitary condition and that the primary impairment relates to behaviour inhibition, with this having a cascading effect on other cognitive functions. This view is countered by Rutter (1995), who suggests that a cognitive deficit specific to ADHD has still to be determined, and even if the majority have cognitive impairments, the trait is not common to all children with ADHD. It is perhaps useful at this point to attempt to place the symptoms and characteristics of ADHD into some form of framework to help understand the different strands and various characteristics that can contribute to ADHD.

To qualify as ADHD the factors that meet the criteria need to have persisted for at least six months to a degree that is maladaptive and inconsistent with developmental level.

Although there has been a considerable amount of literature on ADHD, there is still controversy regarding the unitary model of ADHD as a discrete syndrome. In fact, Cooper (2005) argues that 'a key problem with the DSM diagnostic criteria is that they harbour taken for granted assumptions about the kinds of pupil behaviours that are to be expected in properly functioning classrooms' (p. 128). Many children of course cannot meet these expectations and the spotlight then turns to 'within child' factors as a cause of this.

Framework for attention difficulties

The causal modelling framework used to describe dyslexia in Chapter 1 (Morton and Frith 1995), can also be applied to ADHD.

Although he does not relate ADHD to a framework, such as the causal modelling framework, Levine (1997) ascribes to the following:

Neurological level
At the neurological level, the following factors may be relevant to attention difficulties:

- hemispheric preferences – usually a child with ADHD is a right-hemisphere processor
- saliency determination – that is, recognizing what is relevant. Often a child with ADHD would having difficulty in recognizing the relevant features of conversation or written work
- auditory distractibility – the child is easily distracted by noise of some sort
- tactile distractibility – similarly, touch could be distracting, and often the child with ADHD may want to touch in order to be distracted
- motor inhibition – often, children with ADHD have difficulty in inhibiting a response and may react impulsively in some situations.

Cognitive level

In relation to the cognitive dimensions, the following factors may be significant:

- Depth of processing – if the child is not attending to a stimulus then it is likely that the processing will be at a shallow level. If this is the case then the child will not gain much from the learning experience, either in understanding or in pleasure.
- Information processing – just as in the case of dyslexia, the information-processing cycle of input, cognition and output can be influential in identifying the type of difficulties that may be experienced by children with attention difficulties. This therefore has implications for teaching.
- Metacognitive factors – these are important for reinforcing learning, transferring learning and developing concepts. It is likely the child with attention difficulties will have poor metacognitive skills, and this will make learning less meaningful and have a negative effect on attention span.

Classroom level

In relation to educational or classroom factors, the following can be considered:

- Factors associated with free flight – this means that the child will have little control over the thinking process (essentially what may be described as a right-hemisphere processing style). This means that the individual requires some structure to help to direct their thinking processes.
- Unpredictability, inconsistency and impulsivity – these again indicate that there is little control over learning and that many actions are impulsive.

♦ Pacing skills and on-task factors – lack of pacing skills again means a lack of control over learning, and problems controlling the progress of work. The child may therefore tire easily or finish prematurely.

Identifying and defining attention difficulties

Examining the factors described above would lead one to believe that attention difficulties and ADHD can be confused easily, and the syndrome would be difficult to identify as a discrete syndrome.

It is not surprising therefore that a number of definitions of ADHD are currently used, and a considerable amount of literature on the subject has expounded different views and a variety of interventions. Essentially, however, identification seems to be through the use of diagnostic checklists or observations such as the Brown Rating Scale (Brown 1996) and the Conners scale (Conners 1996). These are widely used but they do demand an element of clinical judgement on the part of the assessor. The important aspect about these is not so much whether they give a diagnosis or not, but rather that they provide a list of definable and observable characteristics that can inform a teaching programme, irrespective of the diagnosis.

It is therefore feasible to identify attention difficulties within an education setting, although in practice much of this type of diagnosis appears to be undertaken by medical professionals – even though the actual 'presenting' difficulties are usually more obvious in school. If a child is said to have attention difficulties then these should be obvious in every subject and in all activities. In practice this is rarely the case, and this must cast some doubt on the validity of the diagnosis.

Assessing for ADHD

At present, no laboratory or imaging test exists to determine if your child has ADD or ADHD. Clinicians base their diagnosis on the signs and symptoms they observe and by ruling out other disorders. In order to get an accurate diagnosis it is important to have a full medical and psychological evaluation.

The American Academy of Pediatrics (AAP) maintain that the professional criteria for a diagnosis of ADD/ADHD requires the following:

♦ Early onset – symptoms must have been present before age seven.
♦ Duration – a combination of symptoms must have been present for at least six months.
♦ Setting – the symptoms must be present in two or more settings, such as home, school and other social settings.

♦ Impact – the symptoms must have a negative impact on the individual's school, family and/or social life.
♦ Developmental level – the symptoms are not due to the child's normal developmental level.
♦ Alternative explanation – the symptoms are not caused by another physical, mental or emotional disorder.

They also recommend that an evaluation for childhood ADD/ADHD should include:

♦ A thorough medical and family history.
♦ A general physical and neurological exam.
♦ A comprehensive interview with the parents, the child and the child's teacher(s).
♦ Standardized screening tools for ADD/ADHD.
♦ Observation of the child.
♦ A variety of psychological tests to measure IQ and social and emotional adjustment.

To be diagnosed with ADD/ADHD, children must exhibit multiple symptoms of hyperactivity, impulsivity or inattention. In addition, the mental health professional assessing the problem will also look at:

♦ *The severity of the symptoms* – to be diagnosed with ADD/ADHD, the symptoms must have a negative impact on the person's education, career, relationships or social life.
♦ *When the symptoms started* – the doctor or therapist will look at how early the symptoms appeared. To receive a positive diagnosis, the symptoms must have been present before age seven.
♦ *How long the symptoms have been present* – the symptoms must have been going on for at least six months before ADD/ADHD can be diagnosed.
♦ *When and where the symptoms appear* – the symptoms of ADD/ADHD must be present in multiple settings, such as at home and school. If the problem only appears in one environment, it is unlikely to be caused by ADD/ADHD.

This list is fairly comprehensive and can provide a guide to an assessor. Most of the guidance on the diagnosis of ADHD in fact stems from the DSM-IV Criteria, which is used by professionals worldwide.

DSM-IV Criteria for Attention Deficit/Hyperactivity Disorder

According to the DSM-IV (American Psychiatric Association 2001), a person with Attention Deficit/Hyperactivity Disorder must have possessed six or more symptoms of either inattention or hyperactivity/impulsivity, as outlined below, for at least six months to a degree that is maladaptive and inconsistent with developmental level:

Inattention

♦ often fails to give close attention to detail or makes careless mistakes in school work, work or other activities
♦ often has difficulty sustaining attention in tasks or play activities
♦ often does not seem to listen when spoken to directly
♦ often does not follow through on instructions and fails to finish schoolwork, chores or duties in the workplace (not due to oppositional behaviour or failure to understand instructions)
♦ often has difficulty organizing tasks and activities
♦ often avoids, dislikes, or is reluctant to engage in tasks that require sustained mental effort (such as schoolwork or homework)
♦ often loses things necessary for tasks or activities (e.g. toys, school assignments, pencils, books or tools)
♦ is often easily distracted by extraneous stimuli
♦ is often forgetful in daily activities.

Hyperactivity/impulsivity

♦ often fidgets with hands or feet or squirms in seat
♦ often leaves seat in classroom or in other situations in which remaining seated is expected
♦ often runs about or climbs excessively in situations in which it is inappropriate (in adolescents or adults, may be limited to subjective feelings or restlessness)
♦ often has difficulty playing or engaging in leisure activities quietly
♦ is often 'on the go' or acts as if 'driven by a motor'
♦ often talks excessively
♦ often blurts out answers before questions have been completed
♦ often has difficulty awaiting turn
♦ often interrupts or intrudes on others (e.g. butts in to conversations or games)

Additionally, DSM-IV indicates the following imperatives:

Dyslexia

- Some hyperactive/impulsive or inattentive symptoms that caused impairment were present before seven years of age.
- Some impairment from the symptoms is present in two or more settings (e.g. at school/work and at home).
- There must be clear evidence of clinically significant impairment in social, academic or occupational functioning.
- The symptoms do not occur exclusively during the course of a pervasive developmental disorder, schizophrenia, or other psychotic disorder and are not better accounted for by another mental disorder (e.g. mood disorder, anxiety disorder, disassociative disorder, or a personality disorder).

Diagnosis

- *Attention Deficit/Hyperactivity Disorder, Combined Type*: If an individual has exhibited both inattention and hyperactivity/impulsivity criteria over the past six months.
- *Attention Deficit/Hyperactivity Disorder, Predominantly Inattentive Type*: If an individual has exhibited the inattention criteria but not the hyperactivity/impulsivity criteria over the past six months.
- *Attention Deficit/Hyperactivity Disorder, Predominantly Hyperactive-Impulsive Type*: If an individual has exhibited the hyperactivity/impulsivity criteria but not the inattention criteria over the past six months.

Factors to consider

A diagnosis of ADHD is multifaceted and should include behavioural, medical and educational data-gathering. This should incorporate an examination of the child's history through comprehensive interviews with parents, teachers and healthcare professionals. Interviewing these people can help to determine the child's specific behaviour characteristics, when the behaviour began, duration of symptoms, whether the child displays the behaviour in various settings and coexisting conditions.

The American Academy of Pediatrics (AAP) stresses that since a variety of psychological and developmental disorders frequently coexist in children who are being evaluated for ADHD, a thorough examination for any such coexisting condition should also be an integral part of any evaluation.

Children aged 6–12 should be evaluated for ADHD if they show symptoms of inattention, hyperactivity, impulsivity, academic underachievement or behaviour problems in at least two settings. Such behaviours should have been harmful for the child academically or socially for at least six months.

The child should meet the official symptom guidelines. A diagnosis requires detailed reports by parents or caregivers. Parents should not be shy about insisting on further evaluation if their experience does not match a doctor's single observation of their child.

Guidelines for primary care doctors emphasize the importance of obtaining direct evidence from the classroom teacher or other school-based professionals about the child's symptoms and their duration, and evidence of functional impairment in the school setting.

The child should also be assessed for accompanying conditions (such as learning difficulties).

Over-diagnosis
Certain factors may lead to the over-diagnosis of ADHD. For instance, the popularity of methylphenidate (Ritalin) has encouraged some parents and teachers to pressure doctors into prescribing the standard ADHD drug for children who are aggressive or who have poor grades. However, some of these children may have other behavioural or emotional problems, or no problems at all.

Other factors that may contribute to misdiagnosis include: children who are young for their grade and therefore socially and intellectually immature; and social and economic problems, such as single-parent households.

Under-diagnosis
On the other hand, certain factors may lead to the under-diagnosis of ADHD. Some evidence suggests that girls with ADHD are under-diagnosed. Research indicates that girls with ADHD are often inattentive but not hyperactive or impulsive. In fact, older girls with ADHD tend to have social problems due to withdrawal and internalized emotions, showing symptoms of anxiety and depression.

Doctors may fail to diagnose some children with ADHD because they behave normally in the quiet doctor's office where there are no distractions to trigger symptoms. In addition, some doctors may be unfamiliar with how to diagnose the condition.

Behaviour and ADHD

Early history of behaviour

It is often helpful if the parents are able to describe the early history. This should include:

♦ specific problems, beginning as early as possible, that they have encountered during the child's development – school reports are very helpful

- sibling relationships
- recent life changes
- a family history of ADHD
- eating habits
- sleep patterns
- speech and language development
- any problems during the mother's pregnancy or during delivery
- any history of medical or physical problems, particularly allergies, chronic ear infections and hearing difficulties.

Behavioural evaluation

Specific questionnaires and rating scales are used to review and quantify the behavioural characteristics of ADHD. ADHD-specific rating scales include:

- CPRS-R:L-ADHD Index (Conners Parent Rating Scale – 1997 Revised Version: Long Form, ADHD Index Scale)
- CTRS-R:L-ADHD Index (Conners Teacher Rating Scale – 1997 Revised Version: Long Form, ADHD Index Scale)
- CPRS-R:L-DSM-IV Symptoms (Conners Parent Rating Scale – 1997 Revised Version: Long Form.

As with all psychological tests, child-rating scales have a range of measurement error. Appropriate scales have satisfactory norms for the child's chronological age and ability levels.

Collecting information about the child's ADHD symptoms from several different sources helps ensure that the information is accurate. Appropriate sources of information include the child's parents, teachers and other diagnosticians, such as psychologists, occupational therapists, speech therapists, social workers and physicians. It is also important to review both the child's previous medical history as well as his or her school records.

Educational evaluation

Behaviours targeted for classroom observation may include:

- problems of inattention, such as becoming easily distracted, making careless mistakes or failing to finish assignments on time
- problems of hyperactivity, such as fidgeting, getting out of an assigned seat, running around the classroom excessively or striking out at a peer
- problems of impulsivity, such as blurting out answers to the

teacher's questions or interrupting the teacher or other students in the class
♦ more challenging behaviours, such as severe aggressive or disruptive actions.

Some characteristics that can alert you to possible ADHD include the following:

♦ restless and overactive – does not stay long with one activity or in one place
♦ fidgety, chatters and interrupts people
♦ easily distracted and does not finish things
♦ inattentive and cannot concentrate on tasks which need thinking through
♦ impulsive, suddenly doing things without thinking first
♦ unable to wait their turn in games, in conversation or in a queue.

Intervention

Intervention can be medical, in the form of drugs such as Ritalin; educational, in relation to classroom adaptations, task analysis and investigation of the student's learning preferences; or even dietary, requiring an examination of children's reactions to certain foods. There is also a view (Lloyd and Norris 1999) that ADHD is a social construction. There is certainly a strong commercial basis to ADHD and this may have fuelled the impetus for acceptance of it as a discrete specific difficulty.

Indeed, there is a view that special educational needs, whatever the particular need might be, can be approached from a situation-centred perspective (Frederickson and Cline 2002). Frederickson and Cline (p. 40) quote Deno (1989), who argues that proponents of this view believe that special educational needs 'can only be defined in terms of the relationship between what a person can do and what a person must do to succeed in a given environment'.

This view indicates that learning difficulties are in fact environmental and a construction of the education system. This would imply that teaching and curriculum approaches hold the key to minimizing the effect on the child of what may be termed a 'special educational need'. Along the same continuum of the environmentally focused approach, one can also view the interactional approach to SEN. Frederickson and Cline suggest that this is the 'complex interaction between the child's strengths and weaknesses, the level of support available and the appropriateness of the education being provided' (p. 420).

Organizing students with attention difficulties

Students diagnosed with ADHD usually have difficulty with organization and the teacher can take an active role in helping the student organize their work programme. Such help could include ensuring that notebooks have dividers and that separate folders are used for different activities and that these folders are clearly labelled in addition to helping the student keep a daily record of tasks to be completed and those that have been completed.

It should be acknowledged, however, that there are different degrees of organization and some students can only tolerate a degree of imposed organization. Nevertheless it should be ensured that the student with attention difficulties is sufficiently aware of materials they will require and how to access the information they need for learning.

Some other suggestions for dealing with ADHD in the classroom are shown below.

♦ Use the child's name in a question or in the material being covered.
♦ Ask a simple question (not even related to the topic at hand) to a child whose attention is beginning to wander.
♦ Stand close to an inattentive child and touch him or her on the shoulder as you are teaching.
♦ Decrease the length of assignments or lessons.
♦ Alternate physical and mental activities.
♦ Increase the novelty of lessons by using films, tapes, flash cards or small group work, or by having a child call on others.
♦ Incorporate the children's interests into a lesson plan.
♦ Structure in some guided daydreaming time.
♦ Teach children self-monitoring strategies.
♦ Use a soft voice to give direction.
♦ Employ peers or older students or volunteer parents as tutors.

Strategies

There are a number of intervention strategies for attention difficulties and these can fit into the different perspectives described earlier in this chapter. However, the points below may be useful as general principles:

♦ avoid confrontational situations
♦ show the student respect
♦ listen to the student's concerns
♦ avoid distraction
♦ keep instructions to a minimum – one at a time

♦ provide reassurance on tasks
♦ split tasks into steps with breaks
♦ enable students to complete tasks themselves
♦ scaffold the student's work
♦ provide routine
♦ provide outlets for active behaviour
♦ provide a clear structure.

Although the above list can be helpful there is, however, no universal formula for dealing with ADHD. Much depends on the support available, the classroom and learning environment and the nature of the difficulties experienced by the student. The perspectives of the practitioner's involved will also have a bearing on the intervention.

Montague and Castro (2004) explain that because of the views held by some regarding the neurobiological nature of ADHD, interventions have tended to focus on pharmacological treatments. They point out that the current trend is moving away from that perspective and professional organizations such as the 'American Academy of Pediatrics, as well as researchers, psychologists, and counsellors advocate a multi-method, multi-informant, and multi-disciplinary approach to treatment . . . and rather than focus on the individual's deficits, emphasis is placed on identifying the strengths of an individual and building on those strengths' (p. 411).

Montague and Castro also suggest that school accommodation plans are the key to intervention and that these should be multifaceted, involving all teachers, parents and children, and that it is important to provide optimal curricular and environmental conditions for learning. They suggest that 'collaboration and cooperation among school, home and community agencies . . . should be the cornerstone of an intervention programme (for ADHD)' (p. 413).

The nature of the provision that is suitable for children with attention difficulties can vary. For some, specialized intervention may be appropriate, but for most differentiation, curriculum and classroom adaptations and acknowledging learning styles will be sufficient. Considering the range of difficulties associated with attention difficulties and the potential behavioural difficulties that can also be associated with attention disorders, this of course provides a challenging situation for teachers.

Learning Styles and Attention Difficulties

In addition to being familiar with ADHD it is also important that teachers are aware of learning theory and how theory can be of practical use in understanding how children learn and particularly how learning can be made more accessible for learners with ADHD. Some factors relating to learning that can have an impact on students with ADHD include the following:

♦ the learners culture
♦ the classroom and school climate
♦ teaching style
♦ classroom dynamics and environment
♦ curriculum expectations.

Co-morbidity and ADHD

It is not surprising that there is a strong view that an overlap exists between ADHD and dyslexia. Many of the cognitive attention-processing mechanisms that children with ADHD seem to have difficulty with, such as short-term memory, sustained attention, processing speed and accuracy in copying, can also be noted in children with dyslexia. Willcutt and Pennington (2000) noted in a large-scale study that individuals with reading disabilities were more likely than individuals without reading disabilities to meet the criteria for ADHD, and that the association was stronger for inattention than for hyperactivity.

However, this notion of co-morbidity has been criticized, and the value of the term questioned, by Kaplan *et al.* (2001). They suggest that the term 'co-morbidity' assumes that the aetiologies of the different specific difficulties are independent. Yet in practice, according to Kaplan *et al.*, it is very rare to see discrete conditions existing in isolation.

In a research study involving 179 children, in order to investigate the notion of co-morbidity, the researchers used criteria to assess for seven disorders – reading disability, ADHD, DCD, oppositional defiant disorder, conduct disorder, depression and anxiety. It was found that at least 50 per cent of the sample tested met the criteria for at least two diagnoses, and the children with ADHD were at the highest risk of having a second disorder. The question presented by Kaplan *et al.* is whether children are actually displaying several co-morbid disorders, or are displaying manifestations of one underlying disorder. This of course raises questions regarding the assessment procedures, and the rationale behind the special needs assessment procedures (SNAP, see below) (Weedon and Reid 2003). The thinking is that children will likely show indicators of other conditions, and the accumulation of descriptive information on the presenting difficulties can be useful for the class teacher. It is important, however, that information is not based solely on clinical assessment or clinical judgement, but also gathered from the evidence of professionals and parents about how the child performs in different situations.

> It is important to obtain descriptive data from observations, interviews and assessments conducted on the child. The usefulness of this data does not lie in the provision of a label, but in the description of the presenting characteristics (which may or may not lead to a label). These should be informative and beneficial in terms of intervention.

Dealing with ADHD in Applied Settings – Policy and Provision

It is important to be aware of how ADHD can impact on families and schools as well as the individual student.

It is important to identify the key issues in formulating policy for students with ADHD and how this can influence the practice in schools. Parents also play an important role in this and you will need to recognize how this role can be made as effective as possible. You will then be asked to translate this to your own school context.

You will note in the article that it indicates that the Individuals with Disabilities Education Act (IDEA) and Section 504 of the Rehabilitation Act of 1973 (Section 504) require schools to provide a special education or to make modifications or adaptations for students whose ADHD adversely affects their educational performance.

Additionally, after it has been determined that a child is eligible for special education and related services under IDEA, an IEP is developed that includes a statement of measurable annual goals, including benchmarks or short-term objectives that reflect the student's needs. The IEP goals are determined with input from the parents and cannot be changed without the parents' knowledge. But at the same time it states that only if it can be demonstrated that a child's ADHD adversely affects his or her learning will the student qualify for services under Section 504. To be considered eligible for Section 504, a student must be evaluated to ensure that the disability requires special education or related services or supplementary aids and services. Therefore, a child whose ADHD does not interfere with his or her learning process may not be eligible for special education and related services under IDEA or supplementary aids and services under IDEA. IDEA and Section 504 require schools to provide special education or to make modifications or adaptations for students whose ADHD adversely affects their educational performance. Such adaptations may include curriculum adjustments, alternative classroom organization and management, specialized teaching techniques and study skills, use of behaviour management and increased parent/teacher collaboration. Eligible children with ADHD must be placed in regular education classrooms, to the maximum extent appropriate to their educational needs, with the use of supplementary aids and services if necessary. The document (IDEA) states that, of course, the needs of some children with ADHD cannot be met solely within the confines of a regular education classroom, and they may need special education.

Identifying Specific Learning Difficulties

The overlap between the different specific learning difficulties can cause some confusion. For that reason Weedon and Reid (2003, 2005, 2009) developed the instrument known as SNAP (special needs assessment profile). This instrument profiles 17 specific learning difficulties. From this, clusters and patterns of weaknesses and strengths help to identify the core features of a child's difficulties: visual, dyslexic, dyspraxic, phonological, attentional or any other of the 17 key deficits (see earlier in this chapter). This can suggest a diagnosis that points the way forward for a teaching programme for that individual child.

SNAP involves four steps:

♦ Step 1 (*Pupil Assessment Pack*): structured questionnaire checklists for completion by teachers and parents give an initial 'outline map' of the child's difficulties.
♦ Step 2 (*CD-ROM*): the learning-support staff chart the child's difficulties, using the CD-ROM to identify patterns and target any further diagnostic follow-up assessments to be carried out at Step 3.
♦ Step 3 (*User's Kit*): focused assessments from a photocopiable resource bank of quick diagnostic 'probes' yield a detailed and textured understanding of the child's difficulties.
♦ Step 4 (*CD-ROM*): the computer-generated profile yields specific guidance on support (including personalized information sheets for parents) and practical follow-up.

The kit helps to facilitate the collaboration between different groups of professionals, and between professionals and parents, which is extremely important in order to attain a full picture of the student's abilities and difficulties. There is a dedicated website that contains a number of ideas on teaching to cover difficulties associated with 17 different specific learning difficulties: www.SNAPassessment.com.

The overlap between the different specific difficulties can be an area of confusion for many teachers and parents. Certainly it can be helpful to obtain a label in many cases but intervention should not necessarily rest on the provision of a label – identifying that there are difficulties and identifying the students needs should in fact be sufficient but unfortunately, in today's resource-driven system, a label is often necessary to access resources. Often this is neither appropriate nor desirable as it can prevent or delay intervention. The key message is that whatever the label, intervention must relate to current need and all should be consulted in the identification of need that will involve teachers, parents and school management.

In summary, this chapter has:

♦ discussed the common issue of overlap between various syndromes
♦ looked specifically at dyspraxia, dyscalculia, ADHD and dysgraphia
♦ provided some suggestions and strategies for identification and showed how the characteristics of the difficulty can overlap with other syndromes
♦ commented on the barriers to learning experienced by children with one or more of the specific learning difficulties and provided suggestions for intervention.

11
Specific Learning Difficulties and Alternative Interventions

There is still no universal agreement on the single-most effective way to deal with dyslexia. However, one area that may have far-reaching consequences and potential comes under the umbrella of 'alternative interventions'. These tend to be popular, new and often have media appeal.

Intervention can be divided into four broad areas. A good approach might be a careful balance between all four. These are the:

♦ neurological/neurophysiological and pharmaceutical (what the child has/has not)
♦ cognitive and learning approach (what the child can/can't do)
♦ child-centered classroom 'hands on' approach (how the child actually performs and how this can be improved)
♦ the curriculum and dyslexia-friendly approach, which includes the learning environment (what the system can do to make the learning experience more effective and efficient for learners with dyslexia).

Effective teaching and differentiation can also be successful with some children with dyslexia.

Regarding alternative or specialized approaches, there are some points to be borne in mind:

♦ Not all approaches are currently evaluated.
♦ Not all evaluations have been carried out using the same criteria for identifying how successful the approach is.
♦ Some approaches may have an advantage over others because of a heavy commercial thrust and a vigorous marketing approach that makes them well known internationally.

There are sometimes significant variations in the approaches suggested by educational authorities and schools. This can cause confusion for parents and also prompt teachers to question their own methods. For this reason, teacher professional development should focus on providing an understanding of dyslexia and other specific difficulties. This can give teachers the confidence that what they are doing is right and help them to defend their case when faced with information about new programmes, sometimes accompanied with exaggerated claims of success.

The current thrust towards inclusive schools can mean that interventions based on individual programmes, for example, involving one-to-one interaction, are not practical but the school may still be able to offer an appropriate form of intervention. It may be good to work with other professionals who have experience in using specialized approaches and incorporate their skills as part of an intervention package.

Nevertheless, the variations in provision and training opportunities available among education authorities and schools can provide an opportunity for some commercial interests to thrive.

What Do We Mean by Alternative Approaches?

Alternative approaches usually refer to the approaches used on a one-to-one basis, which are not usually available in the mainstream classroom. Schools tend to use mainstream approaches that have been tried and tested over a period of time or are recommended by government reports. For example, in the UK the Rose Report (DfES 2005) suggested that schools should be using synthetic phonics following a number of research studies that had been conducted which highlighted the merits of this approach. In the US the No Child Left Behind Act also advocated a number of established practices again using a structured phonics approach.

We are all aware that advertisements try to persuade us to buy a product, and although they are monitored it is possible to make claims that are not backed up by research. This is even more likely when we read material presented on a website, which is not monitored in any way. We can read reports in the media, but these are often based on personal opinion, and the media sometimes has a vested interest in presenting material in a controversial fashion. We can read reports or books, but again these may be partly based on opinion rather than fact, and will not be peer reviewed. The most reliable information we can obtain should be from research published in a peer-reviewed journal, although even here there is a hierarchy, with some journals having a higher impact than others and these are likely to be the sources on which we can best rely. It is important to be aware that some of the material quoted has been more stringently evaluated than others.

Dietary interventions

There has been considerable popular coverage of the use of food additives, and much anecdotal evidence to support the view that these may have an adverse affect on learning, particularly for children with ADHD. Richardson (2001) suggests that there is a wide spectrum of conditions in which deficiencies of highly unsaturated fatty acids appear to have some influence. Further, she argues that fatty acids can have an extremely important influence on dyslexia, dyspraxia and ADHD. Richardson argues that it is not too controversial to suggest that there is a high incidence of overlap between these three syndromes – in fact, she suggests that overlap between dyslexia and ADHD can be around 30 to 50 per cent, and even higher in the case of dyspraxia. She argues that the essential fatty acids (EFAs), which cannot be synthesized by the body, must be provided in the diet – these are linoleic acid (omega-6 series) and alpha-linoleic acid (omega-3 series). She suggests that the longer-chain highly unsaturated fatty acids (HUFA) that the brain needs can normally be synthesized from the EPAs: but this conversion process can be severely affected and limited by dietary and lifestyle factors. Dietary factors which can block the conversion of EFA to HUFA include excess saturated fats, hydrogenated fats found in processed foods, and deficiencies in vitamins and minerals, as well as excessive consumption of coffee and alcohol, and smoking.

Richardson says that the claims connecting hyperactivity and lack of EFA are not new. Studies on dyspraxia have also highlighted the possibility of the links with EFA and suggested that fatty acid supplements can be beneficial (Stordy 1995, 1997). In relation to dyslexia and ADHD, Richardson suggests that fatty acid supplements have been shown to be successful and supplementation has been associated with improvements in reading. Richardson also reports on school-based trials indicating that this intervention can be realistically applied in schools (Richardson 2001; Portwood 2002).

The most recent evidence emerging on fatty acids and dyslexia in adults by Richardson and her colleagues (Cyhlarova *et al.* 2007) shows that reading performance in both dyslexics and controls is linked to higher total omega-3 concentration, and that for dyslexic subjects was negatively related to omega-6 concentration, suggesting that it is the balance between the two which is relevant to dyslexia.

Fast ForWard

Tallal, Miller and Fitch (1993) have claimed that, like language-disordered children, children with dyslexia take longer to process sounds that change rapidly. This is tested with high and low tones, or the sounds ba and da, which are only different in the first few milliseconds. Children with dyslexia (and Specific Language Impairment) cannot tell the difference between the sounds if they are presented close together, and this means that they are likely to have problems with phonological awareness.

The Fast ForWord programme has been designed to train children in just those changes that prove most difficult for them. In order to help them be successful, the sounds they hear are drawn out by 50 per cent so that they sound like whale noises, and with this prolonged presentation children learn to complete the task.

The programme starts at an easy level with slowed down onset and as the children progress the onsets become faster and faster. Children are asked to complete around 10 hours' practice a week in 20-minute sessions for 6–8 weeks, which leads to significant improvements in their ability on the games and also on the Tallal test.

It is claimed, however, that a major drawback is the lack of flexibility in the Fast ForWord system, which means that it is not possible to vary the programme systematically to check which aspects are helpful. A new programme currently under evaluation, Fast ForWord Language to Reading, has now been developed as a second stage to improve reading, based on the use of normal consonants.

Exercise and movement

There has been a longstanding interest in exercise and therapies based on movement for children with specific learning difficulties. Fitts and Posner (1967) provided an account of the learning stages in motor skill development and particularly the development of automaticity. Denckla and Rudel (1976) found that children with dyslexia had a deficit in rapid automatized naming, and suggested that they are characterized by a 'non-specific developmental awkwardness' which is irrespective of athletic ability. In terms of intervention, the work of Ayres (1979) has been developed considerably by Blythe (1992, 2001), Blythe and Goddard (2000) and McPhillips, Hepper and Mulhern (2000). See the website for the Institute for Neuro-Physiological Psychology (INPP), www.inpp. com. The work of Dennison and Dennison (1989, 2001) in relation to Brain Gym©, and that of Hannaford (1995, 1997) on the importance of dominance and laterality and, particularly, the influence of dominance patterns on learning, have also been influential in classrooms and in particular with children with specific learning difficulties.

The inhibition of primitive reflexes

Blythe (1992) found that 85 per cent of children with specific learning difficulties that do not respond to various classroom intervention strategies have a cluster of aberrant reflexes. He argues that as long as these reflexes remain undetected and uncorrected, the educational problems will persist. These reflexes should only be present in a very young baby, and then become redundant after about six months of life. But if they continue to be present, Blythe argued, the development of the mature postural reflexes is restricted, and this will adversely affect writing, reading, spelling, copying, mathematics, attention and concentration.

Blythe (1992) and Goddard-Blythe (1996) have developed the Developmental Exercise Programme, an assessment and intervention programme for assessing the presence of these reflexes, and a series of exercises designed to control the primitive reflexes and release the postural reflexes. A study in Western Australia (Taylor 2002) examined the effects of retention of primitive reflexes in children diagnosed as having ADHD. The results supported the evidence of the importance of this area for cognitive development and learning, and also suggested 'cumulative associations between high stresses, atypical brain lateralization and uninhibited reflexes on scholastic competency' (pp. 216–17).

Educational kinesiology

Educational kinesiology is a combination of applied kinesiology and traditional learning theory, although some aspects of yoga and acupressure are also evident in the recommended programme.

Kinesiology is the study of muscles and their functions, and particular attention is paid to the patterns of reflex activity that link effective integration between sensory and motor responses. Children can develop inappropriate patterns of responses to particular situations, and these can lock the child into inappropriate habits.

Dennison and Hargrove (1985) have produced a series of exercises (Brain Gym©) from which an individual programme can be devised for the child relating to the assessment. Many of these exercises include activities that involve crossing the mid-line, such as writing a figure eight in the air, or cross-crawling and skip-a-cross, in which hands and legs sway from side to side. The aim is to achieve some form of body balance so that information can flow freely and be processed readily. Brain Gym© has been widely and successfully implemented in the school settings.

Dennison and Dennison (1989) developed a system called Brain Organization Profile (BOP) to visually represent their theory. Taylor

(2002) examined the basis and application of this profile with children with ADHD, and was able to develop a useful brain organization profile for each child in the research sample, which found that children with ADHD did show more evidence of mixed laterality processing than the control group.

Other alternative treatments

There are many other alternative treatments that have not been discussed here, but that are popular with parents, such as the Davis Dyslexia Correction methods, which involve orientation and symbol mastery (Davis and Braun 1997), and Sound Therapy (Johanson 1997), which is based on frequency-specific left hemisphere auditory stimulation with music and sounds (Auditory Discrimination Training), and many others, often too many for the parent or teacher to handle or understand. This further underlines the need for collaboration between parents and professionals – the approach that always works is called 'effective communication'.

Comment on alternative treatments

According to Muijs and Reynolds (2005) part of the difficulty is that there is an absence of proof of validity of the existing treatments. If we were able to show that existing interventions were successful then alternative approaches would not need to be developed. Nevertheless it is important to consider all new approaches and programmes and they cannot be dismissed just because they are new. A careful and planned intervention using new and alternative approaches is possible and it is better to work collaboratively with the providers of new approaches than to dismiss them out of hand. So the message is that we need to listen, learn and accommodate our practices to new ideas, particularly those ideas where there is a good body of sound research.

Fawcett and Reid (2009) suggest that the way forward should include setting up a system of benchmarking standards to help inform teachers and parents. The success of the intervention should then be assessed over time – that is: after six months; after one year; and continuous improvement.

The strength of the evidence and the validity of research studies supporting the approach also need to be considered – for example: are they anecdotal or case studies, are there pre- and post-group evaluations and double-blind placebo control groups in the studies? In other words, will the research stand up to scientific scrutiny?

Fawcett and Reid (2009) also point out that children will show different profiles of difficulty, even those who have identified with dyslexia,

Dyslexia

ADHD and dyspraxia. The key point is that the research strongly suggests that early interventions are the most effective in 'accelerating' literacy for many children, but those children who are resistant to intervention will show entrenched problems and may need further intensive one-to-one support, such as a specialized reading approach. A combination of traditional teaching and alternative interventions might prove the most effective in time.

In the meantime, however, it is important that schools and education authorities as well as support groups such as the British Dyslexia Association are consulted and that they seek to equip themselves with information they can readily disseminate to parents and teachers on new and alternative approaches.

> It is interesting to reflect on some of the views highlighted in a recent edition of *Perspectives on Language and Literacy* (winter 2010) on predictions on what the field of dyslexia will resemble in the year 2020. Elbeheri (p. 30) suggests that assistive technology will become more and more involved in the screening and intervention initiatives of dyslexia but will never replace teachers who still need training on how to identify and help individuals with dyslexia. Rosen (2010), in the same periodical (p. 18), suggests that the link between the genetics of dyslexia and the anatomical results of this will become clear, which will result in major breakthroughs in our understanding of dyslexia. He believes this will lead the way in providing innovative and alternative avenues for intervention. He concludes by saying that this 'will allow us to alleviate the burden of dyslexia from our children without affecting the gifts that they bring to other aspects of their lives' (p. 21).

12

Working with Parents

Parents have a key role to play in supporting their child with dyslexia. In fact, dyslexia can be seen as a whole-family responsibility as the impact can be felt by siblings as well as parents, and of course the child him/herself.

Parents can also have a wider role to play within the community. Parents and parent groups have had an impact on policy and practice in the UK, Europe, New Zealand, Australia, Canada and the US. This has provided great impetus to the whole area of dyslexia and it now has a much higher profile than previously. Yet perhaps the most accessible and potentially rewarding means of using the influence of practice is through direct communication with the school. This, without doubt, should be parents' first port of call. Communication at this level has the potential to quell anxieties and maximize use of both the potential support of parents and the skills of teachers. This form of communication can have a two-way beneficial effect – helping both the parents and the school.

In practice, however, this can still be difficult to implement. Some parents are still reluctant to approach the school and may find it difficult to openly consult with the school. It is therefore essential that schools develop proactive and open policies to promote home–school partnerships with parents of children with dyslexia. This will help not only to utilize the skills of parents, but also to avoid the potential legal wrangles and tribunals that have been evident in many countries over the last ten years.

Constructive home–school links are vital to ensure the success of any intervention for children with dyslexia.

Parental Concerns

Diagnosis

One of the concerns experienced by parents can relate to issues of diagnosis. Many parents can have a feeling that their child's educational needs are not being recognized or met and this is not helped if a diagnosis of the difficulties is not available. Understandably there is strong belief among parents that this diagnosis should be in the form of a label. This may be the case in some instances, particularly if the child is significantly lagging in attainments, and additional resources, examination support or a review of provision is needed. In many cases, however, a label is not the most essential factor. The most essential factor is for the school to be aware of the child's progress in all aspects of the curriculum, to communicate this to parents and to discuss together how the school (and parents) plan to deal with any lack of progress in literacy or other areas of learning.

Acceptance

A comment often made by parents is that 'the school does not accept dyslexia'. While this in some situations may unfortunately be the case, it is not the end of the world. All schools need to accept responsibility for the child's progress and they will investigate this by whatever means, and seek to find an explanation for any lack of progress. All this can be done without any recourse to a label. A label of course is helpful and in some situations, such as examination support, essential. Parents often feel considerable relief when the label 'dyslexia' is provided. Often parents remark: 'I was so relieved to know that it had a name'; or 'People had begun to hint he might be mentally retarded because he was illiterate'; or 'The diagnosis helped me to understand exactly why he had difficulties.'

It is important to consider that a label can often be accompanied by acceptance, and this can pave the way for constructive collaboration between home and school.

Anxieties often arise from the potential conflict between the views of individuals and interest groups who may have different agendas. This potential conflict can be noted between parents and teachers, and indeed may place them into opposition with each other. It is important that this form of confrontation is avoided, as anxieties and stresses are usually perceived by the child. It is vital therefore to ensure that the aims of the school in relation to any particular child are made clear to the parents, and that both parents and teachers share a common agenda.

Effective communication between schools and parents can have a positive impact on the child's development. It is important to establish this collaboration at an early stage so that effective partnership with parents can result.

Government involvement

There have been a number of recent government enquiries and reports on dyslexia. This is very encouraging and can be heartening for parents. One example of this comes from Scotland where an investigation on the current status of dyslexia in schools was held. In the subsequent HMI report on dyslexia in Scotland (2008) published as a result of the enquiry, the section on partnership with parents stated that encouragement should be given to parents to be involved in their children's learning. The report also stated that procedures for communicating with parents and for providing information to parents about the school's work, including training, should be a high priority. The report stated that the quality of information parents received on dyslexia varied. Some information was provided on local authority websites and most through leaflets and policies which were available to parents on request. The report also stated, however, that very few parents or pupils were sufficiently informed about the education authority's or school's policy relating to dyslexia.

The report commented a great deal on the need for partnerships with parents and commented that the extent to which schools involved parents in setting targets varied quite a bit, which could be unsettling for parents. Most schools informed parents about the targets rather than involving them in setting targets.

Parents were also critical of long delays in accessing specialist support for their children, in the belief that only with such support could their children progress. Schools were often slow to respond to parents' initial concerns despite provision for assessment being available through additional support for learning legislation. It is interesting that these shortcomings are noted in a country (Scotland) that has been noted for its forward-thinking approaches in policy, training and provision for dyslexia (Reid, Green and Zylstra 2005).

According to the report most primary schools attempted to involve parents in a range of ways to support their children. These included termly attendance at IEP review meetings, additional time at parents' evenings, home-school diaries and opportunities to meet with an educational psychologist, particularly around transition times to secondary school.

A few primary schools shared their support for learning policy with parents and offered information sessions about the difficulties experienced by their children and ways in which parents could provide support. This provides some indication of the types of support that can be made available. It is important that schools seek to involve parents as much as possible into the intervention planning and programmes for students with dyslexia.

US – National Reading Panel

A good example of a government initiative involving parents was the National Reading Panel in the US, which reported in 2000. The panel made an effort to receive written and oral testimony from parents.

The panel report included a section on helping parents to teach phonological awareness, which is generally recognised to be a crucial aspect of dyslexia. None of the studies reviewed by the panel included parents as trainers. One recommendation was that research is needed to address this and that there should be research highlighting the role of parents in informal activities at home that can focus on children's development of sounds in words and teaching letter recognition.

It was no surprise, therefore, that one of the recommendations was to promote an understanding of how to involve parents in cooperative efforts and teaching programmes to help students with reading. This highlights the fact that parents are a valuable resource and they need to be viewed in that way.

Parental Support

It is quite common for parents to volunteer to undertake training in the area of dyslexia. What seems to be the problem is the lack of suitable courses. Many courses are lengthy and detailed although there is now increasing evidence of local dyslexia associations throughout the UK and Ireland running workshops for parents. Many major conferences, such as the IDA conference in the US and the BDA and Dyslexia Scotland Conferences in the UK, which attract vast numbers of delegates, are run and supported largely by parents. A good example of an accessible training course for parents is the distance-learning online course that was developed by the Institute of Child Education and Psychology (Europe) (www.icepe.ie). Some of the aims of this course include the need to provide parents with

♦ the confidence and the advocacy skills needed to ensure their child's needs are met
♦ information on dyslexia and on relevant programmes for teaching reading and spelling

- strategies that can help children with dyslexia deal more effectively with the work at school
- help understanding how dyslexia can impact on their child's learning, and the importance of self-esteem
- supportive suggestions to help them collaborate effectively with the school and to provide pointers that help them look beyond school.

These aims focus to a great extent on parents' needs and it is useful that courses can be made available at local and international levels.

Homework

One of the questions most frequently asked by parents relates to how much homework the child with dyslexia should undertake. This anxiety can stem from the fact that it may take the child much longer than others in the class to complete the same exercise. It is important to maintain the motivation of children with dyslexia, and excessive nightly homework may not be the most effective way to achieve this. Parents, however, should not spend too much time focusing on their child's difficulties, as this can become counter-productive.

A Role for Parents

There are a number of activities that parents can adopt to help their child. Without exception, however, whatever the parent is doing should be communicated to the school and vice versa. Some programmes can be used in conjunction with parents, particularly some reading programmes. Paired Reading is one example of this: this involves the parent and the child reading aloud at the same time.

Reid (2009) points out there are many teaching programmes, many of which will be useful for children with dyslexia. It may be misguided for parents or for teachers to pin their hopes on any one programme.

It is important that programmes and teaching approaches are considered in the light of the individual child's learning profile.

The school should have a good knowledge of both the child and specific teaching approaches. Again, because there is such a wealth of materials on the market, it is important to monitor and evaluate the approach and the progress periodically. It is also important that parents share in this.

Support should not be measured in terms of 'hours' or 'days'. It is difficult to quantify the optimum length of support for any individual young person with dyslexia. Consistency is important, and frequent periodic reviews should provide guidance on the effectiveness of the

Figure 12.1 Paired reading: the child masters the text

approaches being used, and if particular approaches should be continued. It is also important to recognize that such monitoring need not be
in terms of reading and spelling ages. These are important, of course,
but it is also necessary to attain information and assess performances
on particular aspects of curriculum work, such as comprehension,
problem-solving and other curriculum activities that embrace much
more than reading and spelling accuracy.

Parental Perspectives

Reid (2003) interviewed a number of parents on the issues they had to
deal with on discovering their child was dyslexic. The main challenges
in parenting a child with dyslexia included:

♦ helping to maintain the child's self-esteem
♦ helping the child start new work when he or she had not consolidated previous work
♦ protecting the dignity of the child when dealing with professionals/
  therapists
♦ personal organization of the child
♦ peer insensitivity
♦ misconceptions of dyslexia
♦ homework.

These responses are quite interesting because they touch on some
of the key areas, particularly the emotional aspect, of dyslexia. They
also include the misunderstandings and misconceptions that many
can have.

Emotional aspects

It can be too easy to ignore the emotional aspects of dyslexia. Often the child's main difficulty will relate more directly to learning and to literacy, and this can be the main area of concern. If, however, a child is failing in literacy and finds schoolwork challenging, then it is likely that he or she will suffer emotionally. It is important that this feeling is addressed or, preferably, prevented.

Children can be very sensitive, particularly if they feel they are, in any way, different from others. Children with dyslexia usually have to visit psychologists and other specialists. For some children this can indicate that they are different, and they may feel stigmatized as a consequence. Even young adults at college and university can experience these feelings. Assessments and support for students with dyslexia are very often carried out at the 'disability office' within the college or university, and many do not want, or in fact need, the 'disability' label and so may be reluctant to seek help.

This highlights the importance of full, frank and informative feedback, following an assessment with the child or young adult, as well as with the parents. In fact, this initial feedback is as important as the eventual follow-up and intervention.

There are a number of ways of helping to maintain and to boost children's self-esteem, but one of the most obvious and effective ways is to ensure that they achieve some success and are given genuine praise. In order for praise to be effective the child has to be convinced that the praise is worthy of his or her achievements. When children feel a failure it is difficult to reverse these feelings, and often they need to change their perceptions of themselves. This can be a lengthy process, and ongoing support, praise and sensitive handling are necessary.

It is important that the term 'dyslexia' is explained to the child following an assessment and that he or she has a good understanding of what it means. This can become a positive tool for the young person if it is explained in terms of differences rather than in terms of deficits. It is often good for the person to receive an explanation of why he or she is finding some tasks challenging. Try introducing some of the following ideas:

♦ Ensure homework is carried out in an environment that suits your child's learning style. If he/she prefers background music then allow this as it may help with concentration.
♦ Encourage children to explore ideas and concepts through discussion.
♦ Help your child develop his/her own strategies for learning.
♦ Make sure there is a home–school notebook being used on a daily

basis. This keeps parents and teachers in touch with each other.
♦ Look for ways of boosting children's self-esteem – if any strategy seems to be working in class or at home this should be communicated between parents and teachers. A positive self-esteem comes from success so it is important that tasks are accessible for the student.

Developing self-esteem

Some strategies for developing self-esteem are as follows:

Praise
Praise should be given for what the child has *completed*, not what he/she has *succeeded* with. It may be necessary for parents to readjust their perceptions of success, but at the same time keep in mind that the child very likely has abilities that are not being displayed. This can be frustrating for parents and progress can be slower than hoped. This can be a point of discussion between teachers and parents.

Avoid comparisons with others
It is important that parents do not compare their child with others. Children progress at different rates in different ways.

Encourage relationships
Encourage the dyslexic child to develop peer friendships and become a member of clubs outside school. Many children with dyslexia receive a considerable boost to their self-esteem through success in outside-school activities.

Limit homework time
Try to limit time spent on homework – if children are spending too much time on homework it might be wise to discuss this issue at a parent-teacher meeting.

Help child develop learning style
Try to work out the child's particular learning style. Learning styles can be visual, auditory, kinesthetic or tactile, but environmental factors such as sound, light, time of day and even seating arrangements can make a difference. Factors to consider are:

♦ environment (sound, light, temperature, design)
♦ emotions (motivation, persistence, responsibility, structure)
♦ sociological factors (learning by self, pairs, peers, team, with an adult)

♦ physiological aspects (perceptual preferences, food and drink intake, time of day, mobility)
♦ psychological aspects (global or analytic preferences, impulsive and reflective).

Mind Maps©
Mind maps© can be useful for children with dyslexia. They are individually tailored and someone else's mind map may not be meaningful to every learner. It is important, therefore, that children create their own mind map, in order to help both with understanding key concepts and in the retention and recall of facts. Mind maps© can be a learning tool as well as one for retention of information.

Introduce games
Games can be a fun and effective way of reinforcing reading. Although there are a number of commercially produced games, parents themselves can use game-type activities, even board games or games such as scrabble can help the child become more familiar with words and with reading in general.

The Road to Equality and Inclusion

The Salamanca Statement (UNESCO 1994) paved a powerful path towards educational equality and inclusive policies. The statement indicated that 'schools should accommodate to all children regardless of their physical, intellectual, social, emotional, linguistic or other conditions . . . Many children experience learning difficulties and thus have special educational needs at some time during their schooling . . . Schools have to find ways of successfully educating all children, including those who have serious disadvantages and disabilities . . . emerging consensus that children with special educational needs should be included in the educational arrangements made for the majority of children. This has led to the concept of the inclusive school' (UNESCO 1994).

Special Educational Needs and Disability Act (2001) (SENDA)

The Code of Practice is part of the Special Educational Needs and Disability Act (2001) (SENDA). This Act is an amended form of the Disability Discrimination Act (1995) (DDA) that was revised to cover education. The Act provides greater powers to the Special Educational Needs Tribunal and places a duty on Local Education Authorities to provide and advertise both a Parent Partnership Scheme and conciliation arrangements.

Dyslexia

The words 'disability' and 'discrimination' are key words in the Act. The Act states that schools cannot discriminate against disabled pupils (the definition of disability is very broad and dyslexia can be seen in terms of the Act as a disability) in all aspects of school life including extracurricular activities and school excursions.

Parents can claim unlawful discrimination by putting a case to a Special Educational Needs and Disability Tribunal. Under the Act it is unlawful for schools to discriminate in admissions and exclusions and a school cannot deliberately refuse an application from a disabled person for admission to the school. Discrimination is evident when a pupil is treated less favourably and may be at a disadvantage because the school has not made 'reasonable adjustments'. What is meant by 'reasonable' is not explicitly defined in the Act as this depends on individual cases and can be a matter for the Tribunal or an appeal panel to decide.

Essentially the Act aims to incorporate parents as partners in the education of their child. This of course is very important in relation to children with special educational needs and parents need to be informed when a special educational needs provision is made for their child.

Parent Partnership Schemes

In England and Wales, Local Education Authorities are required to set up Parent Partnership Schemes (PPS) on a statutory basis, although there are no national standards set. The aim of PPS is to provide a range of services for parents whose children have SEN so that parents can play an active and informed role in their child's education. This implies that if parents are consulted and their views valued then the educational experience for the child, the parents and the school would be more harmonious and meaningful.

The Scottish Executive (2004) passed new legislation on Additional Support for Learning. The legislation has implications for special needs and for children with dyslexia and their parents. The legislation – Education (Additional Support for Learning) (Scotland) Act arose because it was felt that the existing assessment and recording system for children with special educational needs was outdated and too bureaucratic.

The aim of the legislation is to provide a framework that encompasses all children who may have difficulty in accessing and benefiting from learning, whatever the cause or reason may be for that difficulty. The legislation recognizes that children are individual and that some additional support needs are temporary, while others will present long-term barriers to effective learning. This provides the notion of educational support with a much wider framework than previously was the case.

Republic of Ireland

A major initiative in the Republic of Ireland was the *Task Force Report on Dyslexia in Republic of Ireland* (Government of Ireland 2001). This far-reaching comprehensive government report was the result of delib-erations of a government-appointed Task Force. The Task Force received 399 written submissions from individuals, educational institutions and organizations and 896 oral submissions were received from individuals by telephone. The report noted that parents in particular shared their views and frustrations with the Task Force. The report contains a sum-mary of recommendations of particular interest to parents.

The report said of parents (p. xvii): 'The vast majority of submis-sions came from you, the parents, who have first-hand experience of the learning difficulties arising from dyslexia that are experienced by your children. We thank you for your contributions; we have read your comments carefully and we recognise the complex nature of your experiences and your needs'.

As well as making 61 recommendations the report provides an informative appendix showing indicators of learning differences includ-ing those related to dyslexia for different age groups: 3–5 years, 5–7 years, 7–12 years and 12+.

One of the most influential pieces of legislation that has a potential impact on parents and dyslexia is the No Child Left Behind Act (2001) in the US. It was seen as a landmark in education reform in the US designed to improve student achievement and change the culture of America's schools.

Some of the key points of No Child Left Behind that may help par-ents and children with dyslexia are as follows: it gives schools more money; holds schools accountable for results; provides states and cities with more control and more flexibility to use resources where they are needed most; focuses on teaching methods that have been proven to work; and can allow parents to transfer their child to a bet-ter public school if the state says the school your child attends needs to improve.

Legislation in Canada such as the School Act (British Columbia) is very much rooted in the practice of inclusion. The Learning Difficulties Association of BC and the Canadian Academy for Therapeutic Tutors (CATT) have been very effective in assisting parents and organizing the Parent Advocacy Training and teaching programmes in literacy. They advocate the Orton-Gillingham approach, which is a multisensory struc-tured and sequential approach used effectively in general education as

Dyslexia

well as special education, tutoring and home-school programmes.

The Dyslexia Foundation of New Zealand (DFNZ) was formed in November 2006 to provide a voice for, and services to, the estimated one in ten New Zealanders with dyslexia, as well as to those supporting them. In April 2007, the New Zealand Government recognized dyslexia for the first time. In an accompanying statement, the Ministry of Education said it would be putting greater emphasis on assisting students with dyslexia, and would be implementing a range of initiatives to increase the level and quality of assistance given to these students.

Additionally, an earlier New Zealand government report on an enquiry into the teaching of reading and writing positively noted the work of SPELD, which indicated that the government should work more closely with SPELD and that SPELD teachers should become more involved in mainstream schools. The organization SPELD was set up by parents to help children with dyslexia.

> While many parents experience anxiety over their child's educational provision, there is considerable scope for optimism. Teachers and policy-makers in most countries have now accepted the need to make special and specialized provision for dyslexia, and in general there has been some evidence of teacher training and staff development to ensure that both the acceptance and the recognition of dyslexia are a reality at all stages of education. Practice and provision is still patchy, however, and there are examples of excellent practice but not all parents have access to this. In terms of equality, it is essential that some uniformity in practice and provision becomes more of a reality so that all parents, irrespective of where they live, can have access to good practice in supporting children with dyslexia.

Appendix 1

Suggestions for Follow-up

This book has provided much of the information teachers need to help them understand the key aspects of dyslexia and to plan effective learning programmes for students with dyslexia. Differentiated teaching approaches, insights into individual learning preferences and an understanding of the key issues associated with dyslexia are crucial if teachers are to feel confident and empowered as they deal with the challenges of dyslexia.

One of the most important aspects, however, is that of professional development of all staff in schools. Dealing with dyslexia should not be the sole responsibility of one teacher or even a specialist teacher. It is a whole-school responsibility and the school management needs to be involved in all aspects of practice, provision and training.

Professional Development

Professional development is one of the most effective means of ensuring that dyslexia is understood by all teachers. It is an important area and one that is increasing in importance. For example, the International Dyslexia Association (IDA) regularly has over 3000 attendees at its annual conference, and large influential organizations such as The European Dyslexia Association and the World Dyslexia Federation frequently organize a menu of courses with leading-edge speakers. The Institute of Child Education and Psychology (Europe) has a menu of university-accredited courses for teachers and parents at a range of levels (www.icepe.ie).

The British Dyslexia Association (BDA) has now accredited over 30 certificated courses with university validation on dyslexia. Additionally, many schools and associations in different countries are requesting training in dyslexia. I myself have conducted such training in over 60 countries, in Europe, Africa, Asia, the Middle East, New Zealand, Australia, Canada and the US, all in recent years. This illustrates the growing awareness and the need for training in this area.

Dyslexia

The international awareness of dyslexia is further highlighted by the range of contributors to the *International Book on Dyslexia* (Smythe, Everatt and Salter 2004). Fifty-three countries are represented in this volume, including countries in Europe, Asia, North America, South America and Australasia.

It is important, therefore, that teachers and other professionals have an awareness of dyslexia and that there is someone on the staff who can develop and implement training programmes.

Guidance on training

An example of aims and objectives for a course on dyslexia is shown below.

Aims
◆ To raise the standard of all school students' achievements through improved individual literacy development.
◆ To raise teachers' awareness of the barriers to learning faced by some students as a result of their difficulties in literacy and dyslexia.
◆ To support teachers in exploring and reflecting on appropriate curriculum responses to the needs of students who are dyslexic.
◆ To embrace the concept of an inclusive school, through literacy attainment and parental and pupil participation.
◆ To embrace the notion of dyslexia-friendly practices and provision.

Objectives
◆ To develop an understanding of terminology and controversies evident in the field of specific learning difficulties/dyslexia.
◆ To discuss the different perspectives held by professionals and parents/carers in the field of specific learning difficulties.
◆ To develop competence in using a range of strategies used to assess students' strengths and difficulties.
◆ To develop an awareness of the assessment process in educational settings.
◆ To develop awareness of a range of teaching approaches to overcome the difficulties associated with dyslexia.
◆ To encourage critical reflection on policy, practice and provision in the area of specific learning difficulties and dyslexia.
◆ To develop understanding of the importance of emotional factors for students with dyslexia.
◆ To recognize individual and whole-school approaches to the needs of students with dyslexia.

The point about training in dyslexia is that it should be contextualized for the school. Schools can operate in different ways and it is important that this is taken into account when providing training. It is often a good idea for training needs to be identified by staff. Staff should be in a position to identify which aspects of training they will most benefit from.

While training should be practical, including case studies and examples from the classroom, the latest research should also be provided so that teachers know they are at the cutting edge of practice for dyslexia. This will provide confidence and help in collaboration with parents.

Support at Home

School can be quite an exhausting experience for children with dyslexia. They have to participate in some challenging activities, and these can easily lower their energy and motivation levels. Home should not be a 'second school', but rather a supportive environment. There are activities that can be undertaken at home to reinforce schoolwork.

Reading programmes

Some reading programmes can be carried out at home, as the programme may not require any specialist training. The school will be able to advise on this.

Reading schemes

Reading schemes usually have follow-up readers that can be used at home.

Paired reading

This can be carried out very successfully at home as it is based on the parent and the child reading together. It is intended only for use with individually chosen, highly motivating, non-fiction or fiction books that are *above* the independent readability level of the tutee. One of the important aspects of paired reading is praise – the parent should look pleased when the child succeeds when using this technique.

Discussion

Discussion is also a good reinforcing vehicle. It is important for parents to find out what their child is doing in history or geography and other subjects, as the content of many topics can be incorporated into family outings or discussions. For example, a family trip in the car can be used to reinforce some historical landmarks or the names of crops grown in the area. Similarly, a visit to a castle, museum or art gallery can reinforce names, events and experiences the child may have encountered in some of his or her school subjects.

Reinforcement

At best, any input at home can reinforce what the child is learning at school. This is particularly important for dyslexic children because they have a difficulty with automaticity. This means that even when they have learnt a new word or skill it may not be fully automatized. The implication of this is that they may forget the word or skill after a short while – for example, during a school holiday – if it is not being used. Automaticity is achieved through practice and actually using the new word in as many different settings and ways as possible. Research indicates that dyslexic children take longer than others to achieve automaticity and therefore require over-learning in order to consolidate the new learning. Parents can reinforce the use of a word or skill at home or on family outings without necessarily referring to school work.

Motivation

It is important to ensure that children with dyslexia are motivated to read. This can be challenging, since it may be difficult to find age-appropriate reading material that is at the child's reading level. Books that emphasize high interest and lower levels of vocabulary can be extremely useful, as these can help with reading fluency, reading comprehension and processing speed.

Information for Parents and Teachers

There is a great deal of information available for parents and teachers. Voluntary groups can offer advice and support to parents. It is important, however, that parents recognize that the school should be the first 'port of call', as often at least one member of staff will have some knowledge of dyslexia, and the school may also have suitable resources for parents. Some contact organizations in different countries are shown in Appendix 2.

This book is intended as a reference for both parents and teachers. Although some of it can be seen as quite specialized and more for teachers than parents, it is important that the two groups are linked. Each has an important role to play and it is important that this is carried out in a collaborative and constructive manner. I suggested earlier that the most effective approach in dealing with dyslexia is effective communication between home and school. This helps to ensure that the holistic needs of the child and the family are taken into account. This is crucial as it will ensure that the resources, expertise and strategies described in this book are used in the most effective way. Dealing with dyslexia is not the responsibility of just one person, whether teacher or parent. Rather, it is a whole-school/community concern, and one that is of national and international importance. Supporting students with dyslexia is important in today's inclusive society.

Appendix 2

Contacts

North and South America and Canada

Argentina

APHDA: aphda@hotmail.com

Brazil

Associação Brasileira de Dislexia: www.dislexia.org.br

Canada

International Dyslexia Association British Columbia Branch:
   www.idabc.com
International Dyslexia Association Ontario Branch: www.idaontario.
   com/dyslexia_ONBIDA_resources.html
Canadian Academy of Therapeutic Tutors: www.ogtutors.com
Learning Disabilities Association of Canada: www.ldac-acta.ca

Caribbean

Caribbean Dyslexia Association: Haggart Hall, St Michael, Barbados

USA

International Dyslexia Association (IDA): www.interdys.org
Learning Disabilities Association of America: www.ldanatl.org

Australasia

Australia

SPELD Victoria: www.speldvic.org.au
SPELD South Australia: www.speld-sa.org.au
SPELD New South Wales: www.speldnsw.org.au
SPELD (Tasmania): speldtasmania@bigpond.com
SPELD Western Australia: speld@opera.iinet.net.au; www.dyslexia-speld.com
SPELD Queensland: www.speld.org.au

New Zealand

Dyslexia Foundation of New Zealand: www.dyslexiafoundation.org.nz
SPELD New Zealand: www.speld.org.nz
Learning and Behaviour Charitable Trust: www.lbctnz.co.nz

Europe

Dyslexia International (formerly Dyslexia International – Tools and Technologies (DITT): www.dyslexia-international.org
European Dyslexia Association (EDA): www.dyslexia.eu.com

Croatia

Croatian Dyslexia Association: lencek@antun.erf.hr

Cyprus

Cyprus Dyslexia Association: www.cyprusdyslexia.com

North Cyprus

North Cyprus Dyslexia Association: www.ldncyprus.org

Czech Republic

Czech Dyslexia Association: www.czechdyslexia.cz/eng/index/html

Dyslexia

Denmark

Danish Dyslexia Association: www.ordblind.com

Greece

Greek Dyslexia Association: www.dyslexia.gr
Association of Parents of Dyslexic and with Learning Difficulties
    Children of Thessaloniki and Northern Greece: www.dyslexia-
    goneis.gr
Aggeliki Pappa, Athens: www.ilovedyslexia.gr

Hungary

Dyslexia in Hungary: www.diszlexia.hu
Research in Dyslexia in Hungary: www.diszlexia.hu/Research%20
    on%20Dyslexia%20in%20Hungary.doc
Start dyslexia: Tan Studio, 1118, Hegyalja, UT. 70, Budapest

Republic of Ireland

Dyslexia Association of Ireland: www.dyslexia.ie

Italy

Associazione Italiana Dislessia: www.aiditalia.org

Luxembourg

Dyspel asbl: www.dyspel.org/

Poland

Polskie Towarzystwo Dysleksji: psymbg@univ.gda.pl

Scotland

Dyslexia Scotland: www.dyslexiascotland.org.uk

Sweden

Swedish Dyslexia Association: http://dyslexiforeningen.se/engelska.
    html

UK
British Dyslexia Association: www.bdadyslexia.org.uk

Wales
Welsh Dyslexia Association: www.welshdyslexia.info

Russia
Russian Dyslexia Association: olgainsh@land.ru

Middle East

Egypt
Egyptian Dyslexia Centre: www.dyslexia-egypt.com

Israel
Israel Dyslexia Association: www.orton-ida.org.il

Kuwait
Kuwait Dyslexia Association: www.kuwaitdyslexia.com
Centre for Child Evaluation and Teaching, Kuwait: www.ccetkuwait.
   org

Asia

Hong Kong
Dyslexia Association (Hong Kong): www.dyslexia.org.hk/
Hong Kong Association for Specific Learning Difficulties: www.asld.
   org.hk

Japan
Japan Dyslexia Society: info@npo-edge.jp

Singapore
Dyslexia Association of Singapore: www.das.org.sg

Dyslexia

Taiwan

Dyslexia Global Support: www.dyslexiaglobalsupport.com/

Africa

Gambia

Madonna Jarret Thorpe Trust: PO Box 4232, The Gambia, West Africa. Tel: 00220–9902099. Email: mjtt@airtip.gm

Ghana

Crossroads Dyslexic Centre at U2KAN: PO Box KD525 Kanda, Accra, Ghana, West Africa. Tel: 00233-21-230391/020-811-6198. Email: joybanad@yahoo.com

South Africa

SAALED: PO Box 2404, Cape Town 7740, South Africa, www.saaled.org.za
The Remedial Foundation: PO Box 32207, Braamfontein 2017, Johannesburg, SA

Uganda

Rise and Shine Dyslexia Organization: PO Box 2882 Kampala, Uganda

Other Websites

Dr Gavin Reid

www.drgavinreid.com

Red Rose School

www.redroseschool.co.uk

Provides for the educational, emotional and social needs of up to 48 boys and girls, aged between 7 and 16 years, of average and above average intelligence who experience specific learning difficulties and/ or experiences which cause them to become delicate and vulnerable in a mainstream setting.

ICEP Europe – Institute of Child Education and Psychology (Europe)

www.icepe.ie

The trusted leading provider of high-quality online Continuing Professional Development (CPD) and university-validated diploma programmes in special educational needs for teachers, parents and allied professionals who work with children and young people.

Center for Child Evaluation and Teaching (CCET)

www.ccetkuwait.org

The Center for Child Evaluation and Teaching (CCET) was first established in 1984 in response to the needs of a group of Kuwaiti mothers who realized that their children were having difficulty with schoolwork. As they were unable to find advice locally, they travelled to the UK and, subsequently, to the US, where their children were assessed and intervention programs were recommended. On returning to Kuwait, they decided to set up a centre so that children could be assessed and receive remedial teaching without having to leave the country. The centre is now a source of excellence in research, teaching and test development and evaluations. The CCET believes in the importance of early intervention and most parents and teachers find that early intervention is essential in getting advice and devising treatment strategies to deal with different learning difficulties (LDs) individuals face.

Oak Hill School

www.oakhill.ch

Oak Hill School offers a unique half-day programme to students with diagnosed learning disabilities or attention deficit disorders, who are experiencing difficulties in the mainstream classroom. The language of instruction is English and the school serves the international community in the Lac Léman area in Switzerland. The programme provides students with three highly structured, multisensory instructional periods in reading, written language and mathematics. Students continue to attend their regular school for the remainder of their day, allowing them to participate in the mainstream curriculum, attend extra-curricular activities and maintain normal social interactions.

Oak Hill aims to foster the self-esteem of those students who have failed to thrive in a normal school setting. Achievements are celebrated

Dyslexia

on a daily basis and the programme enables each individual to realise his or her true potential.

> *Having spent a week at Oak Hill School I was extremely impressed by the professionalism of the staff, the structured programme for teaching and learning, the school ethos and the commitment of the school to a high level of professional development. Both I, and the parents who visited me during that week were put fully at ease by the calm atmosphere and the bright and airy environment of the school. It is clear to see why the children at the school are able to develop their full potential – academically and socially. In short, the school is a centre of excellence in the area of teaching and learning.*

> Dr Gavin Reid, Director, Red Rose School for children with specific learning difficulties, UK

ALL Special Kids, (ASK) Geneva

www.allspecialkids.org

A Geneva-based organization, aiming to support the families of children with special needs and learning differences. The network was founded in March of 2003 by a group of parents who were frustrated at the lack of Anglophone support services for children with special needs in the Geneva area and decided to do something about it. One of its first initiatives was to establish a website to provide information on schools, English-speaking specialists, and other local support groups in Geneva and the surrounding area, as well as web links to other useful special-needs organizations and kids-friendly educational websites.

The website serves as an excellent tool in keeping not only the Geneva community informed but also reaching English-speaking parents from other parts of Switzerland and all over Europe as well. In May 2003, ASK began to offer monthly support meetings for parents and educational seminars, which are conducted in English and open to members and non-members alike.

ASK-Bern parents support group was introduced in November 2007. Contact: info.bern@allspecialkids.org

ASK-Vaud parents support group was introduced in September 2008. Contact: info.vaud@allspecialkids.org

ASK-Geneva Francophone parents support group will be introduced in 2010. Contact: info.francais@allspecialkids.org

Fun Track Learning, Perth Western Australia

www.funtrack.com.au/

Contact Mandy Appleyard.

Arts Dyslexia Trust

www.artsdyslexiatrust.org

Learning Works Int.

www.learning-works.org.uk

Focuses on learning and motivating learners whatever their shape, size or ability! Specializes in designing professional development courses, team challenges and learning resources to meet the needs of staff, pupils and parents. Has a great range of publications all of which are practical.

Creative Learning Company New Zealand

www.creativelearningcentre.com

ACLD, Inc.

www.acldonline.org

An Association for Children and Adults with Learning Disabilities

Dyslexia Action (formerly Dyslexia Institute)

www.dyslexia.ie

Working Well Together

www.workingwelltogether.eu
jennieguise@workingwelltogether.eu

Assessing stress at work and work–life balance.

Articles and Reviews About Dyslexia

Dyslexia Online Journal

www.dyslexia-adults.com/journal.html

Articles and research for professionals working in the field of dyslexia.

Dyslexia

Dyslexia Parents Resource

www.dyslexia-parent.com/

Information and resources about dyslexia for parents of children who are, or may be, dyslexic.

Landmark College, Vermont, USA

www.landmark.edu/

Family Onwards

www.familyonwards.com

Helen Arkell Dyslexia Centre

www.arkellcentre.org.uk

I am dyslexic

www.iamdyslexic.com

A site put together by an 11-year-old dyslexic boy.

Institute for Neuro-Physiological Psychology (INPP)

www.inpp.org.uk

Dr Loretta Giorcelli

www.doctorg.org/

A well-known international consultant.

Mindroom

www.mindroom.org

A charity dedicated to spreading much greater awareness and understanding of learning difficulties. Their goal is that by 2020 all children with learning difficulties in the UK will be identified and helped.

Dysguise – dyslexia assessment and consultancy

www.dysguise.com
jennieguise@dysguise.com

SNAP assessment

www.SNAPassessment.com

International Contacts Database

www.wdnf.info/

A series of advice and help sheets have been written by leading experts in their fields.

World of Dyslexia

www.worldofdyslexia.com
www.dyslexia-parent.com/world_of_dyslexia

Adult Dyslexia

www.dyslexia-college.com

Literacy

Buzan Centres Ltd

www.Mind-Map.com

Centre for Early Literacy

www.earlyliteracylearning.org/

Reviews evidence on effective early literacy learning practices.

Crossbow Education

www.crossboweducation.com

Games for learning.

Dyslexia

Iansyst Ltd
www.dyslexic.com

The National Literacy Strategy
www.standards.dfes.gov.uk/literacy/

Orton Gillingham (OG)
Contact Shannon Green – reachshannon@gmail.com

Multisensory language learning. Courses in the Orton-Gillingham approach – parents, teachers, tutors.

Paired reading, writing and thinking
www.dundee.ac.uk/eswce/research/projects/trwresources/reading/

PRO-ED Inc.
www.proedinc.com

Reading Association of Ireland
www.reading.ie/

Bulletin boards, information on associations and links etc.

SEN Marketing
www.senbooks.co.uk

THRASS
www.thrass.co.uk

United Kingdom Literacy Association
www.ukla.org

Newsletter, publications, links worth looking at.

Appendix 3

Tests Used for Dyslexia

Bangor Dyslexia Test

This is a commercially available short screening test developed from work conducted at Bangor University (Miles 1983). The test is divided into the following sections:

- left–right (body parts)
- repeating polysyllabic words
- subtraction
- tables
- months forward/reversed
- digits forward/reversed
- b–d confusion
- familiar incidence.
- www.LDAlearning.com

Cognitive Profiling System

Lucid Creative Ltd, Beverley, Yorkshire, UK

This is a computerized screening programme and constitutes a user-friendly package complete with facilities for student registration, graphic report and print-out of results. It is used in over 3,500 primary schools in the UK and elsewhere in the world.

Comprehensive Test of Phonological Processing (CTOPP)

Richard Wagner, Joseph Torgesen and Carol Rashotte

The Comprehensive Test of Phonological Processing (CTOPP) assesses phonological awareness, phonological memory and rapid naming. Persons with deficits in one or more of these kinds of phonological

Dyslexia

processing abilities may have more difficulty learning to read than those who do not.

DIBELS

http://dibels.uoregon.edu/

The Dynamic Indicators of Basic Early Literacy Skills (DIBELS) is a set of standardized, individually administered measures of early literacy development. They are designed to be short (one-minute) fluency measures used to regularly monitor the development of pre-reading and early reading skills.

Dyslexia Screening Test (DST)

(Fawcett and Nicolson 1996)

The screening instrument can be used for children between 6.6 and 16.5 years of age, although there is also an alternative version developed by the same authors for younger children, *Dyslexia Early Screening Test*, and an adult version (Nicolson and Fawcett 1996). The test consists of the following attainment tests:

♦ one-minute reading
♦ two-minute spelling
♦ one-minute writing.

Additionally, there are the following diagnostic tests:

♦ rapid naming
♦ bead threading
♦ postural stability
♦ phonemic segmentation
♦ backwards digit span
♦ nonsense passage reading
♦ verbal and semantic fluency.

The dyslexia screening tests can be accessed by all teachers and are available from the Psychological Corporation, 24–28 Oval Road, London NW1 1YA. Email cservice@harcourtbrace.com.

Gray Oral Reading Tests, Fourth Edition

J. Lee Weiderholt and Brian R. Bryant

The Gray Oral Reading Tests, Fourth Edition (GORT-4), provides an efficient and objective measure of growth in oral reading and an aid in the diagnosis of oral reading difficulties. Five scores give you information on a student's oral reading skills in terms of:

♦ Rate – the amount of time taken by a student to read a story.
♦ Accuracy – the student's ability to pronounce each word in the story correctly.
♦ Fluency – the student's Rate and Accuracy Scores combined.
♦ Comprehension – the appropriateness of the student's responses to questions about the content of each story read.
♦ Overall Reading Ability – a combination of a student's Fluency (i.e. Rate and Accuracy) and Comprehension scores.

Launch Into Reading Success – Test of Phonological Awareness

Lorna Bennett and Pamela Ottley

Phonological awareness programme designed just for young children. Can prevent reading failure at an early stage if it is identified and intervention with the right programme is used. Launch Into Reading Success is a phonological skills-training programme designed for use by teachers and other professionals in schools and for parents at home. Can provide an effective first step for a child to take in the pursuit of literacy.

PRO-ED Inc.

A leading publisher of nationally standardized tests. www.proedinc.com

Special Needs Assessment Profile

(Weedon and Reid 2003; 2005; 2009)

The Special Needs Assessment Profile (SNAP) is a computer-aided diagnostic assessment and profiling package that makes it possible to 'map' each student's own mix of problems onto an overall matrix of learning, behavioural and other difficulties. From this, clusters and patterns of weaknesses and strengths help to identify the core features of a student's difficulties – visual, dyslexic, dyspraxic, phonological, attentional or any other of the 17 key deficits targeted – and suggests a diagnosis that points the way forward for that individual student. It provides a structured profile which yields an overview at the early stages of 'School Action' in the Code of Practice – and also informs the process of external referral, at 'School Action Plus'. SNAP involves four steps (see p. 188). SNAP (B) refers to SNAP behaviour which is also available and focuses on self-esteem, emotional and behavioural aspects.

The kit helps to facilitate the collaboration between different groups of professionals and between professionals and parents – a collaboration which is vital in order to obtain a full picture of the student's abilities and difficulties.

There is a dedicated website (accessible to anyone) that contains a number of ideas on teaching to cover difficulties associated with the 17 different specific learning difficulties.

www.SNAPassessment.com

Test of Phonological Awareness – Second Edition: PLUS (TOPA-2+)

Joseph K. Torgensen and Brian R. Bryant

This is a group-administered, norm-referenced measure of phonological awareness for children between the ages of five and eight. The scale, which can also be administered individually, has demonstrated reliability and the test yields valid results that are reported in terms of percentile ranks and a variety of standard scores.

TOWRE – Test of Word Reading Efficiency

Joseph Torgesen, Richard Wagner and Carol Rashotte

The *Test of Word Reading Efficiency* (TOWR E) is a nationally normed measure of word reading accuracy and fluency.

WIST (Word Identification and Spelling Test)

Barbara Wilson

Many teachers who are Orton-Gillingham trained use this test. It can pinpoint whether Orton-Gillingham would help the student (can also be done in a group).

Wechsler Individual Achievement Test for Teachers (WIAT-II–T) (PsychCorp™)

This test assesses the following in one assessment:

♦ *Single Word Reading* – includes letter identification, phonological awareness, letter-sound awareness, accuracy and automaticity of word recognition
♦ *Reading Comprehension* – stories and sentences include literal, inferential and lexical comprehension, oral reading accuracy and fluency and word recognition in context
♦ *Reading Speed* – for ages 6 to 16 years 11 months. Words per minute (WPM) can also be recorded for the full age range
♦ *Reading Rate* – this is calculated from the Reading Comprehension subtest. The quartile scores identify the slow and accurate, slow and inaccurate, fast and accurate and fast and inaccurate reader
♦ *Single Word Spelling* – includes letter–sound correspondence for vowels, consonants and consonant blends, regular and irregular words, contradictions and high-frequency homonyms.

www.psychcorp.co.uk/Education/Assessments/Achievement/WIAT-IIUKforTeachers

info@psychcorp.co.uk

References

Allcock, P. (2001) Handwriting Speed Assessment – update PATOSS website: www.patoss-dyslexia.org.

American Psychiatric Association (1994, 2000) *Diagnostic and Statistical Manual of Mental Disorders* (fourth edn). Washington, DC: American Psychiatric Association.

Augur, J. and Briggs, S. (1992) *The Hickey Multisensory Language Course.* London: Whurr.

Ayres, A.J. (1979) *Sensory Integration and the Child.* Los Angeles: Western Psychological Services.

Barkley, R.A. (1997) *ADHD and the Nature of Self-Control.* New York: Guilford Press.

Bell, N. (1991a) 'Gestalt imagery: A critical factor in language comprehension'. Reprint from *Annals of Dyslexia,* vol. 41. Baltimore, MD: Orton Dyslexia Society.

Bell, N. (1991b) *Visualizing and Verbalizing for Language Comprehension and Thinking.* Paso Robles, CA: Academy of Reading Publications.

Bell, N. (2005) 'The role of imagery and verbal processing in comprehension'. Paper presented at the 56th Annual Conference IDA, Denver, 9–12 November 2005.

Berninger, V.W. and Wolf, B.J. (2009) *Helping Students with Dyslexia and Dysgraphia Make Connections: Differentiated Instruction Lesson Plans in Reading and Writing.* Baltimore, MD: Brookes Publishing.

Berryman, M. and Wearmouth, J. (2009) 'Responsive approaches to literacy learning within cultural contexts', in G. Reid (ed.), *The Routledge Companion to Dyslexia.* London: Routledge.

Berryman, M. and Woller, P. (2007) 'RĀPP: Tape-assisted reading to support students' literacy in Māori in two bilingual schools'. SET (2), 19–23. Wellington: NZCER.

Blythe, P. (1992) *A Physical Approach to Resolving Specific Learning Difficulties.* Chester: Institute for Neuro-Physiological Psychology.

Blythe, P. (2001) personal communication.

Blythe, P. and Goddard, S. (2000) *Neuro-Physiological Assessment Test Battery.* Chester: Institute for Neuro-Physiological Psychology.

Bradley, L. (1989) 'Specific Learning Disability: Prediction–intervention–progress'. Paper presented to the Rodin Remediation Academy International Conference on Dyslexia, University College of North Wales.

Bradley, L. (1990) 'Rhyming connections in learning to read and spell', in P.D. Pumfrey and C.D. Elliott (eds), *Children's Difficulties in Reading, Spelling and Writing.* London: Falmer Press.

Bradley, L. and Bryant, P. (1991) 'Phonological skills before and after learning to read', in S.A. Brady and D.P. Shankweiler (eds), *Phonological Processes in Literacy*. London: Lawrence Erlbaum.

Bradley, L. and Huxford, L.M. (1994) 'Organising sound and letter patterns for spelling', in G.D. Brown and N.C. Ellis, (eds), *Handbook of Normal and Disturbed Spelling Development: Theory, Processes and Interventions*. Chichester: Wiley.

Breznitz, Z. (2008) 'The origin of dyslexia: the asynchrony phenomenon', in G. Reid, A. Fawcett, F. Manis and L. Siegel (2008) *The Sage Dyslexia Handbook*. London: Sage Publications.

Breznitz, Z. and Horowitz, T. (2007). 'All the wrong and right moves: a comparison of cerebral activity during accurate and erroneous reading performance among dyslexics and regular readers, an ERP study'. Manuscript submitted for publication.

British Psychological Society (BPS) (1999) *Dyslexia, Literacy and Psychological Assessment* (BPS Working Party Report). Leicester: British Psychological Society.

Brown, A., Armbruster, B. and Baker, L. (1986) 'The role of metacognition in reading and studying', in J. Oraspinu (ed.), *Reading Comprehension from Research to Practice*. Hillsdale, NJ: Lawrence Erlbaum.

Brown, T.E. (1996) *Brown Attention-Deficit Disorder Scales*. London: Psychological Corporation.

Burden, B. (2002) 'A cognitive approach to dyslexia: learning styles and thinking skills', in G. Reid and J. Wearmouth (eds), *Dyslexia and Literacy: Theory and Practice*. Chichester: Wiley.

Butterworth, B. (2003) *Dyscalculia Screener*. London: GL Assessment.

Buzan, T. (1993) *The Mind Map Book: Radiant Thinking*. London: BBC Books.

Came. F. and Reid, G. (2007) *Concern, Assess, Provide, (CAP) It all*. Wiltshire: Learning Works.

Chall, J.S. and Popp, H.M. (1996) *Teaching and Assessing Phonics: Why, What, When, How? A Guide for Teachers*. Cambridge, MA: Educators.

Chinn, S. (2002) '"Count me in". A comparison of the demands of numeracy and the problems dyslexic learners have with maths'. Paper presented at North Kent Dyslexia Association, Conference for Teachers, Greenwich, London (5 October 2002).

Chinn, S. (2009) 'Dyscalculia and learning difficulties in mathematics' in G. Reid (ed.), *The Routledge Companion to Dyslexia*. London: Routledge.

Clay, M. (1985) *The Early Detection of Reading Difficulties: A Diagnostic Survey with Recovery Procedures*. Auckland: Heinemann Educational.

Clay, M. (1992) *Reading: The Patterning of Complex Behaviour*. London: Heinemann.

Clay, M. (1993) *An Observational Survey of Early Literacy Achievement*. Auckland: Heinemann Educational.

Coffield, M., Riddick, B., Barmby, P. and O'Neill, J. (2008) 'Dyslexia friendly primary schools: what can we learn from asking the pupils?', in G. Reid, A. Fawcett, F. Manis and L. Siegel (2008) *The Sage Dyslexia Handbook*. London: Sage Publications.

Conner, M. (1994) 'Specific learning difficulties (dyslexia) and interventions', *Support for Learning* (9)3, 114–19.

References

Conners, C.K. (1996) *Conners' Rating Scale (Revised)*. London: Psychological Corporation.

Cooper, R. (2005) *A Social Model of Dyslexia*. London: South Bank University.

Cooper, R. (2009) 'Dyslexia', in D. Pollak (ed.), *Neurodiversity in Higher Education: Positive Responses to Specific Learning Differences*. Chichester: Wiley-Blackwell.

Cox, A.R. (1985) 'Alphabetic phonics: an organization and expansion of Orton, Gillingham', *Annals of Dyslexia*, 35, 187–98.

Crombie, M. (2002) 'Dyslexia: A new dawn'. Unpublished PhD thesis. Glasgow: University of Strathclyde.

Crombie, M. and McColl, H. (2001) 'Dyslexia and the teaching of modern foreign languages', in L. Peer and G. Reid (eds), *Dyslexia: Successful Inclusion in the Secondary School*. London: David Fulton.

Cudd, E.T. and Roberts, L.L. (1994) 'A scaffolding technique to develop sentence sense and vocabulary', *The Reading Teacher*, 47(4), 34–69.

Culham, R. (2003) *6+1 Traits of Writing: The Complete Guide* (grades 3 and up). New York: Scholastic.

Cyhlarova, E., Bell, J.G., Dick, J.R., Mackinlay, E.E., Stein, J.F. and Richardson, A.J. (2007) 'Membraine fatty acids, reading and spelling in dyslexic and non-dyslexic adults', *European Neuropsychopharmacology*, 17, 116–21.

Dargie, R. (2001) 'Dyslexia and history', in L. Peer and G. Reid (eds), *Dyslexia: Successful Inclusion in the Secondary School*. London: David Fulton.

Davis, R.D. and Braun, E.M. (1997) *The Gift of Dyslexia: Why Some of the Smartest People Can't Read and How They Can Learn*. London: Souvenir Press.

De Bono, E. (1986) *CORT Thinking*. Oxford: Pergamon Press.

Denckla, M.B. and Rudel, R.G. (1976) 'Rapid "automatised" naming (RAN): Dyslexia differentiated from other learning disabilities', *Neuropsychologia*, 14, 471–9.

Dennison, G.E. and Dennison, P.E. (1989) *Educational Kinesiology Brain Organisation Profiles*. Glendale, CA: Edu-Kinesthetics.

Dennison, G.E. and Dennison, P.E. (2001) *Educational Kinesiology Brain Organisation Profiles*. Teachers' training manual, third edn. Glendale, CA: Edu-Kinesthetics.

Dennison, P.E. and Hargrove, G. (1985) *Personalized Whole Brain Integration*. Glendale, CA: Educational Kinesthetics.

Deno, S.L. (1989) 'Curriculum-based measurement and special education services: A fundamental and direct relationship', in M.R. Shinn (ed.), *Curriculum based Measurement: Assessing Special Children*. New York: Guilford Press.

Deponio, P., Landon, J. and Reid, G. (2000) 'Dyslexia and bilingualism – Implications for assessment, teaching and learning', in L. Peer and G. Reid (eds), *Multilingualism, Literacy and Dyslexia. A Challenge for Educators*. London: David Fulton.

DfES (2001) *The National Numeracy Strategy: Guidance to Support Learners with Dyslexia and Dyscalculia*. London: DfES.

DfES (2005, 2009) *Rose Report on the Teaching of Reading*. London: DfES.

Dimitriadi, Y. (2000) 'Using ICT to support bilingual dyslexic learners', in L. Peer and G. Reid (eds), *Multilingualism, Literacy and Dyslexia: A Challenge for Educators*. London: David Fulton.

Dore, W. and Rutherford, R. (2001) 'Closing the gap'. Paper presented at the BDA International Conference on Dyslexia, York.

Dunn, R., Dunn, K. and Price, G.E. (1975, 1979, 1985, 1987, 1989) *Learning Styles Inventory*. Lawrence, KS: Price Systems.

Eadon, H. (2005) *Dyslexia and Drama*. London: David Fulton.

'Education of Children and Young People with Specific Learning Difficulties', report of the task group on dyslexia (2002), www.deni.gov.uk/dyslexia.pdf.

Ehri, L.C. (2002) 'Reading processes, acquisition, and instructional implications', in G. Reid and J. Wearmouth (eds), *Dyslexia and Literacy: Theory and Practice*. Chichester: Wiley.

Elbeheri, G. (2010) '*Researcher Practitioner Perspective* – Literacy is a human right' in *Perspective on Language and Literacy*, winter edition 36(1), 30.

Elliott, J.G. (2005) 'Dyslexia: diagnoses, debates and diatribes'. *Special Children*, 169, 19–23.

Fawcett, A. (1989) 'Automaticity: a new framework for dyslexic research?'. Paper presented at the First International Conference of the British Dyslexia Association, Bath 1989.

Fawcett, A. and Nicolson, R. (2008) 'Dyslexia and the cerebellum', in G. Reid, A. Fawcett, F. Manis and L. Siegel (2008) *The Sage Handbook of Dyslexia*. London: Sage Publications.

Fawcett, A.J. and Nicolson, R.I. (1992) 'Automatisation deficits in balance for dyslexic children', *Perceptual and Motor Skills*, 75, 507–29.

Fawcett, A.J. and Nicolson, R.I. (1996) *The Dyslexia Screening Test*. London: Psychological Corporation.

Fawcett, A.J. and Nicolson, R.I. (2001) 'Dyslexia: the role of the cereballum', in A.J. Fawcett (ed.), *Dyslexia: Theory and Good Practice*. London: Whurr.

Fawcett, A.J. and Nicolson, R.I. (2004) 'Dyslexia: the role of the cereballum', in G. Reid and A.J. Fawcett (eds), *Dyslexia in Context: Research, Policy and Practice*. London: Whurr.

Fawcett, A. and Reid, G. (2009) 'Dyslexia and alternative interventions', in G. Reid (ed.), *The Routledge Companion to Dyslexia*. London: Routledge.

Fife Education Authority in Scotland (2005) *Specific Learning Differences: Guidance for Teachers and Parents*. Fife Council, UK.

Fitts, P.M. and Posner, M.I. (1967) *Human Performance*. Belmont, CA: Brooks Cole.

Flavell, J.H. (1979) 'Metacognition and cognitive monitoring', *American Psychologist*, October, 906–11.

Frederickson, N. and Cline, T. (2002) *Special Educational Needs, Inclusion and Diversity, A Textbook*. Buckingham: Open University Press.

Frederickson, N., Frith, V. and Reason, R. (1997) *Phonological Assessment Battery*. London: NFER Nelson.

Frith, U. (2002) 'Resolving the paradoxes of dyslexia', in G. Reid and J. Wearmouth (eds), *Dyslexia and Literacy: Theory and Practice*. Chichester: Wiley.

Gardner, H. (1983) *Frames of Mind: The Theory of Multiple Intelligences*. New York: Harper and Row.

Gardner, H. (1999) 'Foreword', in D. Lazear, *Eight Ways of Knowing: Teaching for Multiple Intelligences* (third edn). Arlington Heights, IL: SkyLight Professional Development.

Given, B.K. and Reid, G. (1999). *Learning Styles: A Guide for Teachers and Parents*. St Anne's-on-Sea: Red Rose Publications.

References

Goddard-Blythe, S. (1996) *Developmental Exercise Programme*. Chester: Institute for NeuroPhysiological Psychology.

Government of Ireland Department of Education (2001) *Task Force Report on Dyslexia in Republic of Ireland*. Dublin: Department of Education.

Green, S. (2006) 'Reading comprehension and the OG approach'. Presentation at the conference 'From Inclusion to Belonging', SAALD, Johannesburg, 15–17 May.

Guise, J. (2010) 'Higher education written assessment feedback and dyslexic student identity: a discourse analytic study'. Unpublished dissertation, The Open University, UK.

Hales, G. (2001) 'Selfesteem and counselling', in L. Peer and G. Reid (eds), *Dyslexia: Successful Inclusion in the Secondary School*. London: David Fulton.

Hannaford, C. (1995) *Smart Moves: Why Learning Is Not All in Your Head*. Arlington, VA: Great Ocean Publishers.

Hannaford, C. (1997) *The Dominance Factor: How Knowing Your Dominant Eye, Ear, Brain, Hand and Foot Can Improve Your Learning*. Arlington, VA: Great Ocean Publishers.

Hatcher, P. (1994, 2004) *Sound Linkage: An Integrated Programme for Overcoming Reading Difficulties*. London: Whurr.

Healy, J. (1998) *Failure to Connect: How Computers Affect our Children's Minds and What We Can do About It*. New York: Simon and Schuster.

Healy Eames, F. and Hannafin, M.J. (2005) *Switching on for Learning: A Student Guide to Exam and Career Success*. Oranmore, Co. Galway: FHE Learning.

Henderson, S. and Sugden, D. (1992, revised 2008) *Movement Assessment Battery for Children*. Sidcup, Kent.

Henderson, A., Came, F. and Brough, M. (2003) *Working with Dyscalculia*. Wiltshire: Learning Works.

Henry, M. (1996) 'The Orton–Gillingham approach', in G. Reid (ed.), *Dimensions of Dyslexia, vol. 1: Assessment, Teaching and the Curriculum*. Edinburgh: Moray House Publications.

Henry, M.K. (2003) *Unlocking Literacy: Effective Decoding and Spelling Instruction*. Baltimore, MD: Brookes Publishing.

HMI (2008) *Education for Learners with Dyslexia*, Edinburgh: Scottish Executive.

Holmes, P. (2001) 'Dyslexia and Physics', in L. Peer and G. Reid (eds), *Dyslexia: Successful Inclusion in the Secondary School*. London: David Fulton.

Howlett, C.A. (2001) 'Dyslexia and Biology', in L. Peer and G. Reid (eds), *Dyslexia – Successful Inclusion in the Secondary School*. London: David Fulton.

Hunter, V. (2001) 'Dyslexia and general science', in L. Peer and G. Reid (eds), *Dyslexia: Successful Inclusion in the Secondary School*. London: David Fulton.

Hunter, V. (2009) 'Overcoming the Barriers of Transition', in G. Reid (ed.), *The Routledge Companion to Dyslexia*. London: Routledge.

Irish Support for Learning Association (2007) Association conference materials. ISLA, Dublin.

Johanson, K. (1997) 'Left hemisphere stimulation with music and sounds in dyslexia remediation'. Paper presented at the 48th annual conference of the International Dyslexia Association (formerly the Orton Dyslexia Association), Baltimore, MD.

Johnston, R., Connelly, V.D. and Watson, J. (1995) 'Some effects of phonics teaching on early reading development', in P. Owen and P. Pumfrey (eds),

Emergent and Developing Reading: Messages for Teachers. London: Falmer Press.

Jones, N. (2005) 'Children with developmental coordination disorder: Setting the scene', in N. Jones (ed.), *Developing School Provision for Children with Dyspraxia*. London: Paul Chapman.

Joshi, R.M. and Carreker, S. (2009) 'Spelling: Development, Assessment and Instruction', in G. Reid (ed.), *The Routledge Companion to Dyslexia*. London: Routledge.

Kaplan, B.J., Dewey, D.M., Crawford, S.G. and Wilson, B.N. (2001) 'The term comorbidity is of questionable value in reference to developmental disorders: Data and theory', *Journal of Learning Disabilities*, 34(6), 55–65.

Kirby, A. (2003) *The Adolescent with Developmental Co-ordination Disorder*. London: Jessica Kingsley.

Kirby, A. (2006) *Dyspraxia: Developmental Co-ordination Disorder*. Human Horizon Series.

Kirby, A. and Drew, S. (2002) *Guide to Dyspraxia and Developmental Coordination Disorders*. London: David Fulton.

Lannen, S. (1990) Personal correspondence based on PhD study on conflict resolution.

Lazear, D. (1999) *Eight Ways of Knowing: Teaching for Multiple Intelligences* (third edn). Arlington Heights, IL: SkyLight Professional Development.

Levine, M.D. (1997) *All Kinds of Minds*. New York: Educators Publications.

Liberman, I.Y. and Shankweiler, D.P. (1985) 'Phonology and the problems of learning to read and write,' *Remedial and Special Education*, 6(6), 8–17.

Lidz, C.S. (1991) *Practitioner's Guide to Dynamic Assessment*. New York: Guilford Press.

Lloyd, G. and Norris, C. (1999) 'Including ADHD?', *Disability and Society*, 14(4), 505–17.

Macintyre, C. (2009) *Dyspraxia* (second edn). London and New York: Routledge.

Mahfoudhi, A., Elbeheri, G. and Everatt, J. (2009) 'Reading and Dyslexia in Arabic', in G. Reid, G. Elbeheri, J. Everatt, J. Wearmouth and D.K. Knight (eds.) (2009) *The Routledge Companion to Dyslexia*. London: Routledge.

Mahfoudhi, A. and Haynes, C. (2009) 'Phonological awareness in reading disabilities remediation: Some general issues' in G. Reid, G. Elbeheri, G.J. Everatt, J. Wearmouth and D.K. Knight (eds), *The Routledge Companion to Dyslexia*. London: Routledge.

McPhillips, M., Hepper, P.G. and Mulhern, G. (2000) 'Effects of replicating primary-reflex movements on specific reading difficulties in children: A randomised, double-blind, controlled trial.' *The Lancet*, 355, 537–41.

Miles, T.R. (1983) *Dyslexia: The Pattern of Difficulties*. London: Collins Educational.

Moats, L.C. (2005) 'Language Essentials for Teaching of Reading and Spelling, Module 9', *Teaching Beginning Spelling and Writing*. Longmont, CO: Sopris West Educational Services.

Molfese, V.J., Molfese, D.L., Barnes, M.E., Warren, C.G. and Molfese, P.J. (2008) 'Familial Predictors of Dyslexia – Evidence from Preschool Children With and Without Familial Dyslexia Risk', in G. Reid, A. Fawcett, F. Manis and L. Siegel, *The Sage Handbook of Dyslexia*. London: Sage Publications.

Montague, M. and Castro, M. (2004) 'Attention Deficit Hyperactivity Disorder:

References

Concerns and Issues', in P. Clough, P. Garner, J.T. Pardeck and F. Yuen (2004) (eds), *Handbook of Emotional and Behavioural Difficulties*. London: Sage Publications.

Morton, J. and Frith, U. (1995) 'Causal modelling: A structural approach to developmental psychopathology', in D. Cicchetti and D.J. Cohen (eds), *Manual of Developmental Psychopathology*. Chichester: Wiley.

Mosley, J. (1996) *Quality Circle Time*. Cambridge: LDA.

Moseley, D. and Nicol, C. (1995) *ACE (Actually Coded English) Spelling Dictionary*. Cambridge: LDA.

Moseley, D.V. (1988) 'New approaches to helping children with spelling difficulties', *Educational and Child Psychology*, 5(4), 54–8.

Muijs, D. and Reynolds, D. (2005) *Effective Teaching: Evidence and Practice*. London: Sage Publications.

National Reading Panel (2000). *Teaching children to Read: An evidence-based assessment of the scientific research literature on reading and its implications for reading instruction*. www.nichd.nih.gov/research/supported/nrp.cfm accessed 15/4/10 (see also www.nationalreadingpanel.org).

Nicolson, R.I. and Fawcett, A.J. (1990) 'Automaticity: A new framework for dyslexia research?', *Cognition*, 35, 159–82.

Nicolson, R.I. and Fawcett, A.J. (1996) *The Dyslexia Early Screening Test*. London: Psychological Corporation.

Nicolson, R.I. and Fawcett, A.J. (1999) 'Developmental dyslexia: The role of the cerebellum', *Dyslexia: An International Journal of Research and Practice*, 5, 155–177.

Nicolson, R.I. and Fawcett, A.J. (2000) 'Longterm learning in dyslexic children', *European Journal of Cognitive Psychology*, 12, 357–93.

Nicolson, R.I. and Fawcett, A.J. (2008) 'Learning, Cognition and Dyslexia', in G. Reid, A. Fawcett, F. Manis and L. Siegel, *The Sage Dyslexia Handbook*. London: Sage Publications.

Nicolson, R.I., Fawcett, A.J. and Dean, P. (2001) 'Developmental dyslexia. The cerebellar deficit hypothesis', *Trends in Neurosciences*, 24(9), 508–11.

Norwich, B. (2009) 'How compatible is the recognition of dyslexia with inclusive education?', in G. Reid (ed.), *The Routledge Companion to Dyslexia*. London: Routledge.

Norwich, B. and Lewis, A. (2001) 'Mapping a pedagogy for special educational needs', *British Educational Research Journal*, 27(3), 313–31.

Palincsar, A. and Brown, A. (1984) 'Reciprocal teaching of comprehension fostering and comprehension-monitoring activities', *Cognition and Instruction*, 1(2), 117–75.

Peer, L. (2009) 'Dyslexia and Glue Ear: A Sticky Educational Problem', in G. Reid, A. Fawcett, F. Manis and L. Siegel (2008) *The Sage Handbook of Dyslexia*. London: Sage Publications.

Peters, M.L. (1970) *Success in Spelling* (Cambridge Monographs on Education No. 4). Cambridge: Cambridge Institute of Education.

Peters, M.L. (1975) *Diagnostic and Remedial Spelling Manual*. London: Macmillan Education.

Peters, M.L. (1985) *Spelling: Caught or Taught – A New Look*. London: Routledge.

Portwood, M. (2000) *Understanding Developmental Dyspraxia. A Textbook for Students and Professionals*. London: David Fulton.

References

Portwood, M. (2001) *Developmental Dyspraxia: A Practical Manual for Parents and Professionals.* London: David Fulton.

Portwood, M. (2002) 'School based trials of fatty acid supplements'. Paper presented at Durham County Council Education Conference.

Portwood, M. (2006) 'School based trials of fatty acid supplements'. Paper presented at Durham County Council Education Conference.

Pringle-Morgan, W.P. (1896) 'A case of congenital word-blindness', *British Medical Journal*, 2, 137–8.

Reason, R., Brown, P., Cole, M. and Gregory, M. (1988) 'Does the "specific" in specific learning difficulties make a difference to the way we teach?', *Support for Learning*, 3(4), 230–36.

Reddington, R.M. and Wheeldon, A. (2002) 'Involving parents in baseline assessment: employing developmental psychopathology in the early identification process', *Dyslexia*, 8(2), 119–22.

Reid, G. (2001) 'Specialist teacher training in the UK: Issues, considerations and future directions', in M. Hunter-Carsch (ed.), *Dyslexia: A Psychosocial Perspective.* London: Whurr.

Reid, G. (2003) *Dyslexia: A Practitioner's Handbook* (third edn). Chichester: Wiley.

Reid, G. (2004) *Dyslexia: A Complete Guide for Parents.* Chichester: Wiley.

Reid, G. (2005a) 'Dyslexia and learning styles'. Presentation at the European Independent Schools Council, The Hague, the Netherlands, 20 November.

Reid, G. (2005b) 'Specific learning difficulties: the spectrum', in N. Jones (ed.), *Developing School Provision for Children with Dyspraxia.* London: Paul Chapman.

Reid, G. (2006) 'Managing attention difficulties in the classroom: a learning styles perspective', in G. Lloyd and J. Stead (eds), *Critical New Perspectives on AD/HD.* London: Routledge.

Reid, G. (2007) *Motivating Learners: Strategies for the Classroom.* London: Sage Publications.

Reid, G. (2009) *Dyslexia: A Practitioners Handbook*, fourth edn. Chichester: Wiley-Blackwell.

Reid, G. and Green, S. (2007) *100 Ideas for supporting pupils with dyslexia.* London: Continuum.

Reid, G. and Green, S. (2007) *The Teaching Assistants Guide to Dyslexia.* London: Continuum.

Reid, G., Green, S. and Zylstra, C. (2005) 'Parents and dyslexia: Issues, concerns and successes: experiences from both sides of the Atlantic'. Presentation at the IDA 56th Annual Conference, Denver, 9–12 November.

Richardson, A.J. (2001) 'Dyslexia, dyspraxia and ADHD – Can nutrition help?', paper presented at fourth Cambridge Conference, Helen Arkell Dyslexia Association.

Riddick, B. (2006) 'Dyslexia Friendly Schools in the UK', *Topics in Language Disorders*, 26(1), 142–54.

Riddick, B. (2009) 'The implications of students' perspectives on dyslexia for school improvement', in G. Reid (ed.), *The Routledge Companion to Dyslexia.* London: Routledge.

Robertson, J. and Bakker, D.J. (2002) 'The balance model of reading and dyslexia', in G. Reid and J. Wearmouth (eds), *Dyslexia and Literacy: Theory and Practice.* Chichester: Wiley.

References

Rohl, M. and Tunmer, W. (1988) 'Phonemic segmentation skills and spelling acquisition', *Applied Psycholinguistics*, 9, 335–50.

Rosen, G.D. (2010) 'Dyslexia, genes, and the brain: 10 years and beyond', in *Perspective on Language and Literacy*, winter edition 2010, 36(1), 18–21.

Rubie-Davies, C., Hattie, J. and Hamilton, R. (2006). 'Expecting the best for students: teacher expectations and academic outcomes', *British Journal of Educational Psychology*, 76, 429–44.

Russell, S. (1992) *Phonic Code Cracker*. Glasgow: Jordanhill College Publications.

Rutter, M. (1995) 'Relationships between mental disorders in childhood and adulthood', *Acta Psychiatrica Scandinavica*, 91, 73–85.

Scottish Executive (2004) The Education (Additional Support for Learning) (Scotland) Act 2004. Edinburgh: Scottish Executive.

Silverman, L. (2005) personal correspondence.

Slingerland, B.H. (1993) *Specific Language Disability Children*. Cambridge: Educators Publishing Service.

Smith, P., Hinson, M. and Smith, D. (1998) *Spelling and Spelling Resources*. Tamworth, UK: NASEN Publications.

Smith, D. (1997) *Spelling Games and Activities*. Tamworth, UK: NASEN publications.

Smits-Engelsman, B.C.M. and Van Galen, G.P. (1997), 'Dysgraphia in Children: Lasting psychomotor deficiency of transient developmental delay?' *Journal of Experimental Child Psychology*, 67, 164–84.

Smythe, I., Everatt, J. and Salter, R. (eds) (2004) *International Book of Dyslexia*. Chichester: Wiley.

Snowling, M.J. (1994) 'Towards a model of spelling acquisition: The development of some component skills', in G.D.A. Brown and N.C. Ellis (eds), *Handbook of Spelling: Theory, Process and Intervention*. Chichester: Wiley, pp. 111–28.

Snowling, M.J. (2000). *Dyslexia* (second edn). Oxford: Blackwell.

Snowling, M.J. (2005) 'Language skills and learning to read: risk and protective factors'. Presentation at the 56th Annual Conference IDA, Denver, 9–12. November 2005.

Stein, J. (2008) 'The Neurobiological Basis of Dyslexia', in G. Reid, A. Fawcett, F. Manis, L.Siegel, *The Sage Dyslexia Handbook*. London: Sage Publications.

Stordy, B.J. (1995) 'Benefit of docosahexaenoic acid supplements to dark adaptation in dyslexia', *The Lancet*, 346, 385.

Stordy, B.J. (1997) 'Dyslexia, attention deficit hyperactivity disorder, dyspraxia do fatty acids help?', *Dyslexia Review*, 9(2).

Stanovich, K.E. (1991) 'Discrepancy definitions of reading disability: has intelligence led us astray?', *Reading Research Quarterly*, 26(1), 7–29.

Sugden, D. (2008) 'Movement in Learning' lecture presented to the Centre for Child Evaluation and Teaching, Kuwait, January.

Tallal, P., Miller, S. and Fitch, R. (1993) 'Neurobiological basis of speech: a case for the preeminence of temporal processing', in Temporal Information Processing in the Nervous System: Special Reference to Dyslexia and Dysphasia, P. Tallal, A.M. Galaburda, R.R. Llinas and C. von Euler (eds), *Annals of the New York Academy of Sciences*, v. 682, pp. 27–47.

Taylor, M.F. (2002) 'Stress-induced atypical brain lateralization in boys with attention-deficit/hyperactivity disorder. Implications for scholastic performance', Unpublished PhD thesis. University of Western Australia.

Thomson. M (2006) 'Dyslexia Friendly Guidance for the Secondary School, Series produced and distributed by Dyslexia Scotland, Stirling.

Topping, K.J. (1992) 'Cued Spelling Training Tape'. London: Kirklees Metropolitan Council.

Topping, K.J. (2001a) 'Peer Assisted Learning, A Practical Guide for Teachers', www.dundee.ac.uk/ psychology/kjtopping/plearning.html. Cambridge, MA: Brookline Books.

Topping, K.J. (2001b). 'Thinking reading writing: A practical guide to paired learning with peers, parents & volunteers'. New York/London: Continuum.

Topping, K. Nixon, J., Sutherland, J., Yarrow F. (2000) 'Paired writing: a framework for effective collaboration', in *Reading*, 34(2), 51–98.

Treiman, R. (1993) *Beginning to Spell: A Study of First Grade Children*. New York: Oxford University Press.

Ulmer, C. and Timothy, M. (2001) 'How does alternative assessment affect teachers' practice? Two years later'. Paper presented at the 12th European Conference on Reading, Dublin, 1–4 July.

UNESCO (1994) 'Salamanca Statement: Network for Action for Special Needs in Education'. UNESCO Paris www.inclusion.com/artsalamanca.html

Usmani, K. (1999) 'The influence of racism and cultural bias in the assessment of bilingual children', *Educational and Child Psychology*, 16(3), 44–54.

Vellutino, F.R., Fletcher, J.M., Snowling, M.J. and Scanlon, D.M. (2004). 'Specific reading disability (dyslexia). What have we learned in the past four decades?', *Journal of Child Psychology and Psychiatry*, 45, 2–40.

Vygotsky, L.S. (1986a) *Mind in Society: The Development of Higher Psychological Processes*. Cambridge, MA: Harvard University Press.

Vygotsky, L.S. (1986b) *Thought and Language*. Cambridge, MA: MIT Press.

Wagner, R.K., Torgesen, J.K. and Rashotte, C.A. (1999). *Comprehensive Test of Phonological Processing*. Austin, TX: PRO-Ed.

Weedon, C. and Reid, G. (2001) *Listening and Literacy Index*. London: Hodder and Stoughton.

Weedon, C. and Reid, G. (2002) *Special Needs Assessment Profile Pilot Version*. Edinburgh: George Watson's College.

Weedon, C. and Reid, G. (2003, 2005, Version 3, 2009) *Special Needs Assessment Profile (SNAP)*. London: Hodder Murray.

West, T.G. (1997) *In the Mind's Eye: Visual Thinkers, Gifted People with Learning Difficulties, Computer Images and the Ironies of Creativity* (second edn). Buffalo, NY: Prometheus Books.

Willcutt, E.G. and Pennington, B.F. (2000) 'Comorbidity of reading disabilty and attention-deficit/hyperactivity disorder: Differences by gender and subtype', *Journal of Learning Disabilities*, 33(2), 179–91.

Williams, F. and Lewis, J. (2001) 'Dyslexia and geography', in L. Peer and G. Reid (eds), *Dyslexia: Successful Inclusion in the Secondary School*. London: David Fulton.

Wolf, M. and O'Brien, B. (2001) 'On issues of time, fluency and intervention', in A. Fawcett (ed.), *Dyslexia, Theory and Good Practice*. London: Whurr.

Wray, D. (2009) 'Extending Literacy Skills: Issues for Practice', in G. Reid (ed.), *The Routledge Companion to Dyslexia*. London: Routledge.

Yoshimoto, R. (2005) 'Gifted dyslexic children: characteristics and curriculum implications'. Presentation at the 56th Annual Conference IDA, Denver, 9–12 November.

Web links

Introduction

Rose report: http://search.publications.dcsf.gov.uk/kbroker/dcsf/dcsfpubs/search.
ladv?sr=0&cs=UTF-8&sc=dcsfpubs&nh=10&sb=0&ha=144&hs=0&fl1=publica
tionshop%3A&op1=1&ty1=0&tx1=2986&fl0=&op0=1&ty0=0&ucSearchContro
l%3ASimpleSearchButton=Search&fl8=contributor%3A&op8=1&ty8=0&tx0=D
yslexia&tx8=)

New Zealand literacy benchmarks: www.dyslexiafoundation.org.nz/index_flash.php

In Western Australia, the innovative learning centre 'Fun Track Learning' under the
direction of Mandy Appleyard: www.funtrack.com.au/

Fraser Academy in Vancouver: www.fraseracademy.ca/

The Kenneth Gordon Maplewood School: www.kennethgordon.bc.ca/

The Center for Child Evaluation and Teaching (CCET) *in Kuwait*: www.ccetkuwait.
org/

The Institute for Child Education and Psychology (ICEP) Europe: www.icepe.ie/

Red Rose School: www.redroseschool.co.uk

Chapter 3

No to failure project: www.notofailure.com/

The screening phase of the study (reported on in 2008): www.notofailure.com/
article/2/interim-evaluation-reports-groundbreaking-research

Learning Works, UK: www.learning-works.org.uk

Chapter 4

National Reading Panel (2000): www.nationalreadingpanel.org

OG: www.OrtonAcademy.org

Alphabetic Phonics: www.ALTAread. org

Association Method: www.usm.edu/dubard

Language!: www.SoprisWest.com

Lexia-Herman Method: www.Hermanmethod.com

Lindamood–Bell: www.Lindamoodbell.com

Project Read: www.Projectread.com

Slingerland: www.Slingerland.org

Sonday System: www.SondaySystem.com

Spalding Method: www.Spalding.org

Wilson Fundations and Wilson Reading: www.wilsonlanguage.com

IDA: www.interdys.org

Dyspraxia Foundation: www.dyspraxiafoundation.org.uk

Linda Silverman's websites: www.gifteddevelopment.com and: www.visualspatial.org.
Crossbow Education: www.crossboweducation.com

Chapter 6

Resources developed around the Trait model: www.teachcanada.ca/Merchant2/
merchant.mvc?Screen=CTGY&Category_Code=trait
and: http://educationnorthwest.org/traits.

Chapter 7

Good examples of tutorial and extended teaching and learning centres:
Red Rose School in England: www.redroseschool.co.uk
Fraser Academy in Vancouver, Canada: www.fraseracademy.ca
Fun Track Learning in Perth, Australia: www.funtrack.com.au

A variety of software is available from: www.dyslexic.com
www.cricksoft.com/uk/ has created many high-quality resources for use with
Clicker 5. The Clicker Writer is a talking word processor – you can write by using
the keyboard, or by selecting letters, words or phrases in the Clicker Grid.
http://xavier.bangor.ac.uk/xavier/sounds_rhymes.shtml has a very comprehensive
range of software for dyslexic pupils.

There is also a wide range of software on study skills and memory training. Two
such programs developed by Jane Mitchell include Mastering Memory and Time
2 Revise/Timely Reminders: www.calsc.co.uk/

R-E-M software also produce computer materials aimed at those with dyslexia,
and have produced a specific catalogue: www.r-e-m.co.uk

A considerable range can also be found in the Educators Publishing Service
website: www.epsbooks.com

Chapter 10

A useful general web link is: www.dyscalculia.org
Details of the dyscalculia screener can be found at: www.gl-assessment.co.uk
Further information can also be seen in the government website (UK): www.
standards.dfes.gov.uk/numeracy/about
A dedicated website that can be accessed by anyone and contains a number
of ideas on teaching to cover difficulties associated with 17 different specific
learning difficulties: www.SNAPassessment.com

Chapter 11

Institute for Neuro-Physiological Psychology (INPP): www.inpp.org.uk

Appendix 2

Africa

Madonna Jarret Thorpe Trust: mjtt@airtip.gm
Crossroads Dyslexic Centre at U2KAN: joybanad@yahoo.com

Web links

Asia

Dyslexia Association (Hong Kong): www.dyslexia.org.hk/
Hong Kong Association for Specific Learning Difficulties: www.asld.org.hk
Japan Dyslexia Society: info@npo-edge.jp
Dyslexia Association of Singapore: www.das.org.sg
Learning Disability Association in Taiwan: www.dale.nhctc. edu.tw/ald

Australia

SPELD Victoria: www.speldvic.org.au
SPELD South Australia: www.speld-sa.org.au
SPELD New South Wales: www.speldnsw.org.au
SPELD (Tasmania): speldtasmania@bigpond.com
SPELD Western Australia: speld@opera.iinet.net.au; www.dyslexia-speld.
  com
SPELD Queensland: www.speld.org.au

Canada

International Dyslexia Association Ontario: www.idaontario.com
Canadian Academy of Therapeutic Tutors: www.ogtutors.com
Reach O-G Learning Center, Vancouver: www.reachlearningcenter.com

Europe

DITT: www.dyslexia-international.org
Dyslexia International – Tools and Technologies (DITT) aims to bring full awareness
  of the problems associated with specific learning difficulties into the education
  systems of all EU member states.
European Dyslexia Association (EDA): www.dyslexia.eu.com
Croatian Dyslexia Association: lencek@antun.erf.hr
Cyprus Dyslexia Association: dyslexiacy@cytanent.com.cy
Czech Dyslexia Association: zelinkova@mymail.cz
Danish Dyslexia Association: www.ordblind.com
www.dyslexia.gr
www.diszlexia.hu
www.dyslexia.ie
Associazione Italiana Dislessia: www.dislessia.it
Dyspel asbl: www.dyspel.org/
Polskie Towarzystwo Dysleksji: psymbg@univ.gda.pl
www.dyslexiascotland.org.uk
Swedish Dyslexia Association: www.ki.se/dyslexi
www.bda-dyslexia.org.uk
www.welshdyslexia.info

Middle East

www.orton-ida.org.il
www.kuwaitdyslexia.com
Egyptian Dyslexia Centre: www.dyslexia-egypt.com

Web links

New Zealand
SPELD New Zealand: www.speld.org.nz
Learning and Behaviour Charitable Trust: www.lbctnz.co.nz

South America
APHDA: aphda@hotmail.com
Associação Brasileira de Dislexia: www.dislexia.org.br, e-mail: info@dyslexiaassociation.ca

Russia
olgainsh@land.ru

USA
International Dyslexia Association (IDA): www.interdys.org
Learning Disabilities Association of America: www.ldaamerica.org

Appendix 3
www.LDAlearning.com
DIBELS: http://dibels.uoregon.edu/

PRO-ED Inc.
A leading publisher of nationally standardized tests: www.proedinc.com

Special Needs Assessment Profile: www.SNAPassessment.com

Other Websites
Dr Gavin Reid: www.drgavinreid.com
www.redroseschool.co.uk

ICEP Europe – Institute of Child Education and Psychology (Europe): www.icepe.ie/
The trusted leading provider of high quality online Continuing Professional Development (CPD) and University validated Diploma programmes in special educational needs for teachers, parents and allied professionals who work with children and young people.

Oak Hill School, Chemin de Précossy, 31 1260 Nyon, Switzerland: www.oakhill.ch.
Oak Hill School offers a unique half-day programme to students with diagnosed learning disabilities or attention deficit disorders, who are experiencing difficulties in the mainstream classroom.

ALL Special Kids, (ASK) Geneva: www.allspecialkids.org
A Geneva-based organization, aiming to support the families of children with special needs and learning differences.

Fun Track Learning: www.funtrack.com.au/
Learning Works Int: www.learning-works.org.uk
Creative Learning Company New Zealand: www.creativelearningcentre.com
Dyslexia Association of Ireland: www.dyslexia.ie

243

Web links

Dyslexia Action (formerly Dyslexia Institute): www.dyslexiaaction.org.uk
Dyslexia Online Magazine: www.dyslexia-parent.com/magazine.html

Dyslexia Online Journal: www.dyslexia-adults.com/journal.html
Articles and research for professionals working in the field of dyslexia.

Dyslexia Parents Resource: www.dyslexia-parent.com/
Information and resources about dyslexia for parents of children who are, or may
   be, dyslexic.
Family Onwards: www.familyonwards.com
Helen Arkell Dyslexia Centre: www.arkellcentre.org.uk

I am dyslexic: www.iamdyslexic.com
A site put together by an 11-year-old dyslexic.

Institute for Neuro-Physiological Psychology (INPP): www.inpp.org.uk

Dr Loretta Giorcelli: www.doctorg.org/
A well-known international consultant.

Mindroom: www.mindroom.org
A charity dedicated to spreading greater awareness and understanding of learning
difficulties. Goal is that by 2020 all children with learning difficulties in the UK are
identified and helped.

Dysguise – dyslexia assessment and consultancy
www.dysguise.com

World Dyslexia Network Foundation: www.wdnf.info
A series of advice and help sheets have been written by leading experts in their
fields.
World of Dyslexia: www.worldofdyslexia.com, www.dyslexia-parent.com/
   world_of_dyslexia
Adult Dyslexia: www.dyslexia-college.com
Buzan Centres Ltd: www.Mind-Map.com

Crossbow Education: www.crossboweducation.com
Games for learning.

Iansyst Ltd: www.dyslexic.com

International Reading Organization: www.reading.org
Bulletin boards, information on associations and links, etc.

The National Literacy Strategy: www.standards.dfes.gov.uk/literacy/

Index

Index

Index